Ecclesiastes

Peter Enns

WILLIAM B. EERDMANS PUBLISHING COMPANY

GRAND RAPIDS, MICHIGAN / CAMBRIDGE, U.K.

Published 2011 by
Wm. B. Eerdmans Publishing Co.
2140 Oak Industrial Drive N.E., Grand Rapids, Michigan 49505 /
P.O. Box 163, Cambridge CB3 9PU U.K.

Printed in the United States of America

17 16 15 14 13 12 11   7 6 5 4 3 2 1

Library of Congress Cataloging-in-Publication Data

Enns, Peter, 1961-
    Ecclesiastes / Peter Enns.
        p.   cm. — (The Two Horizons Old Testament commentary)
    Includes bibliographical references.
    ISBN 978-0-8028-6649-3 (pbk.: alk. paper)
    1. Bible. O.T. Ecclesiastes — Commentaries.   I. Title.

BS1475.53.E56   2011
223'.807 — dc23

                                                        2011026656

www.eerdmans.com

THE TWO HORIZONS OLD TESTAMENT COMMENTARY

J. GORDON MCCONVILLE and CRAIG BARTHOLOMEW, *General Editors*

Two features distinguish THE TWO HORIZONS OLD TESTAMENT COMMENTARY series: theological exegesis and theological reflection.

Exegesis since the Reformation era and especially in the past two hundred years emphasized careful attention to philology, grammar, syntax, and concerns of a historical nature. More recently, commentary has expanded to include social-scientific, political, or canonical questions and more.

Without slighting the significance of those sorts of questions, scholars in THE TWO HORIZONS OLD TESTAMENT COMMENTARY locate their primary interests on theological readings of texts, past and present. The result is a paragraph-by-paragraph engagement with the text that is deliberately theological in focus.

Theological reflection in THE TWO HORIZONS OLD TESTAMENT COMMENTARY takes many forms, including locating each Old Testament book in relation to the whole of Scripture — asking what the biblical book contributes to biblical theology — and in conversation with constructive theology of today. How commentators engage in the work of theological reflection will differ from book to book, depending on their particular theological tradition and how they perceive the work of biblical theology and theological hermeneutics. This heterogeneity derives as well from the relative infancy of the project of theological interpretation of Scripture in modern times and from the challenge of grappling with a book's message in Greco-Roman antiquity, in the canon of Scripture and history of interpretation, and for life in the admittedly diverse Western world at the beginning of the twenty-first century.

THE TWO HORIZONS OLD TESTAMENT COMMENTARY is written primarily for students, pastors, and other Christian leaders seeking to engage in theological interpretation of Scripture.

Hans Enns
  1920-2006
Ingrid Enns
  1931-2009

Who knows if the human spirit rises upward and if the spirit of the animal goes down into the earth? — QOHELET

In my Father's house are many rooms. — JESUS

We do not want you to be uninformed about those who sleep, so that you do not grieve like the rest who have no hope. — PAUL

Contents

Acknowledgments

The more I write, the more I understand the many ways I am dependent on many others.

I am indeed grateful for the many students I taught at Westminster Theological Seminary during my fourteen years on the faculty. My thoughts began to take shape in teaching "Poetry and Wisdom Literature" to M.Div. and M.A.R. students, and then benefited greatly from the Th.M. and Ph.D. students in the Ecclesiastes seminar I led for ten years. The fruit of those intimate, interactive settings are plain to me, even if hidden to general readers.

Two former teachers in particular have had a significant influence on how I approach Ecclesiastes. Tremper Longman III was first my teacher at Westminster, then a colleague, and now a trusted collaborator and lifelong friend. James L. Kugel, my doctoral advisor at Harvard University, introduced me to early Jewish and rabbinic exegesis, and from him I learned what a truly close reading of the Hebrew text entails. It is fair to say that my own academic journey is a synthesis of the two influences represented by these men.

I am deeply indebted to the work of three student assistants: Art Boulet (Princeton Theological Seminary), David Griffin (Westminster Theological Seminary), and Rob Kashow (Dallas Theological Seminary). All three worked through the manuscript at various stages and made many corrections, offered numerous suggestions (all with superhuman speed and accuracy), and helped secure copious amounts of secondary literature. It is truly a "grievous task" I have laid upon them, and their work not only sped up the completion of this volume by many months, but kept me from mirroring Qohelet's sense of despair over living. I am also thankful to Rob Kashow for preparing the Scripture index and Steve Bohannon (Princeton Theological Seminary) for preparing the name index. Russell Schaffner proofread the manuscript in its final stages.

As always, my wife Sue and children Erich, Elizabeth, and Sophie are never far from me — quite literally — no matter what I write. Throughout my career, they have typically been walking about above my basement study, and it is hard to imagine it otherwise, although departures to college have interrupted this familiar rhythm. There is no more palpable influence on my life than Sue, my wife of now twenty-seven years, and our (nearly all adult) children, and I hope this commentary reflects some of my own growth as the husband and father of this wonderful little family.

This volume is dedicated to my parents, Hans and Ingrid, Russian-German and Polish-German immigrants, respectively, who built from scratch a life in the United States beginning in the late 1950s, and who provided for my sister Angelika and me far more than they ever dreamed of in their own early lives. My father passed away as I began this commentary and my mother passed away just a few weeks after I completed the first draft. It has not escaped my notice that their deaths frame my work on a biblical book whose author railed against the inviolability of death, and I have heard the echo of his voice more clearly and deeply than I might like.

June, 2011

Abbreviations

AB	Anchor Bible
AnBib	Analecta biblica
ANETS	Ancient Near Eastern Texts and Studies
AUUSSU	Acta Universitatis Upsaliensis. Studia Semitica Upsaliensia
b. Shab.	Babylonian Talmud, *Shabbat*
BBB	Bonner biblische Beiträge
BEATAJ	Beiträge zur Erforschung des Alten Testaments und des antiken Judentum
BETL	Bibliotheca ephemeridum theologicarum lovaniensium
BibInt	*Biblical Interpretation*
BSac	*Bibliotheca sacra*
BZAW	Beihefte zur Zeitschrift für die alttestamentliche Wissenschaft
CBQ	*Catholic Biblical Quarterly*
CurTM	*Currents in Theology and Mission*
ErIsr	*Eretz-Israel*
HAT	Handbuch zum Alten Testament
HUCA	*Hebrew Union College Annual*
IBHS	*Introduction to Biblical Hebrew Syntax,* ed. B. K. Waltke and M. O'Connor (Winona Lake, IN: Eisenbrauns, 1990)
Int	*Interpretation*
JANES	*Journal of the Ancient Near Eastern Society*
JBL	*Journal of Biblical Literature*
JETS	*Journal of the Evangelical Theological Society*
JPS	Jewish Publication Society
JQR	*Jewish Quarterly Review*
JSOT	*Journal for the Study of the Old Testament*
JSOTSup	Journal for the Study of the Old Testament: Supplement Series
JTS	*Journal of Theological Studies*

KJV	King James (Authorized) Version
LXX	Septuagint
m. ʿEd.	Mishnah, *ʿEduyyot*
m. Yad.	Mishnah, *Yadayim*
MT	Masoretic Text
NASB	New American Standard Bible
NICNT	New International Commentary on the New Testament
NICOT	New International Commentary on the Old Testament
NIV	New International Version
NIVAC	New International Version Application Commentary
NRSV	New Revised Standard Version
OLA	Orientalia lovaniensia analecta
OTL	Old Testament Library
OTWSA	*Ou-Testamentiese Werkgemeenskap van Suid-Afrika*
PSB	*Princeton Seminary Bulletin*
RSV	Revised Standard Version
SBLDS	Society of Biblical Literature Dissertation Series
TD	*Theology Digest*
TNIV	Today's New International Version
TynBul	*Tyndale Bulletin*
VT	*Vetus Testamentum*
VTSup	Vetus Testamentum Supplements
WBC	Word Biblical Commentary
WTJ	*Westminster Theological Journal*
WW	*Word and World*
ZAW	*Zeitschrift für die alttestamentliche Wissenschaft*

Introduction

To introduce a book of the Bible is often seen as a preliminary necessity, almost a courtesy to ease readers into the content of the book. This is not the case with the book of Ecclesiastes, for which it is precisely the standard introductory questions — who wrote the book, when, and for what purpose — that continue to prove challenging for any commentator. Not only will one find widely divergent answers to these questions documented throughout the history of interpretation of Ecclesiastes, but the difficulty is that how one answers these questions will ultimately affect one's interpretation of the book as a whole.

There is, in other words, a vicious circle in interpreting Ecclesiastes. How one understands the overarching message of Ecclesiastes as a whole will affect how one handles the details of the book itself, yet the book's overall message cannot be determined apart from the book's details. Of course, on one level, this circle is operative with any biblical book, but the problems are augmented in the case of Ecclesiastes: it is not only the introductory questions that prove elusive, but the very details of the book, the data by which a plausible model of the whole must be constructed, likewise suffer from difficulties and ambiguities, and thus challenge any attempt to harness its overall message. It is a common experience when reading Ecclesiastes that, just when it seems the book's train of thought has been apprehended and some firm conclusion is forthcoming, a verse or two later the author says something that turns it all on its head. One begins to suspect that this is precisely what he has in mind, a point we will have a chance to observe throughout this commentary.

Although the introductory matters that follow represent my own view on how I see the pieces of Ecclesiastes fitting together, they nevertheless are developed in conversation with a wide spectrum of scholarly opinions, to which I am greatly indebted, even where I disagree. My general goal, in keeping with the purpose of this commentary series, is to allow the tensions and ambiguities of Ecclesiastes to stand, while also, at every point, working toward an articulation of the theological message of the book as a whole. In this respect, I have been most influenced by the observation of Michael V. Fox concerning the self-contradictory statements of Qohelet. He argues that these contradictions are not oddities to be adjusted here and there. Rather, they reflect the author's *intention* for how he wishes to communicate his theological message. I quote Fox here at length, who takes

> Qohelet's contradictions as the starting point of interpretation. My primary thesis is a simple one: The contradictions in the book of Qohelet are real and intended. We must interpret them, not eliminate them. . . . Qohelet's persistent observation of contradictions is a powerful cohesive force, and an awareness of it brings into focus the book's central concern: the problem of meaning in life. The book of Qohelet is about *meaning:* its loss and its (partial) recovery. . . . Qohelet's contradictions are the starting point but not the message of the book. He marshals them to *tear down* meaning, but he does not stop there. He is not a nihilist. He also *builds up* meaning, discovering ways of creating clarity and gratification in a confusing world.[1]

I am not suggesting that this is the most important observation one can make concerning Ecclesiastes, only that I have found its utter simplicity to provide a dynamic point of departure for allowing the words of Ecclesiastes to have their say. Whatever resolution there may be to specific exegetical issues or to the overall message of the book, interpreters of Ecclesiastes must first do the hard work of trying to think the author's thoughts after him. It is my sincere hope that this commentary will contribute to that goal by providing a meaningful theological framework within which students, church leaders, lay readers, and scholars can bring the message of Ecclesiastes to bear on Christ's church.

What Is Ecclesiastes About and Why Was It Written?

What can we say about the overall purpose of Ecclesiastes, the reason for which it was written? This issue catapults us to the very crux of the interpretive challenges of Ecclesiastes. Two major points are quickly apparent. First, various passages in the book seem to be at odds with other portions of the

---

1. Fox, *Time to Tear Down*, 3. Fox develops this notion throughout pp. 1-26 of his commentary. His present views on the matter there represent a further development of his earlier work *Qohelet and His Contradictions*.

OT.[2] Hence the degree to which one feels that the overall message of any one biblical book should be in harmony with any other will significantly affect how one handles these tensions. Second, Ecclesiastes is dotted with internal inconsistencies (e.g., 1:18 and 2:13; 5:10[3] and 10:19; 7:3 and 8:15). Here too the degree to which one can accept significant internal tensions in a biblical book will play itself out, knowingly or unknowingly, in the nuts and bolts of exegesis. But this is not simply a modern dilemma. Discussions reaching back at least to rabbinic times document the theological problems encountered in reading Ecclesiastes.[4] An overview of standard commentaries and introductions will quickly demonstrate the broadly contrasting opinions held, today and in the past.

Indeed, perhaps no other book of the Hebrew Scriptures has had the history of counterunderstandings as Ecclesiastes. Of nearly any other biblical book, one can make coherent statements as to its basic content and purpose that would find general agreement (Song of Songs and Job being two other notable exceptions). If any ten knowledgeable readers of Genesis were asked what Genesis is about, one might get ten diverse answers, but those answers would likely still accent legitimate and generally agreed upon aspects of the book, for example, creation, estrangement from God, the beginnings of Israel as a people, and so on. But no one capable of coherent thought would say that Genesis is about God's destruction of the universe, his blessing of the tower of Babel project, or his rejection of Abraham.

Yet Ecclesiastes, fueled in large part by its internal tensions, is a book that is amenable to conflicting and even contradictory interpretations, and so respected interpreters throughout history have struggled with the basic message of the book. Is Qohelet[5] coherent or incoherent, insightful or confused?

---

2. Perhaps foremost among them is the book's rather negative view of God's role in human affairs (e.g., 1:13-15). See also: death (3:19-20), righteousness (7:16), God's judgment (9:1-2), pleasure (2:10; compare Num 15:39).

3. The versification of the Hebrew text of Ecclesiastes corresponds to that of English translations at every point except ch. 5. Whereas ch. 4 in English translations ends with 4:16, the Hebrew continues to 4:17, which is 5:1 in the English. Hence, throughout ch. 5, English translations are one verse ahead of the Hebrew (Heb. 4:17 = Eng. 5:1, etc.). The versification is aligned once again in 6:1. English versification will normally be given throughout this commentary; to avoid confusion, I will include the Hebrew versification when referring to Hebrew terms.

4. The rabbis argued over whether Ecclesiastes "made the hands unclean," i.e., was inspired (*m. Yad.* 3:5; *'Ed.* 5:3). See the summary of the debate in Beckwith, *Old Testament Canon*, 274-304. See also Hirshman, "Qohelet's Reception"; Dell, "Ecclesiastes as Wisdom"; Sandberg, *Rabbinic Views of Qohelet*, 18-27.

5. Qohelet, announced in 1:1, is the speaker of the book from 1:12 through 12:7. The issue of authorship will be treated in more detail below.

Is he a stark realist or merely faithless? Is he orthodox or heterodox? Is he an optimist or a pessimist? Is the ultimate message of the book, "Be like Qohelet, the wise man," or "Qohelet is wrong, make sure you don't fall into his trap"? Discovering the meaning and purpose of Ecclesiastes will likely continue as a back-and-forth journey between overarching concepts and smaller exegetical details, balancing the forest and the trees. In the end, the theory that presents the most cohesive picture of Ecclesiastes will gain assent, at least for the time being.[6] What is disconcerting, however, is that confusion about the book's basic message may dissuade preachers and teachers from bringing its theology to bear on the life of the church. Or, perhaps more problematic, ill-informed or even reckless interpretation of the book — that which expects a certain kind of cohesion, or expects only certain things from biblical authors — could do more damage than simply avoiding the book altogether. It is for this reason that a credible explication of the basic message of the book of Ecclesiastes is necessary. Our investigation into that basic meaning takes as its point of departure the macrostructure of the book, to which we now turn.

The Frame Narrator

Ecclesiastes begins as a third person narrative in 1:1-11, where the narrator introduces the words of Qohelet. Beginning at 1:12 and extending through 12:7, the narrator's voice gives way to allow Qohelet's own voice to speak (with the curious exception of 7:27). In the epilogue (12:8-14),[7] the narrator's voice resumes, providing a summary and evaluation of Qohelet's words. The book's intentional design is underscored by comparing 1:2 and 12:8. After the general introduction of 1:1 ("The words of Qohelet, son of David, king in Jerusalem"), we read the narrator's summation of Qohelet's words in 1:2:

הֲבֵל הֲבָלִים אָמַר קֹהֶלֶת הֲבֵל הֲבָלִים הַכֹּל הָבֶל/*hăbēl hăbālîm 'āmar qōhelet hăbēl hăbālîm hakkōl hābel*, "Absolutely absurd!" says Qohelet, "Absolutely absurd! Everything is absurd."[8]

6. In saying this, I do not mean to create the impression that theological presuppositions do not affect how one approaches the text. Still, one's presuppositions are not so easily delineated, and the challenge remains to be self-reflective of what they are and to let Qohelet have his fair say to the greatest extent we can.

7. The epilogue is often considered to begin at 12:9 because this is where the explicit evaluation begins (e.g., Seow, *Ecclesiastes*; Fox, *Time to Tear Down*). I prefer to locate the beginning at v. 8 (see also Longman, *Ecclesiastes*), since this is where the third person narrative of the frame narrator resumes.

8. The phrase הֲבֵל הֲבָלִים/*hăbēl hăbālîm*, which appears twice in 1:2, is translated in the

This verse is repeated with minor variation in 12:8:

הֲבֵל הֲבָלִים אָמַר הַקּוֹהֶלֶת הַכֹּל הָבֶל/*hăbēl hăbālîm ʾāmar haqqôhelet hakkōl hābel*, "Absolutely absurd!" says Qohelet. "Everything is absurd!"

Since 1:2 and 12:8 frame Ecclesiastes in this way, 1:1-11 and 12:8-14 are often referred to as the frame of the book, and the speaker of these sections as the "frame narrator." How one understands the relationship between this third person frame and the first person body of Ecclesiastes will determine how one understands the message of the book as a whole.

It is clear that these bookends of Ecclesiastes suggest a fully intentional macrostructure to the book: a narrator framing the words of a certain "Qohelet." This structure, however, should not suggest that Ecclesiastes was originally composed as the wholly skeptical discourse of Qohelet (1:12–12:7) to which was added a later, orthodox framework. Despite the presence of first and third person discourses, positing two originally separate texts strikes me as an unhelpful and unnecessary conjecture. I can appreciate that some of Qohelet's words are simply too much at odds with the general testimony of the OT, and so a second author, the frame narrator, looks to provide an orthodox counterpoint. Still for others, there may be an additional theological or doctrinal motivation to posit, if not two originally distinct texts, then at least two distinct perspectives, thus providing a means of obviating the unorthodox implications of Qohelet's observations.

But it is precisely at this point that we must allow the frame narrator's introduction to speak for itself. The frame narrator makes very clear what Ecclesiastes is about. We are told directly in 1:1-2 that Qohelet sees everything as "absolutely absurd." This is a blunt and succinct summation of Qohelet's words that will occupy the remainder of the book up to 12:8. We should take careful note that there is no indication here (or elsewhere in 1:1-11) of any attempt to correct or sanitize the tone of what will occupy the middle section of the book. The problems in interpretation arise at the very outset when we presume that the frame narrator's words, even here, are a negative evaluation rather than simply a succinct summary of Qohelet's words.

This brings us to the role of the epilogue in our understanding of the

---

NIV as "Meaningless! Meaningless!" in the first instance but then "Utterly meaningless!" in the second. The grammatical construction is emphatic, so the latter is certainly correct, although the translation of *hebel* as "meaningless" is debatable and will be addressed elsewhere.

Throughout the commentary, I use the NIV as a base text, often as a point of departure for suggesting alternative translations of certain words or phrases. At times I simply offer my own translation of the Hebrew.

book as a whole. Unlike the introduction, the epilogue has an overt evaluative force, and so its importance for addressing the issue at hand is apparent. The basic question is: Does the epilogue give a fundamentally negative or positive evaluation of the words of Qohelet? Is the purpose of the epilogue to *correct* the errant theology of Qohelet or to *confirm* his observations? I take the view that the epilogue fundamentally supports Qohelet's observations while at the same time offering a mild "corrective" by placing Qohelet's observations in a broader (and traditional) theological context. In other words, there are elements of both confirmation and correction, but the latter is undertaken within the overall context of the former.[9]

Such an understanding of the function of the narrative frame encourages the view that the frame narrator is the *author* of the book, regardless of whatever independent prehistory there might have been for the middle section, although this too is a conjecture.[10] Qohelet may be (1) a fictional character created out of whole cloth, (2) the frame narrator's own alter ago (the vehicle by which he recounts his own struggles), or (3) a literary product that in some sense had an "independent" existence before its adaptation by the frame narrator (which is not to imply it would have existed in the precise form in which we see it in 1:12–12:7). I do not think this issue can be settled, nor is it vital to do so. In any case, Qohelet represents a point of view that the frame narrator apparently feels strongly enough about to lay out patiently for his readers over 203 of the 221 total verses in the book. There is clearly something

---

9. There is a growing consensus that the frame narrator does not simply contradict the words of Qohelet. Bartholomew goes so far as to say that it is "naïve" to think otherwise (Bartholomew, *Reading Ecclesiastes*, 95-96). According to Fox, "the author of the epilogue basically supports Qohelet's teachings. . . . [There is no] ideological conflict between Qohelet's teachings and the epilogue. Both express the author's views, but with different tones and emphases" (*Time to Tear Down*, 371, 373; see also Seow, *Ecclesiastes*, 38, and Provan, *Ecclesiastes*, 33 n. 13, 36). Shields argues: "In essence, Qohelet is the epilogist's 'straw man.' But the epilogist does not go to great lengths to knock down the straw man, for — to employ a different illustration — the epilogist has given Qohelet sufficient rope, and he has hung himself. To the reader familiar with the remainder of the Old Testament, it is clear that the wisdom of Qohelet has gone astray — much as Solomon himself had gone astray — and is ultimately incompatible with the message of the remainder of the canon" ("Ecclesiastes and the End of Wisdom," 138-39). Although this is not the place to engage Shields's argument in any detail, his summary of Ecclesiastes fails to address some important questions surrounding any explanation of the book, namely, how a book that is "critical of the wisdom movement" (138), which is itself a rather flat description of Israel's diverse wisdom tradition, could have been embraced in the Jewish canon. Shields's analysis also fails to consider that creating tension with "the message of the remainder of the canon" may be quite intentional on the part of the author of Ecclesiastes and compatible with the wisdom quest overall.

10. See Longman, *Ecclesiastes*, 21.

worthwhile his readers are expected to discern. Understanding Ecclesiastes as being *a book*, the product of an intentional, skilled, creative, and above all sagely (12:9-10) mind, encourages readers today to presume the book's coherence, which is seen precisely through the tensions in the book and amid the conflicting struggles of life that are recounted for us there.

To help reinforce this general approach to reading Ecclesiastes, the discussion on the epilogue below will focus on the last two verses of that passage, 12:13-14.[11] Doing so, even in an introduction to a commentary, will necessarily lead us to touch on several other points of the book as a whole that will need to be treated more fully in the relevant sections of this commentary. Yet this is a valuable point to mention here at the outset: reading Ecclesiastes is an exercise in paying very close attention to recurring, and often confusing, mixtures of themes and phrases that drive forward the theology of the book. It is virtually impossible, and certainly unwise, to read any portion of Ecclesiastes in isolation from whatever echoes of that passage might be found elsewhere in the book.

The End as a Key to the Whole

The book of Ecclesiastes ends as follows:

> [13]The end of the matter; everything has been heard: Fear God and keep his commandments, indeed, this is the whole of man (כָּל-הָאָדָם/*kol-hā'ādām*). [14]For God will bring every activity into judgment, including every hidden thing, whether it is good or evil.

Our focus here will be on כָּל-הָאָדָם/*kol-hā'ādām*, the last two words of v. 13, literally "all the man," translated in the NIV as "the whole duty of man."[12]

It is widely recognized that the epilogue intentionally picks up on the language and themes of Qohelet's discourse.[13] The phrase *kol-hā'ādām* is

---

11. Some commentators do not include vv. 13-14 as part of the epilogue beginning at v. 8 (or v. 9). Rather, they posit a final redactor to the book who is responsible for bringing the errant theology of Ecclesiastes into line with orthodoxy. See, for example, Siegfried, *Prediger;* McNeile, *Introduction to Ecclesiastes.* Fox refers to 12:9-12 as the epilogue and vv. 13-14 as the "postscript," where "A new voice enters, one which probably belongs to a later scribe," whose addition "undoubtedly succeeded in promoting the book's acceptance for public use, on the grounds that it 'end with the words of Torah' (b. Shab. 30b)" (*Time to Tear Down*, 359, 373-74).

12. The following points can be found in more detail in Enns, "כל-האדם."

13. For example, see Shead, "Reading Ecclesiastes 'Epilogically'"; Bartholomew, *Reading Ecclesiastes*, 237-53.

found three other times in Ecclesiastes (3:13; 5:18 [Eng. 19]; 7:2).[14] My suspicion is that the author's use of this phrase in 12:13 was meant by him to be read in light of these previous occurrences. Briefly put, in 3:13 and 5:18, the so-called carpe diem passages, Qohelet affirms that *kol-hā'ādām* ("everyone") is to find enjoyment in their daily existence. In 7:2 Qohelet observes that death is the end (סוֹף/*sôp*) of *kol-hā'ādām*. Enjoyment and death are two important, indeed, dialectical and pivotal, theological themes in Qohelet's discourse, and the phrase כִּי-זֶה כָּל-הָאָדָם/*kî-zeh kol-hā'ādām* in 12:13 should be understood as the final reflection on these themes.

The first instance of *kol-hā'ādām* is in 3:13, where Qohelet considers the value of pleasure and enjoyment.[15]

> [12]I know that there is nothing better for men to do than to be happy and to do good[16] while they live. [13]That everyone (וְגַם כָּל-הָאָדָם/*wĕgam kol-hā'ādām*) may eat and drink and find[17] satisfaction in all this toil — this is a gift from God.

The NIV translation in v. 13 ("That everyone") is fine, but perhaps a better way of translating it here, at least for the purpose of drawing out its theological connections with other passages in Ecclesiastes, is: "Moreover, *the whole*

---

14. The phrase occurs another fourteen times in thirteen verses in the OT: Gen 7:21; Exod 9:19; Num 12:3; 16:29 (bis), 32; Josh 11:14; Judg 16:17; 1 Kgs 8:38; Jer 31:30; Ezek 38:20; Zech 8:10; Ps 116:11; 2 Chr 6:29. These occurrences have no bearing on our topic. In all of these instances, the meaning is typically (and rather unambiguously) rendered "every man/everyone," "any man/anyone," "all mankind/humanity," or something similar. The syntax also presents no challenges: the phrase is found as the object of a preposition (e.g., Num 12:3; Judg 16:17; 1 Kgs 8:38), the subject of a clause (e.g., Ezek 38:20), and the object of the verb (e.g., Zech 8:10). The syntax of Eccl 3:13 and 5:18 (Eng. 19) is a bit more challenging. The phrase occurs in a verbless clause, וְגַם כָּל-הָאָדָם/*wĕgam kol-hā'ādām*, in 3:13 and גַם כָּל-הָאָדָם/*gam kol-hā'ādām* in 5:18, followed by the relative pronouns שֶׁ/*še* in 3:13 and אֲשֶׁר/*'ăšer* in 5:18. Isaksson argues, however, that *'ăšer* and *še* do not function as relative pronouns in 3:13 and 5:18 but as demonstratives marking out "the following sentence as being the subject of a nominal clause" (*Studies in the Language*, 120). His translation, however, does not differ significantly from conventional translations.

15. At various junctures in the book, Qohelet counsels his readers concerning the matter of pleasure. We meet this topic first in 2:1-11, where Qohelet determines that pleasure (שִׂמְחָה/*śimḥâ*) and amusement (שְׂחוֹק/*śĕḥôq*) are ultimately "meaningless" (הֶבֶל/*hebel*); see also 7:4.

16. The phrase לַעֲשׂוֹת טוֹב/*la'ăśôt ṭôb* does not imply moral behavior, i.e., the doing of what is right, as NIV "do good" may imply. It is better understood as doing what is "enjoyable." The same goes for the use of *ṭôb* in v. 13, which NIV translates "satisfaction."

17. The root ראה/*r'h* (NIV "find"), normally meaning "to see," means more than simply optical activity in Ecclesiastes. Qohelet often uses the verb to speak of things he has *experienced*, or, as in this case, things that one should experience. See also Schoors, "Words Typical of Qohelet," 26-33.

[duty] of man is that he should eat, . . ." When we handle this phrase here the way in which it is typically understood in 12:13, the contrast between them becomes apparent: which exactly is *kol-hā'ādām*? Is it to enjoy the simple pleasures of life as 3:13 has it, or is it to fear God and keep his commandments as in 12:13?

The contrast between the two is underscored when we consider the tone of resignation that surrounds 3:12-13. Verse 12 states, "there is nothing better than . . ." (טוֹב אֵין/'ēn ṭôb; see also 2:24; 3:22; 8:15). This section follows 3:1-9, which likewise, despite Pete Seeger's hopeful folk song ("Turn, Turn, Turn"), reflects Qohelet's resignation to the inevitability of the cycles of life.[18] In fact, Qohelet is revisiting here the theme already introduced in 1:1-11. The recurring cycles of life demonstrate that there is no יִתְרוֹן/yitrôn, no surplus or profit (NIV "gain" in v. 2),[19] and it is this fact that renders all of life *hebel*;[20] that is, all human activity is ultimately *hebel* because no human activity produces *yitrôn*. This is the lesson so clearly illustrated in 1:5-7. The sun, wind, and streams labor, but in the end they are no better off than when they started. There is no profit or surplus to their struggles. This drama of nature outlined in the introduction is, according to Qohelet, played out mercilessly on the human stage: since death levels the playing field for all, and since you cannot take it with you, it is the inevitability of death that ensures that no human activity will provide *anyone* with *any* profit or surplus (e.g., 3:19-22). This is what renders life "under the sun"[21] *hebel*.

The larger section in which 3:13 is found, 3:10-15,[22] continues this mood

---

18. Note the pessimistic evaluation of 3:1-9 given in 3:9, "What does the worker gain from his toil?" See commentary at 3:9 and Rudman, *Determinism*, 89-91.

19. Seow discusses *yitrôn* as one of several examples in Ecclesiastes that indicate that the author "presumes an audience that is deeply concerned with economic terms" ("Socioeconomic Context," 173). See also the more detailed discussion in Seow, *Ecclesiastes*, 21-36.

20. The precise meaning of *hebel* in Ecclesiastes has been a matter of much musing in modern scholarship. It is a central concept in Ecclesiastes, and so will come up again and again in the commentary. For summaries of the issue see Christianson, *Time to Tell*, 79-91; Fox, *Time to Tear Down*, 27-49. I would like to say already at this point, however, that "meaningless" can sometimes blunt the force of Qohelet's observations on life. Fox's translation of *hebel* as "absurd" seems more consistent with Qohelet's intended meaning (Fox, *Time to Tear Down*, 133).

21. I understand this recurring phrase in Ecclesiastes to refer to the "land of the living" and not in contrast to a "heavenly" perspective. The former is an expansive reading of the phrase, the latter restrictive. See commentary at 1:3 and Seow, *Ecclesiastes*, 104-5; Lohfink, *Qoheleth*, 37. For the latter position see Longman, *Ecclesiastes*, 66.

22. This section can be treated as a coherent unit because it is set off by the use of רָאִיתִי/rā'îtî, which appears in 3:10 and 3:16, and is frequently used in Ecclesiastes to introduce a new or subsequent observation, or to summarize an evaluation for an observation just made. See 1:14;

of resignation. Echoing 1:13, Qohelet remarks that God has given humanity a "task" or "occupation" (עִנְיָן/'*inyān*) to occupy them (v. 10). The specific nature of that task is not made clear, but in view of the use of the word in 1:13 ("What a heavy burden ['*inyān*] God has laid on men!") it likely cannot be viewed positively. Moreover, the tone of 3:11 is likewise relevant. God has made everything "fitting" or "appropriate" in its "time" (יָפֶה בְעִתּוֹ/*yāpeh bě'ittô*). To be sure, the use of עֵת/'*ēt* in 3:11 is to be understood in light of the recurrent use of this word in 3:1-8 (a time for this, a time for that), which is a statement of resignation (hence the translation "fitting" or "appropriate" for *yāpeh* rather than the NIV's more positively construed "beautiful").[23] Moreover, not only has God ordered the times in such a way, but he has also given to humanity the ability to ponder the fact that such order extends throughout all earthly time (3:11, הָעֹלָם/*hā'ōlām*, not "eternity"),[24] even though they cannot understand (ponder, plan, predict, control) what God does "from beginning to end." In view of such observations, Qohelet draws the conclusion that there is nothing better than the experience of enjoyment in this life (v. 12).

It is within this larger context of resignation that כָּל-הָאָדָם/*kol-hā'ādām* in v. 13 must be understood. He is not offering praise to God but is *resigning* himself to the fact that eating, drinking, and "experiencing what is good" (v. 12, לַעֲשׂוֹת טוֹב/*la'ăśôt ṭôb*) are what God gives everyone to do. It is God's "gift" (v. 13, מַתַּת/*mattat*), not a "present," wrapped in festive paper and tied in a bow, putting joy in the heart of humanity, but what God has *assigned* for humanity to do. It is for everyone *(kol-hā'ādām)* to procure mundane benefits, such as eating, drinking, and getting some simple pleasures out of life. Even though there is no "profit," these are the things that everyone can and should do the days of their existence. *These* are the activities that counter the absurdity of life "under the sun," albeit in the face of death's inexorable final blow. Finally, vv. 14-15 continue Qohelet's rather pessimistic appraisal of the human situation. What God has done, the recurring cycle of times and humanity's meager lot in life, are God's doing and cannot be changed. Things will *always* be this way (לְעוֹלָם/*lě'ôlām*).[25] They cannot be added to (יסף/*ysp*) or taken away from

---

2:13; 3:22; 4:4, 15; 5:12, 17 (Eng. 13, 18); 6:1; 7:15; 8:9, 10, 17; 9:13; 10:5, 7. The imperfect אֶרְאֶה/'*er'eh* is also used in this way (2:3; 4:1, 7). On the value of *rā'îtî* and '*er'eh* for discerning units in Ecclesiastes, however, see below, "On Dividing Ecclesiastes into Logical Units" (pp. 22-23).

23. The JPS translation puts it well: "He brings everything to pass *precisely* in its time."

24. Bartholomew, *Reading Ecclesiastes*, 243. See the note to 3:11 in the JPS translation: "He occupies man with the attempt to discover the times of *future events*."

25. This expression refers to the lengthy duration of earthly time, not to "eternity" as modern readers sometimes assume.

(גרע/*grʿ*). The purpose for which God has done it so is "so that they [humanity] will fear (ירא/*yrʾ*) him." Precisely what Qohelet means by "fear" can be debated, but it certainly seems to be bound up in the frustrating incomprehensibility of the inevitability that there is nothing new, a point aptly made in v. 15a: "What is already was, and what will be already was."[26]

The rhythm of life under the sun does not change, which is the summation of Qohelet's thoughts in 1:1-11. Amid the timing of the circumstances of life, known only by God, the summation of humanity's existence is to accept as God's gift the simple pleasures that come from one's labor. *This* is what, according to 3:13, is for "everyone" *(kol-hāʾādām)*.

As with 3:13, 5:18 (Eng. 19) is also a carpe diem passage set within a larger context.

> Moreover, everyone *(kol-hāʾādām)* to whom God gives wealth and possessions[27] he gives him the ability to partake of them, to accept his lot, and rejoice in his labors. This is a gift from God.

As with 3:10-15, 5:17-19 (Eng. 18-20) is set off by the marker רָאִיתִי/*rāʾîtî* in 5:17 and 6:1. The sentiment expressed here is very similar to that of 3:10-15, a point borne out by a number of similarities in wording. Verse 17 repeats the triad "eat, drink, experience good" of 3:13. Moreover, this activity is what Qohelet calls "fitting" *(yāpeh)*, thus echoing the notion of God's fitting activity of ordering the rhythms of life (3:11). This passage also speaks of what God has given *(mattat)* to humanity (5:18), although here it is summed up a bit differently. Whereas 3:13 speaks simply of eating, drinking, and experiencing good as *kol-hāʾādām*, in 5:18 the thought is added that God gives humanity wealth (עֹשֶׁר/*ʿōšer*), possessions (נְכָסִים/*nĕkāsîm*), and the ability (הִשְׁלִיטוֹ/*hišlîṭô*) (1) to partake of these things (לֶאֱכֹל מִמֶּנּוּ/*leʾĕkōl mimmennû*), (2) to accept one's lot (לָשֵׂאת אֶת-חֶלְקוֹ/*lāśēʾt ʾet-ḥelqô*), and (3) to rejoice in one's labor (לִשְׂמֹחַ בַּעֲמָלוֹ/*liśmōaḥ baʿămālô*).

Qohelet's admonition to his readers to content themselves with the pleasures of this life as their portion (חֵלֶק/*ḥēleq*) is his attempt to construct meaning in a world where meaning, at least for him, has collapsed. But his calls to seize the day, however sincere, are repeatedly relativized by the universal inevitability of death. It is the fact of death that renders all human activity

---

26. On this see Muntingh, "Fear of Yahweh," esp. 143-44. Muntingh cites Pfeiffer, "Gottesfurcht," 133.

27. Fox (*Time to Tear Down*, 238) and Isaksson (*Studies in the Language*, 96) make the conditional sense of this sentence explicit, i.e., "If God should give to anyone wealth and possessions, he gives them. . . ."

without profit *(yitrôn)*. There is no payoff ultimately to anything we do, since we, like the animals, will die (3:19).

The juxtaposition of death and carpe diem in Ecclesiastes creates a tension that is not resolved until the epilogue. In the meantime, 7:2 explicitly ties the theme of death to *kol-hā'ādām*.

> It is better to go to the house of mourning than to the house of feasting, because[28] that is the end of everyone (סוֹף כָּל-הָאָדָם/*sôp kol-hā'ādām*); the living should take this to heart.

Death is a dominant theme in Ecclesiastes. It is, as Shannon Burkes puts it, the "driving theme and main concern of Qohelet."[29] This is not an exaggeration, for it is the specter of death that routinely nullifies whatever positive conclusions Qohelet might draw. Although it is only in 7:2 that Qohelet laments that death is specifically *kol-hā'ādām*, the notion is implied throughout the book.[30] This focus on death is out of proportion with what is found elsewhere in the Hebrew Scriptures. As Burkes puts it, "With Qohelet . . . death makes its entrance into the Hebrew traditions as a phenomenon to be reckoned with."[31]

Burkes attempts to locate Qohelet's preoccupation with death in the context of larger paradigm shifts in the postexilic world.[32] Specifically, Burkes focuses on Egyptian biographies that share certain themes with Ecclesiastes. Both Ecclesiastes and these Egyptian biographies are part of a larger paradigm shift fueled by "permutations" in the "power structures of the ancient world . . . that were felt far and wide."[33] For the author of Ecclesiastes, who passed his days in such a time of upheaval, death "represents the chief flaw that embraces and subsumes all other problems in the world."[34]

In the exile the Israelites began to struggle to come to grips with their

---

28. Although not true for every instance, the relative אֲשֶׁר/*'ăšer* here preceded by the preposition בּ/*b* is causal (Isaksson, *Studies in the Language*, 152). See also 8:4.

29. Burkes, *Death in Qoheleth*, 1. Similarly, see Lo, "Death in Qohelet," who understands death to permeate the entire book, beginning at 1:4-8 and culminating at 12:1-7, with 1:2 and 12:8 forming the frame that supports this thematic structure.

30. The explicit references to death in Ecclesiastes are 2:14-16; 3:2, 19-21; 4:2-3; 5:15-16; 6:3-6; 7:1-2, 4, 17, 26; 8:8; 9:2-12; 11:8; 12:5-6.

31. Burkes, *Death in Qoheleth*, 75.

32. The reasons for attributing Ecclesiastes to the postexilic period will be considered below.

33. Burkes, *Death in Qoheleth*, 6. Burkes is very careful not to argue for any direct dependence.

34. Ibid., 2.

lost glory. The status of the group was uncertain, and so the question of the individual's fate began to present itself. To put it another way, whatever national hope there might have been for Israel is transferred to the individual.[35] God's perpetual covenant fidelity to a *nation* had been demonstrated (indeed, promised; see 2 Sam 7:5-16) in the form of possession of land, performance of cult, and an unbroken line of kings. Such things ceased for Israel in the early sixth century B.C. But to transfer these promises to the individual is no easy task, for how can an individual experience the perpetual covenant? The reality and finality of death call into question the applicability of God's ancient promises to the individual. Moreover, "The symbolic immortalities offered elsewhere in the Bible, the memory and endurance of a good name, survival through one's children and people, even the qualitative good life that negates the 'death' of folly and unrighteousness, fail utterly in Qohelet's opinion."[36] Death is that which, for Qohelet, ultimately renders futile humanity's "quest for meaning." All, human and animal alike (3:19-21), come to the same end. What punctuates Qohelet's theology, then, is that which is the activity of "everyone": to enjoy the pleasures that God has given (3:13 and 5:18) and then to die (7:2).

The book as a whole, however, does not let the matter rest there. A broader perspective to the tension is provided in 12:13, where *kol-hā'ādām* appears again. It seems highly unlikely to me that *kol-hā'ādām* in 12:13 can be treated in isolation from the theology espoused in the previous uses of the phrase. Further, it seems most unlikely to me that the purpose of 12:13-14 is simply to contradict Qohelet, that is, that the teachings of Qohelet, which are expressed very deliberately over the span of roughly twelve chapters, are there merely to be dismissed in the closing verses of the book. Moreover, the epilogue has a decidedly positive flavor (see commentary on those verses). Despite legitimate ambiguities in the closing section of the book, the epilogue clearly presents Qohelet as a wise teacher (12:9). There is no indication that the epilogue is to be seen in *fundamental* contrast to Qohelet's words. It seems, rather, that *kol-hā'ādām* contributes to our understanding of the epilogue as a mild corrective to the teachings of Qohelet, by accepting Qohelet's observations as wise but then going one step further.

Two points are worth noting concerning the use of *kol-hā'ādām* in 12:13. First, this phrase is emphatic: כִּי־זֶה כָּל־הָאָדָם/*kî-zeh kol-hā'ādām*. Through-

---

35. Burkes (ibid., 111) cites Fox (*Qohelet and His Contradictions*, 294) that Qohelet has "no sense of the nation or community." This may be a bit of an overstatement, however, if we think of Ecclesiastes as being written *to* an Israelite community.

36. Burkes, *Death in Qoheleth*, 111.

out Ecclesiastes, the demonstrative pronoun זֶה/זוֹ/זֹה/*zeh/zōh* is used in a number of climactic statements.[37] In fourteen instances it is used to introduce Qohelet's conclusion, "this is הֶבֶל/*hebel*": 2:15, 19, 21, 23, 26; 4:4, 8, 16; 5:9 (Eng. 10); 6:2, 9; 7:6; 8:10, 14. Similarly, it is used as a concluding statement of some sort in twelve other instances:

זֶה חָדָשׁ/*zeh ḥādāš*, "This is new," 1:10

שֶׁגַּם-זֶה הוּא רַעְיוֹן רוּחַ/*šeggam-zeh hû' ra'yôn rûaḥ*, "This, too, is a chasing after the wind," 1:17

וְזֶה-הָיָה חֶלְקִי מִכָּל-עֲמָלִי/*wĕzeh-hāyâ ḥelqî mikkol-'ămālî*, "This was my portion from all my labors," 2:10

גַּם-זֹה רָאִיתִי/*gam-zōh rā'îtî*, "This, too, I have seen," 2:24; 8:9; 9:13

וְגַם-זֹה רָעָה חוֹלָה/*wĕgam-zōh rā'â ḥôlâ*, "This, too, is a grievous evil," 5:15 (Eng. 16)

זֶה מַתַּת אֱלֹהִים הִיא/*zeh mattat 'ĕlōhîm hî'*, "This is a gift from God," 5:18 (Eng. 19)

כָּל-זֹה נִסִּיתִי בַחָכְמָה/*kol-zōh nissîtî baḥokmâ*, "All this I tested by wisdom," 7:23

זֶה מָצָאתִי/*zeh māṣā'tî*, "This I have found," 7:27, 29

זֶה רָע/*zeh rā'*, "This is evil," 9:3

When we keep in mind the rather obvious fact that 12:13-14 are themselves the concluding verses of the concluding section of Ecclesiastes, the "concluding" force of *zeh* in 12:13 seems self-evident. Further, in light of this observation, it is reasonable to suggest that *kî* should be understood emphatically (indeed, truly), yielding the following translation: "Fear God. Keep the commandments. Indeed *(kî), this (zeh)* is *kol-hā'ādām*."[38] Further, whereas גַם כָּל-הָאָדָם/*gam kol-hā'ādām* in 3:13 and 5:18 (Eng. 19) is followed by the relative particle אֲשֶׁר/שֶׁ/*'ăšer/še*, in 12:13 the phrase *concludes* the sentence, thus

---

37. Perry argues, somewhat tersely, that the demonstrative "is intended to denigrate . . . what follows" (*Dialogues with Kohelet*, 173). He cites Job 14:3 in support. It is not entirely clear to me what is meant by this comment, but I would prefer to assign to *zeh* an emphatic force.

38. The use of *kî* in Ecclesiastes is outlined in Michel, *Untersuchungen zur Eigenart*, 200-212. Unfortunately, he does not consider 12:13 in his investigation. In discussing this phrase, the comment by Gordis is commonly cited that *zeh kol-hā'ādām* is "a pregnant idiom, characteristically Hebrew, for 'this is the whole duty of man'" (*Koheleth*, 355). It is not immediately clear what Gordis means by a "pregnant idiom." Moreover, to suggest that the idiom is "characteristically Hebrew, for 'this is the whole duty of man,'" does not seem to square with the fact that this specific phrase in Eccl 12:13 is unique to the Hebrew Bible. The examples he cites (Pss 109:4; 110:3; 120:7; Isa 28:12; Job 5:25; 8:9; 29:15; Num 10:31) do not, in my opinion, clarify the matter.

adding to its emphatic force. The translation offered by Fox comes close to reading 12:13 as the final word on 3:13, 5:18, and 7:2: fearing God and keeping the commandments are "the substance, the 'material' of every person. There should be no alloy."[39] If I may put it differently, fearing God and keeping the commandments, *this* is what truly "summarizes the human experience," or as the JPS translation puts it, "For this applies to all mankind." Qohelet is correct in taking to heart the pleasures and rewards of life (3:13 and 5:18) and facing the stern reality of death (7:2). These are central components of the human drama for each Israelite, for "everyone." But more foundational and central is each Israelite's fear of God and obedience to God's law.

The conclusion to the book does not pit the frame narrator against Qohelet, but rather places Qohelet's flesh-and-blood struggles into their larger and theologically ultimate context and perspective. Qohelet was indeed wise in his observations (12:9-11), but the frame narrator encourages his readers to view their daily struggles, which are a legitimate and expected element of life, from a broader perspective. To refer back to Burkes's historical observations, 12:13-14 is an attempt to answer the crisis of Israel's exile and the resulting paradigm shift. But the epilogue does not answer this crisis by encouraging the readers to continue the debate. Indeed, 12:12-13 cuts off debate entirely. And here we may find an indication of why the author adopts a royal persona. A king — no less one presented as "Solomon" — is the paragon of wisdom, and has at his disposal the necessary resources and time to investigate the meaning of life under the sun (see esp. 2:1-11). His readers do not. Qohelet's investigation takes him to dark places where his readers cannot, and need not, tread. It is up to the reader, therefore, to heed the frame narrator's words, that (1) Qohelet is wise (12:9-11), (2) nothing can be added to his words (12:12-13a), (3) the proper response is never to dismiss Qohelet's words or revel in them but to move beyond them by acknowledging one's duty to fear God and keep the commandments (12:13b), and trust that God is still about the business of setting all things aright (12:14).

Despite the reality of the struggles so eloquently outlined by Qohelet, the answer is still as it always was. Qohelet was indeed wise in his observations of the inconsistencies, even contradictions, of life, as the epilogue points out. But there is something more, and the "more" is not a new twist, but the tried and true formula of "fear and obedience," what was central to Israel's tradition. Such a solution to the newer problems that beset postexilic Israelites serves as an appeal to Israel to see their historical vicissitudes from the point of view of traditional categories, thus encouraging a sense of continuity

39. Fox, *Time to Tear Down*, 362.

between Israel's past and present, despite the circumstances. The emphatic phrase in 12:13 is intended to direct the reader's attention toward a higher goal that sums up Israel's quest for meaning. To paraphrase 12:13:

> Qohelet is wise, to be sure. As he says, pleasure and death are real and are the portion of everyone *(kol-hā'ādām)*. But there is a deeper, more fundamental obligation upon this earth, which is to fear God and keep his commandments. *This* is *truly* everyone's portion *(kî-zeh kol-hā'ādām)*.

The disjunction with other portions of the OT as well as internal tensions assures that Ecclesiastes will continue to challenge interpreters. The book's macrostructure provides a context within which these tensions are respected rather than hastily adjusted. In the closing verses of the epilogue, the author resolves the tensions of the book, not by dismissing Qohelet's observations, but by acknowledging the wisdom they contain and then bringing them under the broader (more traditional) umbrella of fearing God and keeping his commandments. The force of this resolution will not be fully appreciated apart from the necessary and challenging work of reading Ecclesiastes patiently and allowing the author to present the case in his time and in his way. But as I see it, the friction created by Qohelet's unorthodox speculations and the frame narrator's declaration of Qohelet's wisdom is the daring yet also comforting theological message the author wishes to communicate, and which has interesting implications for biblical theology and contemporary application, as we shall explore later.

Date and Authorship

As we have seen above, at the very beginning of the book the frame narrator ascribes the words to follow as those of "Qohelet," which raises two questions: Who is Qohelet? What is the relationship between him and the frame narrator? How one answers these questions will directly affect how one handles the book.

The meaning and identity of Qohelet have eluded biblical interpreters for centuries and will continue to do so for the foreseeable future. The word is from the Hebrew root קהל/*qhl*. The verb means "to assemble or summon," and the noun (קָהָל/*qāhāl*) denotes an "assembly or convocation." Qohelet (קְהֶלֶת *qōhelet*) is a Qal feminine participle, and may denote a speaker in an assembly. The Septuagint title reflects this understanding *(ekklēsiastēs),* "assembly" or "church," and the Vulgate *(Liber Ecclesiastes)* and English titles follow suit. Such translations as "Preacher" (Martin Luther, *Prediger*) or "Teacher" (NIV) further reflect such an understanding of "Qohelet." Such attributions, however, are highly interpretive and cannot claim clear — or even likely — support from the Hebrew. That the word neither occurs outside Ecclesiastes nor is defined in Ecclesiastes renders any translation inconclusive. It is best to leave it untranslated, treating it as an alias, rather than assigning to it a conjectural etymology.

One thing seems certain, however: Qohelet is not someone's name. The person in question is referred to as "king over Israel in Jerusalem" (1:12; see also 1:16; 2:7, 9). No king is known by that name, so we can safely assume that it is a pseudonym. This does not mean, however — and it is important to bear this in mind — that the author wishes to deceive his readers. It simply means that the main character of the book is referred to as Qohelet, for reasons that still elude interpreters to this day.[40] The more pressing question is whether this person referred to as Qohelet was indeed an actual king of Israel, or whether the references to his kingship are likewise, for whatever reason, part of the author's literary construction. For many this is the crux of the matter. To disguise the identity of the king by naming him Qohelet is one thing, but to refer to him as "son of David, king in Jerusalem" (1:1), when he was neither is problematic for some interpreters, although it need not be, since there is no reason to assume that adopting a literary persona is an act of deception.

It is my opinion that Qohelet is a character created by the author to make his theological point,[41] that is, a nickname adopted by the writer to maintain a Solomonic connection for his character while also distancing his character from the actual person.[42] Conversely, the name "Qohelet" is not intended to be a veiled reference to an actual Israelite king, designed either to keep his identity secret or to communicate some cryptic quality. Indeed, the traditional reference to Solomon specifically would be quite odd, given what we see in 1:16, "Look, I have grown and increased in wisdom *more than anyone who has ruled over Jerusalem before me.*" Only one king, David, was before Solomon ruling in Jerusalem. One could argue that this reference to many kings ruling in Jerusalem should not be restricted to *Israelite* kings but could apply to other occupants (e.g., Melchizedek [Gen 14:18], Adoni-zedek [Josh 10:1]), but such an argument has the air of desperation about it.

One could adduce, however, 1 Chr 29:25, in support of 1:16 being compatible with Solomonic authorship: "The LORD highly exalted Solomon in

---

40. See Provan, *Ecclesiastes*, 26-31.
41. Fox, *Time to Tear Down*, 372-73.
42. See Longman, *Ecclesiastes*, 4.

the sight of all Israel and bestowed on him royal splendor *such as no king over Israel ever had before.*" This phrase is similar to what we see in Eccl 1:16. (The designation "in Jerusalem" is missing, which would now allow the inclusion of Saul along with David.) Since the reference here in Chronicles is clearly to Solomon, it lends a certain weight to reading Eccl 1:16 as likewise referring to Solomon. But the relevance of 1 Chr 29:25 for supporting the Solomonic identity of Eccl 1:16 is more superficial than substantive. One must explore the ideological and theological themes in Chronicles in order to determine how such a designation would have functioned *in Chronicles.*[43] It is not a question, therefore, of refusing to take the Chronicler's words at "face value." It is a question of how this verse functions in the Chronicler's overall purpose, which *is* to take 1 Chr 29:25 at "face value."

As with Ecclesiastes, a reference to ancient non-Israelite kings is out of place for the Chronicler's ideology. This is even more the case since one of the central theological foci of Chronicles is *all Israel.* An isolated (and somewhat cryptic) reference to non-Israelite kings seems a bit of a stretch. The author's purpose for designating Solomon in this way is not so much an exercise in reviewing objectively the history of Solomon, but of reviewing Solomon's reign for the benefit of the author's postexilic community. The reference to Solomon in 1 Chr 29:25 is meant to evoke in the *postexilic* community a sense of Israel's strong *and ancient* royal tradition that they *now* are summoned to recapture. In other words, the past is recast in terms of present concerns.[44]

The Chronicler is using the ancient image of Solomon to get across his contemporary theological point that Israel's reconstructed monarchy, their return to Solomonic glory (however inchoate it might be at the time), will likewise be exalted "in the sight of all Israel" like none before. First Chronicles 29:25 is part of the Chronicler's theology of Israel's return to its glorious past. Indeed, in view of 1 Chr 29:25, one could just as well, and perhaps more easily, argue precisely the opposite of what a more "plain" reading of Eccl 1:16 suggests. This verse is not a proof text for Solomonic authorship, but an indication that Ecclesiastes likewise participates in a postexilic theological program similar to what we see in Chronicles.[45] Ecclesiastes, too, is a book that appeals to Israel's ancient past (12:13, fear God, keep the commandments) in order to address contemporary concerns (the challenges the exile poses to maintain-

---

43. Overviews of the ideology of the author of Chronicles can be found in Japhet, *Ideology,* and more briefly in her *I and II Chronicles,* 43-49.

44. Recasting the past to speak to present concerns is a recurring concern among Second Temple biblical interpreters, of which the Chronicler is one. See Kugel and Greer, *Early Biblical Interpretation,* 12-102, esp. 34-39.

45. On the issue of dating see below.

ing faith). In other words, reading Eccl 1:16 in light of 1 Chr 29:25 fits well with the final words of the book in 12:13, as seen above.

At least as early as the rabbinic commentary *Qohelet Rabbah* (composed sometime after the fifth century A.D.), appeal was made to 1 Kgs 8:1 and 22 in support of Solomonic authorship, where the verbal and nominal forms (respectively) of קהל/*qhl* are used in reference to Solomon's "assembling" of the leaders of Jerusalem. Hence it was thought that "Qohelet" is a cryptic allusion to this episode in Solomon's life, thus *identifying* Qohelet with Solomon. Such a midrashic solution attests to the mystery surrounding the name, but there is no reason to assume that this oblique allusion — if that is indeed what it is — is intended to identify Qohelet as Solomon any more than it could be intended simply to anchor the Solomonic *persona*. In other words, it may be that the intention of this alleged allusion is to get the perceptive reader to "think Solomon when you read this."[46]

Or it is perfectly conceivable that the allusion is not the result of the author's own literary creativity intended only for the most perceptive readers; it may have already become an accepted designation for Solomon by the time Ecclesiastes was written — although we should readily admit that this is highly conjectural and ultimately has no exegetical payoff. Similarly one could argue that the words of the book are Solomon's, and that the words have been recast in the postexilic period, by which time "Qohelet" had already — for whatever reason — become an accepted nickname for ancient Solomon, and so the author has Solomon referring to himself as such. But at some point an unbiased reader has to appeal to Occam's razor. Such layered and hypothetical explanations have the ring of desperation, and sooner or later weaken the point of the argument itself: Solomonic *authorship*.

Ecclesiastes does not claim to be authored by Solomon, and the non-Solomonic authorship of Ecclesiastes is the least problematic position in view of the points made above.[47] In addition, two other general sets of arguments are typically adduced to support a non-Solomonic and postexilic authorship of Ecclesiastes. The first concerns the book's attitude toward kingship. It has

---

46. Reasons why this is an important reading strategy will be discussed further in the commentary beginning at 1:12.

47. Provan's observation is most pertinent here: "It is one of the great ironies of modern biblical scholarship (of whatever theological and confessional complexion) that what the originators of Old Testament tradition have thus themselves pronounced unimportant about the text, its modern readers have pronounced crucial for its understanding, expending enormous and futile effort in an attempt to trace the erased footsteps across the sands of time and exhume their alleged owners' corpses from their self-sealed tombs" (*Ecclesiastes*, 30). Provan is content to date Ecclesiastes to the postexilic period generally (26).

long been pointed out that the royal persona seems to recede into the background quite quickly.[48] We read of kingly activities in 1:12–2:16, but by the time we get to chapter 3 the theme of Qohelet's royal explorations is forgotten.[49] In 4:13-16 the author seems aloof toward kingship. By the time we get to 5:8 he is critical. In 8:2-4 and 10:20 we see a not-too-veiled reference to the king being a threat. It is in my view generally sound reasoning to conclude that a king would not commit such an idea to writing. The kingly persona, however, serves another function, to which we will return later.

The second argument concerns specifically the style of Hebrew in Ecclesiastes. The language and style of Ecclesiastes have instigated considerable debate among linguists, although it is fair to say that a postexilic date, based on linguistic factors, is the most common position, and it is held by scholars across the ideological spectrum. Franz Delitzsch is often cited in this regard: "If the Book of Koheleth were of old Solomonic origin, then there is no history of the Hebrew language."[50] The point expressed is that the language of Ecclesiastes is, by all standards of our knowledge of the historical development of Hebrew, unambiguously of later origin. Likewise, the nineteenth-century Princeton OT scholar William Henry Green, of no mean conservative pedigree, although ambivalent about the matter for some time, conceded later in his career that the language of Ecclesiastes "stands alone in the Bible," and then (reluctantly) concurred with Delitzsch: "After all that has been said, however, we do not see how the argument from the language can be met. We conclude, therefore, that it is decisive. . . . It is alleged, and the fact seems to be, that the Hebrew of this book is so Aramean [i.e., Aramaic] that it must belong to a period later than Solomon."[51] Indeed, the similarities between the Hebrew of Ecclesiastes and Aramaic, which did not begin to exert an international influence until about the seventh century B.C., had led scholars at one time to suppose an Aramaic original to Ecclesiastes, which was then translated into Hebrew.[52] Although this theory has not gained wide scholarly assent, it illustrates perhaps the depth of the problem.

48. Longman, *Ecclesiastes*, 4-8. For a different view see Shields, "Qohelet," 635-40.

49. Fox, *Ecclesiastes*, x. For a contrary view see the full discussion in Christianson, *Time to Tell*, 128-47.

50. Delitzsch, *Song of Songs and Ecclesiastes*, 190.

51. Green, *Old Testament Literature*, 56.

52. A fair amount of debate surrounded this topic in the early part of the twentieth century. For example, see Burkitt, "Is Ecclesiastes a Translation?"; Zimmermann, "Aramaic Provenance of Qohelet"; Gordis, "Original Language of Qohelet"; Torrey, "Question of Original Language." Burkitt, Zimmermann, and Torrey defend an Aramaic original while Gordis argues against it.

A number of linguistic indicators in Ecclesiastes suggest a postexilic date.[53] (1) The increased use of vowel letters in Ecclesiastes is more consistent with exilic and postexilic developments as seen in their dramatic increase by the time of the Dead Sea Scrolls. (2) The Persian words *pardēs* (garden, 2:5) and *pitgām* (sentence, 8:11) suggest a time when the Persian language influenced Hebrew. Although this does not necessarily indicate a postexilic setting, Persian loanwords occur elsewhere in the Bible only in books of demonstrably postexilic date (e.g., Chronicles, Ezra, Nehemiah, Esther, Daniel). (3) As mentioned above, there is significant Aramaic influence on Ecclesiastes. As with the Persian words, Aramaic influence in isolation does not necessarily prove a late date, but the sheer frequency of these terms suggests more than just bare international "influence"; it suggests a historical *setting* for the book. (4) Certain grammatical elements are more consistent with an exilic or postexilic date, such as frequency of the relative pronoun שֶׁ/*še-;* exclusive use of the first person pronoun אֲנִי/*ʾănî* instead of אָנֹכִי/*ʾānōkî;* expanded use of אֶת/אֵת/*ʾēt/ʾet-* beyond that of direct object marker; the feminine demonstrative זֹה/*zōh*, rather than זֹאת/*zōʾt;* use of third person masculine pronominal suffix for feminine plural antecedents; negation formed by אֵין/*ʾēn* plus the infinitive in 3:14 instead of לֹא/*lōʾ* plus the imperfect. (5) C. L. Seow also notes that the abundance of economic terms (e.g., money, riches, profit, account, salary, success; see commentary throughout) bespeaks a postexilic monetary and commercial economy, since the minting of coins (daric) only began under Darius I in 515 B.C.[54]

Although a postexilic date for Ecclesiastes is the consensus position, this is not to say that arguments to the contrary have not been adduced.[55] Perhaps one of the more respected, and often cited (by both supporters and detractors), positions is that offered by Daniel C. Fredericks.[56] His main observation is that the linguistic evidence places Ecclesiastes no later than the exilic period and possibly preexilic. A general preexilic date, however, still leaves us

53. A clear and concise discussion of the following indicators may be found in Seow, *Ecclesiastes*, 11-21. Seow dates Ecclesiastes to the Persian period (fifth century B.C.). See also Seow, "Linguistic Evidence."

54. Seow, *Ecclesiastes*, 21-36. Rudman does not see the economic terms being restricted to the Persian period, and so argues for a Hellenistic date (*Determinism*, 15-16). Likewise, Pixley is convinced of Ecclesiastes being composed during the Ptolemaic period ("Qoheleth"), as is Crenshaw (*Ecclesiastes*, 49-50). Prior suggests, "Ecclesiastes mirrors the general ethos and culture of middle and upper class circles who cultivated a pragmatic, intellectual culture. Ecclesiastes was written about and for merchants, small-holders, homesteaders, fellow bureaucrats, rulers, elders, prophets, priests, legislators" ("When All the Singing Has Stopped").

55. For a judicious appreciation of these arguments, see Longman, *Ecclesiastes*, 11-15.

56. Fredericks, *Qoheleth's Language*. See also Young, ed., *Biblical Hebrew*.

very far from a demonstration of Solomonic authorship (which is not Fredericks's aim), or even a date roughly compatible with Solomon's time. Although Fredericks's arguments have not achieved a consensus,[57] they should still be allowed to stand or fall on their own merits. If anything, Fredericks provides a possible balance to those who require a second- or even first-century B.C. date, bearing the marks of Mishnaic Hebrew.[58] Debates will certainly continue concerning a more precise dating of Ecclesiastes, but it is not likely that arguments for authorship in Solomon's time will be able to gain academic support. Any arguments for an early date would only gain acceptance if the linguistic arguments were first met. Until such time, the positions expressed above by Delitzsch and Green can be considered a base for subsequent discussion.

On Dividing Ecclesiastes into Logical Units

One of the genuine difficulties with interpreting Ecclesiastes is dividing the book into "logical" sections.[59] This is a particularly acute problem when one considers a preacher's or teacher's need to focus on a bite-sized segment for a sermon or lesson. As noted above, there is a significant amount of interweaving and revisiting of themes. Sometimes they seem to come almost out of nowhere: Qohelet seems to be on one topic, then he takes a dramatic shift to another, only to return a few verses later to the previous topic. This phenomenon proves challenging for any interpreter. The author of Ecclesiastes does not seem overly concerned to accommodate our penchant for thinking that all meaningful communication must adhere to certain strictures.

A number of what appear to be larger structural syntactic markers in the book look promising. For example, the verb רָאָה/r'h (to see), mentioned earlier, often seems to introduce a new section, especially in the perfect (רָאִיתִי/rā'îtî, "I saw/observed"), but this holds more consistently for the earlier sections of the book (e.g., 1:14; 2:13; 3:10, 16). Conversely, הֶבֶל/hebel seems to function as some sort of concluding comment/evaluation at a number of important junctures (e.g., 1:14; 2:1, 11, 15, 17, 19, 21, 23, 26), but this use of *hebel* is concentrated in the first two chapters, lessens in frequency in chapters 3–8, and then disappears altogether until the epilogue. Of these two, the former is

---

57. For example, see Schoors, *Preacher Sought*, 221-24.

58. See the argument by Whitley (*Koheleth*, esp. 119-48) and the contrary argument by Isaksson (*Studies in the Language*, e.g., 193-97).

59. A very helpful overview of different attempts may be found in Murphy, *Ecclesiastes*, xxxv-xxxix.

the more promising, but applying this criterion rigidly would quickly devolve into artificiality.

The simplest logical structure for Ecclesiastes may also be the least useful pedagogically: prologue (1:1-11), words of Qohelet (1:12–12:7), epilogue (12:8-12). The challenging question, of course, concerns the middle section. James Crenshaw divides the middle into no less than twenty sections, some as short as two verses (9:11-12), others spanning across two chapters (1:12–2:26).[60] No attempt is made, however, to bring these smaller units under various larger headings as almost every other commentator does (see below). Crenshaw's scheme leaves one with the impression that the sections are not tied together in some purposeful sequence. There is certainly interpenetration throughout the book (themes and concepts are regularly revisited), but Crenshaw seems content to let the units stand more or less on their own, dividing them simply according to where the treatment of a particular concept seems to begin and end, regardless of their relative length. Still, there is a certain wisdom in this straightforward approach, as it resists artificiality and oversimplification.

Other approaches are a bit more intentional in organizing the content of Qohelet's discourse. For example, Tremper Longman groups thirty-eight sections of 1:12–12:7 into four main sections: Autobiographical Introduction (1:12); "Solomon's" Quest for the Meaning of Life (1:13–2:26); The Quest Continues (3:1–6:9); Qohelet's Wise Advice (6:10–12:7).[61] These divisions meaningfully suggest a flow to Qohelet's discourse, although placing a major division between 2:26 and 3:1 may not be convincing to all. Seow's organization is perhaps the most creative.[62] Building on the work of F. J. Backhaus,[63] Seow divides Ecclesiastes into four main blocks of alternating emphases, the first of which begins at 1:2: Reflection (1:2–4:16), followed by Ethics (5:1–6:9; English versification); then Reflection (6:10–8:17), followed by Ethics again (9:1–12:8).[64] Each main section is divided into between two and four subsections.

60. Crenshaw, *Ecclesiastes*, 5-6. Crenshaw's thorough analysis is on pp. 34-49, where he discusses various schemes and patterns. Likewise, Krüger has twenty-six separate sections, including 1:1, 1:2, and 12:8, which he treats individually *(Qoheleth)*. Krüger, however, collates these smaller sections under five larger headings: 1:3–4:12, The King and the Wise Man; 4:13–5:8 (Eng. 5:9), The King and the Deity; 5:9 (Eng. 10)–6:9, Poverty and Wealth; 6:10–8:17, Critical Discussion of Conventional Wisdom; 9:1–12:7, Life in View of Chance and Transitoriness.

61. Longman, *Ecclesiastes*, viii-ix. Fox's scheme is similar in its simplicity: 1:1-18, Introduction; 2:1–4:16, Reflections and Meditations; 4:17–11:6, Counsels and Teachings; 11:7–12:8, Conclusion; 12:9-14, Epilogue.

62. Seow, *Ecclesiastes*, 46-47.

63. Backhaus, *Denn Zeit*.

64. Lohfink has a similar but more elaborate structure. He recognizes the following ma-

There are a pleasing simplicity and rhythm to this arrangement, but, as with all such attempts, much of the material seems to resist such classification (as Seow himself hints).

Any attempt to divide Ecclesiastes should be done in an effort to elucidate the book's contents for modern readers. I continue to have the nagging suspicion, however, that such divisions are often an imposition that the book resists at every turn.[65] An approach such as Crenshaw's seems to offer the least problems so long as we do not allow these sections to stand in isolation from one another. In other words, if by dividing Ecclesiastes into sections we give the impression that these units are anything other than vitally interconnected with one another, we will miss the "structure" that the author himself seems intent to communicate.

As with all other commentators, my own divisions of the book reflect my attempt to allow the units to arise as naturally as I can, taking into account indicators of segmentation as they arise, be they lexical, grammatical, thematic, or any combination of these (which is typically the case). More simply put, I begin and end each section where I think Qohelet has more or less completed a train of thought, although I am always eager to remember the regular interweaving of concepts throughout the book as a whole, a style that seems to represent the author's own literary architecture. Even so, the artificiality of any organizational scheme will occasionally surface precisely due to the echoes in the book. Each larger section can certainly be thought of as containing several smaller units; but, for reasons to be discussed at the appropriate junctures, I feel that thinking in terms of the larger sections is justified because of the near proximity of recurring words and/or themes. (One comes to what one thinks, on the basis of certain markers that elsewhere in the book have proved helpful, is clearly the end of a section, only to see that a key word or concept is picked up again two verses later.) Still, remaining as sensitive as one can to such structural markers is the best way I can see to keep from forc-

---

jor divisions, with numerous subsections: 1:1-3, Title and Prologue; 1:4-11, Cosmology; 1:12–3:15, Anthropology; 3:16–4:16, Social Critique I; 4:17–5:6 (Eng. 5:1-7), Religious Critique; 5:7 (Eng. 5:8)–6:10, Social Critique II; 6:11–9:6, Deconstruction; 9:7–12:8, Ethic; 12:9-14, Epilogue.

65. For other attempts at outlining the logical structure of the book, see de Jong, "Book on Labour." He provides some interesting insights, but they still amount to a more general observation of Qohelet's repetitions, more or less, and not an explanation of the actual structure of the book. Also, although I certainly agree that human labor is an important theme of the book, I do not think it is the central theme. Rather, it is a subtheme, a state of affairs that leads readers to other conclusions, namely, the futility of all of life and God's role in making it so. Another organizational strategy is argued by J. S. Reitman, who thinks that attention to Qohelet's structuring principles can help alleviate the problems of apparent contradiction and nihilism ("Structure and Unity of Ecclesiastes"). While he makes some helpful insights along the way, I am not persuaded by Reitman's case.

ing the issue of "organization." But again, what is far more important than dissecting the book into sections is allowing the portions of Ecclesiastes to echo throughout as loudly as possible. This makes grasping the whole a complicated endeavor, but it is well worth the energy expended. Hence, wherever warranted, I will indicate such echoes and connections between the units.

Some Recurring and Important Lexemes for the Theology of Ecclesiastes

The major theological themes of Ecclesiastes will be treated elsewhere in this commentary. A related matter is the author's use of recurring lexemes that help move these theological themes forward. These words are particularly helpful in moving us toward an understanding of the whole, as they alert us to important themes and concepts in the book. The further significance of these words will be illustrated at the relevant points in the commentary. I should like to make clear, however, that the list below should not be misunderstood as perpetuating some distinction between words and concepts.[66] Quite the opposite. The importance of these words is in how they are *used* in Ecclesiastes to *point* to concepts. In preparation both for the exegetical portion of the commentary to follow and the subsequent section on theology, it is profitable to list here these key words in Ecclesiastes.

> אֱלֹהִים/*'ĕlōhîm* (God — 1:13; 2:24, 26; 3:10, 11, 13, 14, 15, 17, 18; 4:17 [Eng. 5:1]; 5:1, 3, 5, 6, 17, 18, 19 [Eng. 2, 4, 6, 7, 18, 19, 20]; 6:2; 7:13, 14, 18, 26, 29; 8:2, 12, 13, 15, 17; 9:1, 7; 11:5, 9; 12:7, 13, 14)
>
> בקשׁ/*bqš* (seek — 3:6, 15; 7:25, 28, 29; 8:17; 12:10)
>
> הֶבֶל/*hebel* (meaningless, absurd — 1:14; 2:1, 11, 15, 17, 19, 21, 23, 26; 3:19; 4:4, 7, 8, 16; 5:6, 9 [Eng. 7, 10]; 6:2, 4, 9; 7:6; 8:10, 14; 9:9; 11:8, 10; 12:8)
>
> הָלַךְ/*hālak* (walk, go; sometimes a metaphor for death — 1:4, 6, 7; 2:1, 14; 3:20; 4:15, 17; 5:14, 15; 6:4, 6, 8, 9; 7:2; 8:3, 10; 9:7, 10; 10:3, 7, 15, 20; 11:9; 12:5)
>
> חָכְמָה/*hokmâ* (wisdom — 1:13, 16, 17, 18; 2:3, 9, 12, 13, 14, 15, 16, 19, 21, 26; 4:13; 6:8; 7:4, 5, 7, 10, 11, 12, 16, 19, 23, 25; 8:1, 5, 16, 17; 9:1, 10, 11, 13, 15, 16, 17, 18; 10:1, 2, 10, 12; 12:9, 11)
>
> חֵלֶק/*hēleq* (portion — 2:10, 21; 3:22; 5:17, 18 [Eng. 18, 19]; 9:6, 9; 11:2)
>
> חֵפֶץ/*hēpeṣ* (pleasure/delight; matter — 3:1, 17; 5:3, 7 [Eng. 4, 8]; 8:3, 6; 12:1, 10)

---

66. Silva, *Biblical Words and Their Meaning*, esp. 17-32.

טוֹב/*ṭôb* (good — 2:1, 3, 24, 26; 3:12, 13, 22; 4:3, 6, 8, 9, 13; 5:4, 10, 17 [Eng. 5, 11, 18]; 6:3, 6, 9, 12; 7:1, 2, 3, 5, 8, 10, 11, 14, 18, 20, 26; 8:12, 13, 15; 9:2, 4, 7, 16, 18; 11:6, 7; 12:14)

ידע/*yd'* (know, knowledge — 1:17; 2:14, 19; 3:12, 14, 21; 4:13, 17 [Eng. 5:1]; 6:5, 8, 10, 12; 7:22, 25; 8:1, 5, 7, 12, 16, 17; 9:1, 5, 11, 12; 10:14, 15; 11:2, 5, 6, 9)

יוֹתֵר/יִתְרוֹן/*yitrôn/yôtēr* (profit, excess — 1:3; 2:11, 13, 15; 3:9; 5:8, 15 [Eng. 9, 16]; 6:8, 11; 7:11, 12, 16; 10:10, 11; 12:9, 12)

כֹּל/*kōl* (all — 1:2, 3, 7, 8, 9, 13, 14, 16; 2:5, 7, 9, 10, 11, 14, 16, 17, 18, 19, 20, 22, 23; 3:1, 11, 13, 14, 17, 19, 20; 4:1, 4, 8, 15, 16; 5:8, 15, 16, 17, 18 [Eng. 9, 16, 17, 18, 19]; 6:2, 6, 7; 7:2, 15, 18, 21, 23, 28; 8:3, 6, 9, 17; 9:1, 2, 3, 4, 6, 8, 9, 10, 11; 10:3, 19; 11:5, 8, 9; 12:4, 8, 13, 14)

כְּסִיל/*kěsîl* (fool — 2:14, 15, 16; 4:5, 13, 17 [Eng. 5:1]; 5:2, 3 [Eng. 3, 4]; 6:8; 7:4, 5, 6, 9; 9:17; 10:2, 12)

לֵב/*lēb* (heart, intensive referent to one's "inner" self — 1:13, 16, 17; 2:1, 3, 10, 15, 20, 22, 23; 3:11, 17, 18; 5:1, 19 [Eng. 2, 20]; 7:2, 3, 4, 7, 21, 22, 25, 26; 8:5, 9, 11, 16; 9:1, 3, 7; 10:2, 3; 11:9, 10)

מִשְׁפָּט/*mišpāṭ* (judgment — 3:16; 5:7 [Eng. 8]; 8:5, 6; 11:9; 12:14)

סְכְלוּת/*siklût* (fool — [שִׂכְלוּת/*śiklût* in 1:17]; 2:3, 12, 13; 7:25; 10:1, 13)

עוֹלָם/*'ôlām* (great expanse of time — 1:4, 10; 2:16; 3:11, 14; 9:6; 12:5)

עמל/*'ml* (labor — 1:3; 2:10, 11, 18, 19, 20, 21, 22, 24; 3:9, 13; 4:4, 6, 8, 9; 5:14, 15, 17, 18 [Eng. 15, 16, 18, 19]; 6:7; 8:15, 17; 9:9; 10:15)

עֵת/*'ēt* (time — 29 times in 3:1-8; 3:11, 17; 7:17; 8:5, 6, 9; 9:8, 11, 12; 10:17)

צדק/*ṣdq* (righteous — 3:17; 7:15, 16, 20; 8:14; 9:1, 2)

קרה/*qrh* (fate — 2:14, 15; 3:19; 9:2, 3, 11; 10:18)

ראה/*r'h* (see, observe, experience — 1:8, 10, 14, 16; 2:1, 3, 12, 13, 24; 3:10, 13, 16, 18, 22; 4:1, 3, 4, 7, 15; 5:7, 12, 17 [Eng. 8, 13, 18]; 6:1, 5, 6; 7:11, 13, 14, 15, 27, 29; 8:9, 10, 16, 17; 9:9, 11, 13; 10:5, 7; 11:4, 7; 12:3)

רעה/רע/*r'/r'h* (evil, unjust; see רשע/*rš'* below — 1:13; 2:17; 4:8, 17 [Eng. 5:1]; 5:12, 13, 15 [Eng. 13, 14, 16]; 6:1, 2; 7:14; 8:3, 5, 11, 12; 9:3, 12; 10:5, 13; 11:2, 10; 12:14)

רשע/*rš'* (evil, unjust; see רעה/רע/*r'/r'h* above — 3:16, 17; 7:15, 17, 25; 8:8, 10, 13, 14; 9:2)

שמח/*śmḥ* (joy — 2:1, 2, 10, 26; 3:12, 22; 4:16; 5:18, 19 [Eng. 19, 20]; 7:4; 8:15; 9:7; 10:19; 11:8, 9)

תַּחַת הַשָּׁמֶשׁ/*taḥat haššāmeš* (under the sun — 1:9, 14; 2:11, 17, 18, 19, 20, 22; 3:16; 4:1, 3, 7, 15; 5:12 [Eng. 13]; 6:1, 12; 8:9, 15, 17; 9:3, 6, 9, 11, 13; 10:5)

Bearing these words in mind — even looking for them — will alert the reader to the interconnectedness of Qohelet's major themes and concepts. And observing such interconnections will force the reader to allow Qohelet himself to set the agenda for how he wishes to be understood.

Reading Ecclesiastes Christianly

The entire introduction to this point has assumed what can now be stated plainly: proper interpretation of any biblical book must commence by paying close attention to the words in front of us understood in their historical context, at least as best as it can be determined. At times one can discern a particular or general historical setting in which the book was written. In the case of Ecclesiastes, mainly because of linguistic factors, a postexilic context is presumed — although it is hardly fair to expect such a general affirmation to have significant exegetical payoff at every turn. Nevertheless, assuming a postexilic context will, I hope to show at relevant points, yield some very profitable readings. And where no specific historical setting can be clearly affirmed, one is still bound to handle the book in such a way that each part interacts with the whole, so as to come away satisfied that one has grappled with the contents of the book, not simply privileged certain favorite passages to the exclusion of others.

But we do not read Scripture simply for the sake of reading. We read Scripture as members of Christ's church, as a book for Christ's church. We are asking questions of significance, the nexus between "what it meant" and "what it means," or, if you will, the overused word "application." How one gets from then to now has in my experience proved to be a complex interpenetration of factors both obvious and subtle.[67] But to speak of the significance of a biblical book is to say that the setting of the interpreter (whether individual or community, however defined) presents itself as an influential factor in interpretation.

The Bible does not have contemporary "significance" for anyone apart from a conceptual framework within which one makes sense of anything.[68] This certainly entails one's individual time and place in world history. For Christians, however, that conceptual framework is centered first and foremost not on our particular or personal life settings, but on the gospel, on what God has done for his people and the world in and through the person

67. I explore some of these issues, albeit briefly, in "Apostolic Hermeneutics," esp. 279-87.

68. See, e.g., the comment by McCartney: "When a person within a certain social context, who shares with the culture a certain way of thinking about reality, comes to a text, he or she understands that text in categories drawn from an already-extant understanding of everything" ("New Testament's Use," 104).

and work of Christ. I am not attempting to mount an argument here for a so-called Christological or Christocentric reading of Ecclesiastes. I have no real objection to these terms, other than they have sometimes come to represent an approach to Christian hermeneutics that can hold a book like Ecclesiastes at a safe distance rather than engage it. For the gospel to form our grid for understanding Ecclesiastes is not a call to "see Christ" in every verse, or even every passage of the book. This is not what it means to see Christ as the "center" of Ecclesiastes. Rather, the gospel forms our basic hermeneutical posture, that point of view from which we read and to which the meaning of Ecclesiastes will be applied. It is to acknowledge that the very questions we raise, the very way in which we interact with Ecclesiastes, is profoundly shaped by our having been raised and united with the crucified and risen Christ. It is, in my view, precisely a failure to recognize this vital hermeneutical posture that has fostered the notion that a faithful, Christian reading of Ecclesiastes is demonstrated by deriving some immediate moral lesson from the book — an approach that can drive one to ignore, brush aside, or actually mishandle portions of the book. Our outlook must rather be shaped by the knowledge that, on the one hand, Ecclesiastes has something to say, and on the other hand, how we hear it will be shaped in a most fundamental way by our living in the privileged setting of the post-resurrection cosmos.

All this is to say that any Christian interpreter of any OT book, including Ecclesiastes, must purposefully endeavor to allow the two horizons of then and now to be in conversation with each other. And they must be in *conversation*. I do not think that the cross and resurrection mean that the challenging peaks and valleys of Ecclesiastes can now be made level. But it is still a conversation that embraces the powerful and liberating realization that we are living in the age of the inaugurated eschaton. It is from this final, climactic stage in the drama of redemption that we now look back and say, "Now that we know where Israel's story ends up, what difference does that knowledge make in how we understand previous stages in the story?" In other words, the "now" with which the "then" must be in conversation is not primarily the private now of my personal experiences (although the personal dimension is certainly in play), but the eschatological now of the new age (2 Cor 6:2) that dawned when Christ, the climax of God's covenant with Israel, was crucified and raised from the dead. Only after this eschatological posture is allowed to exert its proper force do we as Christians bring Ecclesiastes to bear on the particular circumstances of our individual and corporate lives.

This attitude toward reading Ecclesiastes (and the OT as a whole) is what can be referred to as a Christotelic reading.[69] Rather than placing Christ "in" the book of Ecclesiastes, a Christotelic reading sees Christ as the climactic end (Greek *telos*) of Israel's story, which is the vantage point from which we today engage the book. This is analogous, perhaps, to how one engages a well-told tale in a good novel. The first time through you let the story hit you as the plot unfolds and the characters develop. Then when you get to the climax of the story, the various peaks and valleys of the previous chapters begin to be seen in light of the whole. The end of the story does not render those chapters null and void, merely a prop to bring you to the end. But now, having read the story once and seen where it winds up, you go back and read it again. It is precisely because you know where the story is going that you can have a deeper connection with the various parts: "Oh, *now* I know how that part fits. . . . I didn't see that before, and now that I do, it seems pretty important. How could I have missed it before? . . . That part isn't nearly as straightforward as I once thought it was. Maybe I need to pay more careful attention to it this time."

For this reason a theological reading of Ecclesiastes for the church is ultimately a synthesis of the first and second readings. We must allow its own prominent peaks and valleys to define our hermeneutical landscape, while at the same time bearing in mind that there is another, grander landscape beyond the immediate horizon, against which Ecclesiastes can be seen in a different light. Interestingly, an analogy with the book of Ecclesiastes itself may illustrate the point. Just as reading the epilogue brings us to say to Qohelet, "Yes, you are right, but there is something more," so too does our post-resurrection vantage point bring us to look at Ecclesiastes as a whole and say, "Yes, you are right, but there is something more." The difference, of course, is that the "something more" of the epilogue is a reiteration of Israel's traditional categories of fear and obedience. For us, the "something more" is the complex realization that, however bound we are to traditional categories, they are now reconfigured in the crucified and risen Christ, who paradoxically embodies *and* transforms Israel's story. In the final chapters of this volume I will attempt to draw the contours of Ecclesiastes into a conversation with relevant portions of the OT as well as God's final word in Christ.

---

69. For a fuller, yet still brief, explication of this notion, see Enns, *Inspiration and Incarnation*, 113-63, esp. 152-63. See also Enns, "Apostolic Hermeneutics."

Commentary

1:1-11: Prologue: Summary of Qohelet's Quest

As mentioned in the introduction to this commentary, 1:1-11, written in the third person, forms the frame narrator's introduction to the words of Qohelet. Beginning at 1:12 and going to 12:7, we read a first person discourse from Qohelet himself, only to return to the frame narrator's third person summation in 12:8-14.

The purpose of the opening verses is to summarize the content of Qohelet's observations in 1:12–12:7, thereby introducing the reader to what he/she should expect in the chapters to follow. The narrator does this first by announcing whose words we are about to read, namely Qohelet's (v. 1). Second, he provides a summary of Qohelet's entire discourse in vv. 2-4. Third, he illustrates and expands on this summary by appealing to analogies from the natural world (vv. 5-7). Fourth, he describes in more direct language the lesson derived from these analogies (vv. 8-10). Fifth, he homes in on what will prove to be a dominant theme throughout the book: the inevitable meaninglessness of life is seen most clearly and most decisively in the specter of death (v. 11).

In these eleven verses the narrator provides the reader not so much with an introduction to ease us into the blunt observations of Qohelet, but a summary — a first round, square blow to the chin — of what will be seen on page after page in what follows. In a way, there is no mystery whatsoever concerning what Ecclesiastes is about, despite the long history of diverse interpretation (see the introduction). Of course, I am not suggesting that there are no interpretive challenges throughout the book — far from it — but the overall message is being handed to us by the frame narrator on a silver platter. To paraphrase:

30

This is what Qohelet is saying: At the end of the day, life is frustratingly absurd. The cycles of nature are screaming that message to you. You live. You exert a lot of energy, but nothing new happens. Just like the sun, wind, and rivers. Then you die. And one other thing: after you die, you will be quickly forgotten.

Not the best way to make friends and influence people, but that is neither the narrator's nor Qohelet's purpose.

This entire message is itself summarized in v. 2, where the narrator quotes Qohelet. The precise meaning of the Hebrew word הֶבֶל/*hebel* continues to elude us. The NIV translates it "meaningless," which moves us further along the way, but I much prefer "absurd," as Michael Fox has argued.[1] Hence v. 2 can be translated "'Absolutely absurd,'[2] says Qohelet. 'Absolutely absurd. Everything is absurd.'" We should allow the force of this declaration to hit us. This is not an academic observation, made from a distance. It is more a cry — perhaps shout — of a desperate man at the end of his rope. To paraphrase the force of the Hebrew: "*Everything* is *absolutely* — I said *absolutely* — *absurd.*"[3]

I prefer the word "absurd" because other translation options for *hebel* are either too familiar to us or do not get at what, I trust, a close reading of the remainder of the book will amply demonstrate. What "absurd" communicates better than "meaningless" is well put by Fox: by *hebel* Qohelet means to say that life as he sees it is "an affront to reason."[4] A fitting biblical analogy is a lament psalm like Psalm 73. There, too, the psalmist is struck with the disjunction between what he knows should be the case (God rewards the

---

1. Fox, *Time to Tear Down*, 133.

2. The Hebrew phrase is the singular construct הֲבֵל/*hăbel* followed by the plural הֲבָלִים/*hăbālîm*. This is a way of forming an emphatic construction, hence the famous KJV translation, "vanity of vanities."

3. An interesting, although ultimately limited, article is that of Jarick, who exploits the visual similarity between הַכֹּל/*hakkōl* (everything) and הֶבֶל/*hebel* (which he translates "nothing") ("Hebrew Book of Changes"). We have in these two words, according to Jarick, "the most compact form of parallelism to be found in the Hebrew Bible" (81), i.e., הכל הבל/*hkl hbl*. This is a stimulating notion, although I do not find that Jarick's suggestion about the Chinese *Book of Changes (I Ching)* is of much concrete help in discerning the meaning of Ecclesiastes.

4. Fox, *Time to Tear Down*, 31. In this light, however, it is important to keep before us the observations of Miller, who regards *hebel* as a symbol of insubstantiality (no advantage or profit), transience (short and fragile life), and foulness (affront to justice) ("Qohelet's Symbolic Use of הבל"). Miller's analysis is extremely helpful and helps avoid simplistic definitions, and so helps readers dig deeper into the subtleties of Qohelet's thought. I do feel, however, that "absurd" (which corresponds best to Miller's third use) as a base translation of *hebel* incorporates all these symbolic uses. I do not suggest that such a base definition should cover over the nuances of Qohelet's argument, as I hope the subsequent commentary will show.

righteous and punishes the wicked) and what is indeed the reality of the matter (the wicked prosper and the righteous languish), as vv. 1-14 make clear. Where the analogy breaks down is at the end of the psalm (vv. 23-28). There a fairly standard solution presents itself: be patient, God will be just in the end. There is little, if any, such sentiment in Ecclesiastes. Even the epilogue, although generally supportive of Qohelet's words (see the introduction), hardly provides such a straightforward answer. It has struck me more than once over the years that Qohelet's (let's call it for the time being "less-than-orthodox") outburst is not a result of his not knowing such passages as Psalm 73. Rather, it stems from his observations that the theology expressed therein does not actually touch the here-and-now world.

The introduction to the book, therefore, is summarized nicely in v. 2, and the remaining verses (vv. 3-11) serve to support that point. Verse 3 introduces three vital and recurring concepts in Qohelet's thinking: "profit" (יִתְרוֹן/*yitrôn*), "labor" (עָמָל/*ʿāmāl*), and "under the sun" (תַּחַת הַשָּׁמֶשׁ/*taḥat haššāmeš*).[5] "Under the sun" does not mean "on earth, as opposed to heaven." Some have found in such an interpretation an early indication of Qohelet's skewed perspective: "You see! That is Qohelet's problem! If only his eyes were *in heaven* and not simply on earth, then he would not get himself into so much trouble!" Such a position might make it easier to chastise Qohelet for his brazen observations, but surely Qohelet's observations cannot be so lightly dismissed as a faulty this-worldly perspective. For one thing, we must keep in mind, as we saw in the introduction, that the epilogue (12:8-14) lends support to Qohelet's observation — not without some qualification, but the epilogue is not a condemnation of Qohelet's words as being restricted by an earthly outlook. Second, as Seow points out, the phrase, also found in Phoenician inscriptions of the fifth century B.C., refers simply to "the realm of the living"[6] as opposed to the netherworld, the land of the dead. In other words, the meaning of the phrase is not to imply that Qohelet's search is restricted in any way, but the exact opposite: his gaze is *everywhere,* throughout all the land of the living. We are told here that Qohelet searched high and low, far and wide; he left no stone unturned.

By "labor" he means the things with which humans occupy and busy themselves on this earth, that is, that which we do. By "profit," Qohelet means "the payoff." Here Seow is very helpful in pointing out how Qohelet employs a number of economic terms to make his theological point (money, riches,

---

5. On these three see "Some Recurring and Important Lexemes for the Theology of Ecclesiastes" (p. 26) in the introduction.

6. Seow, *Ecclesiastes,* 105.

inheritance, salary, wealth, etc.).[7] "Profit" can be understood as "advantage," but a sharper definition would be more economical: "surplus," that is, payoff, profit. In other words, what Qohelet is asking rhetorically here in v. 3 is, "What payoff is there in any activity I could possibly engage in throughout the land of the living?" As we will see below, the prime reason that Qohelet arrives at such a conclusion is his blunt and relentless observation that death is the end of everyone.

Indeed, we see hints of this dominant theme not only in v. 11, as mentioned earlier, but already in v. 4. Although this will not prove to be consistent throughout the book, the root הלך/*hlk* is often used as a metaphor for death, and that appears to be the case in v. 4. It is best to translate the beginning of the verse, "A generation *goes* (הלך/*hlk*) and a generation *comes* (בוא/*bw'*)" rather than what might flow more naturally from our lips, "a generation comes and a generation goes." What Qohelet is saying is that (v. 3) there is no profit to anything we do here on earth, *because* (v. 4) one generation dies off and another simply takes its place. It is the specter of death that ultimately renders all of our activity as pointless.

Therefore I take v. 4b to be explanatory rather than contrastive. Rather than translating v. 4, "A generation goes and a generation comes, *but* the earth remains forever," I prefer, "A generation goes and a generation comes: the earth remains forever." He is not saying, "Don't worry. Although people come and go, the earth is here to stay." He is saying, "People die and others are born to take their place, and this *situation* does not change. It remains forever."[8]

To illustrate the point, Qohelet provides three analogues from nature: the sun, wind, and rivers in vv. 5-7. These three natural phenomena demonstrate one of Qohelet's central concerns, that, despite the occasional and temporary appearance of things, there is ultimately no payoff, no "profit" in anything we do because no matter what we do, nothing changes. (To jump ahead a bit, this theme continues on through v. 10 and then in v. 11, the final verse in the prologue, which tantalizingly begins to home in on the ultimate expression of absurdity: after all we do in this life, we die and are forgotten.) Every morning the sun rises and every evening it sets, only to "pant"[9] back to its place and start the unending cycle all over again the next day (v. 5). Likewise, the wind rides its circuit, round and round, south to north, again and again (v. 6). Rivers flow into the ocean, but no matter how hard the rivers work, the

---

7. Ibid., 22.

8. I certainly agree here with Fox that "the earth" (הָאָרֶץ/*hā'āreṣ*) in v. 4b refers not to the physical universe but to "humanity as a whole" (*Time to Tear Down*, 166).

9. The Hebrew root is שאף/*š'p*, which can mean panting or stomping, and "conveys vigorous activity, but also tiredness" (Seow, *Ecclesiastes*, 107).

ocean is never full (v. 7). The rivers' strivings have no profit.[10] This is a very different view than is presented in the Psalms, where God is extolled for the wonders of creation. For Qohelet, the very fabric of creation demonstrates that life is absurd because there is no payoff when all is said and done. The cycle just keeps on going.

Beginning in v. 8, Qohelet moves from analogues taken from the natural world to human activities — speaking, seeing, and hearing — and the result is the same: they amount to nothing. The first two words of v. 8, כָּל-הַדְּבָרִים/*kol-haddĕbārîm,* can mean "all things" but this is unlikely in Ecclesiastes. First, הַכֹּל/*hakkōl* is the typical expression Qohelet uses for "every*thing*" (e.g., 1:2, 14; 2:11, 16, 17; 3:1; it can mean "everyone," e.g., 3:20). Second, דבר/*dbr* in Ecclesiastes everywhere else pertains to words or speaking.[11] Hence the beginning of v. 8 does not summarize the previous observation but introduces a new one.

It is difficult to read these opening words apart from 12:12: "much study *wearies* the flesh." The root יגע/*ygʿ* is used in 1:8 and 12:12 (elsewhere only in 10:15), and seems to form a sort of frame for the book as a whole: "words/study will not get you anywhere." Words just make you weary, and so, as v. 8 continues, "one is not able to speak." It is not entirely clear what "not able" (לֹא-יוּכַל/*lōʾ-yūkal*) means, but it certainly does not refer to the mechanical inability to utter words. It likely should be understood in the same vein as the two other sensual activities that follow: neither the eye nor ear is satisfied/full, no matter how much they go about doing their business. "Not able" to speak, therefore, seems to mean something like, "the wearisomeness of words makes speaking ineffective; talk is incessant and gets nowhere — neither do seeing and hearing." Or to borrow the imagery of nature above, speaking, seeing, and hearing are never "full" because the cycle never ceases.

Verses 9-10 make the same point but more directly, without recourse to natural or physical imagery. Indeed, we may say that vv. 9-10 summarize in plain language the points made thus far: "Whatever has happened[12] is what will happen. Whatever has been done is what will be done. There is nothing at all new under the sun" (see also 3:15). This summary notion is very strong: "There is nothing at all new (אֵין כָּל-חָדָשׁ/*ʾēn kol-ḥādāš*)" anywhere on earth ("under the sun"; see v. 3 above), not in the past, present, or future. The "cir-

10. It is worth mentioning that הלך/*hlk* is used in vv. 6 and 7 to describe the absurdity of the cycles of the wind and rivers. Just as generations die and are replaced, so too do the wind and rivers "die" only to rise again.

11. On this see Seow, *Ecclesiastes,* 109; Fox, *Time to Tear Down,* 167.

12. The Hebrew interrogative מָה/*mâ* (or מֶה/*meh*) followed by the relative particle שֶׁ/*še* plus the verb הָיָה/*hāyâ* occurs in the OT only in Eccl 1:9; 3:15, 22; 6:10; 7:24; 8:7; 10:14, although it is common in Mishnaic Hebrew. It means "whatever has happened." See Seow, *Ecclesiastes,* 110.

cle of life" is for Qohelet not a source of stability or comfort, but the very expression of the absurdity of life, since "the cycle" ensures that nothing that
happens or nothing we do will amount to anything.[13] "Oh sure," Qohelet
continues in v. 10, "someone might look at something and say, 'Look, this is
new,' but it really is not. It is just the same old thing. It has been here forever
(לְעֹלָמִים/*lĕ'ōlāmîm*)."[14]

Verse 11 concludes the prologue and brings us to another summary
statement of sorts, one that will become a dominant theme throughout Ecclesiastes: death. Not only is there no *thing* new under the sun — no permanent
deed or human activity — but this holds for us as well. The words רִאשֹׁנִים/
ri'šōnîm and אַחֲרֹנִים/*'aḥărōnîm* refer not to first and latter things (in which
case the feminine ending would be expected) but to people.[15] It is not only
things and events that suffer, but humans as well. The very existence of previous generations is forgotten (root זכר/*zkr*). Likewise, those who are yet to be
born will eventually, after their own death, be forgotten by generations who
will come after them.

This is no throwaway line, as its sentiment should echo with anyone familiar with the OT, for it is precisely a blessed memory that is the hope and
comfort for God's people. To live in such a way as to live on in the memories
of one's descendants is a mark of a life lived in communion with God and
God's covenant faithfulness to his people (e.g., Prov 10:7, "The memory [זֵכֶר/
zēker] of the righteous will be a blessing, but the name [שֵׁם/*šēm*, i.e., reputa-
tion] of the wicked will rot"; Ps 112:6, "Surely he will never [לְעוֹלָם/*lĕ'ôlām*] be
shaken; a righteous man will be remembered forever [לְזֵכֶר עוֹלָם/*lĕzēker
'ôlām*]"). At least in 1:11, Qohelet does not seem to leave room for the memory
of the righteous: nonremembrance is the lot of *all* the living. The point is

---

13. Taking note of this observation here will allow the meaning of 3:1-8 to emerge naturally. That passage is sometimes misunderstood as extolling the rhythms of life, but that is
hardly Qohelet's intention, as 3:9 makes clear (see below).

14. By this expression Qohelet certainly does not conceive of "eternity" in the Western
sense of the word (i.e., before creation). It is better understood as "from time immemorial," i.e.,
as far back "under the sun" as one can conceive. The preposition ל/*l* does not require a future
meaning (e.g., "*to* the ages") as it is used of past time elsewhere in Scripture, e.g., לְעֹלָם/*lĕ'ōlām*
in Exod 3:15.

15. On this point see Seow, *Ecclesiastes*, 111. Fox, however, sees v. 11 as continuing the
theme of things/events (*Time to Tear Down*, 169). Seow's position is preferable in that (1) a clear
reference to such a dominant theme as death is fitting in the instruction, especially as v. 11 represents the personal application of the phenomenon of absurdity that has occupied the previous
ten verses; (2) the biblical precedent for the masculine plural ending referring to former and latter *generations* (Lev 26:45; Deut 19:14; Ps 79:8; not to mention Eccl 4:16, הָאַחֲרוֹנִים/*hā'aḥărônîm*,
where it clearly refers to people).

made more clearly in 2:16: "There is no memory (אֵין זִכְרֹון/*'ēn zikrôn*) for the wise man, like the fool, forever (לְעֹולָם/*lě'ôlām*); in days to come both will be forgotten. Like the fool, the wise man too must die!" At any rate, in 1:11 Qohelet has already turned his attention to the topic of death: we all die and no one will remember you.

With this thought we come to the end of the prologue and begin the words of Qohelet. Whatever winding path Qohelet chooses to take to arrive at his points of destination, we must keep before us the fact that the frame narrator has already pointed us in the ultimate direction in which Qohelet is headed: The cycle of life, as illustrated even in nature itself, assures that *there is no payoff* (יִתְרֹון/*yitrôn*) for any of our activities and efforts. All (הַכֹּל/*hakkōl*) that we do in any corner of our existence (תַּחַת הַשָּׁמֶשׁ/*taḥat haššāmeš*) collapses to *absurdity* (הֶבֶל/*hebel*). Moreover, the ultimate indication of absurdity is the fact that *we will all die,* and even the hope of being remembered by our descendants is an empty one.

The thought process behind the summary of 1:1-11 will now be laid out for us in Qohelet's own words from 1:12 through 12:7.

1:12-15: Qohelet's Own Summary of His Quest

Before getting into the particulars of his own quest in 2:1, Qohelet summarizes for us bluntly the results of that quest. In a manner of speaking, 1:12-18 is a second introduction to the book, the first being by the frame narrator in 1:1-11. Here too we are given very valuable information concerning what we as readers should expect to find in the chapters that follow. It will be our reflex, perhaps, to want to judge Qohelet's orthodoxy — even emotional stability — as we come across some stunning statements. We must bear in mind that, although evaluating Qohelet's words is certainly in order, we must first enter into Qohelet's conversation as a participant, not a judge. Furthermore, it bears repeating that the frame narrator himself has provided a canonical evaluation in 12:8-14, which, as mentioned in the introduction to this commentary, has a demonstrably positive dimension to it. In other words, we should not rush to evaluation and judgment, but be patient in allowing Qohelet to make his case in his own terms, however jumbled and belabored it might appear at times, and then bring the totality of Qohelet's words into conversation with the frame narrator's evaluation. Only after that groundwork is laid can Christians readers (the primary focus of this commentary series) begin to work through the challenging yet exciting task of bringing the message of Ecclesiastes as a whole — not just isolated statements by Qohelet

— to bear on the gospel, and ultimately begin to see the theological interchange between faith in Christ and the theology of Ecclesiastes.

Qohelet begins by announcing his identity in 1:12. Such an announcement reflects an ancient Near East genre of literature sometimes referred to as "royal testament," which is aimed at a king's self-glorification.[1] In keeping with its ancient counterparts, 1:12 should probably be translated as a declaration: "I am Qohelet. I have been king . . ." (rather than "I, Qohelet, have been king . . ."). The name is announced, followed by a list of the king's accomplishments, all of which are geared toward securing the king's reputation. What is most interesting about Qohelet, however, is that, although he parrots the literary style, his conclusion is not at all aimed at self-glorification. As the following verses make clear, Qohelet's quest, which includes his many kingly accomplishments (2:1-11), eventually comes to naught. They do *not* secure his memory, but, like everything else under the sun, demonstrate the exact opposite. Qohelet employs an ancient literary device and then subverts it.

This is where an understanding of the genre of Ecclesiastes becomes very important. Qohelet identifies himself as king *over Israel in Jerusalem.* Only David and Solomon fit this description (reigning over a united Israelite kingdom with the throne in Jerusalem). And since Qohelet is referred to as David's son in 1:1, the implication is that Qohelet is to be identified with Solomon. Now, as discussed in more length in the introduction, this identification is not to be understood as providing the historical identity of the author as the third king of Israel. Nor is the author trying to pull the wool over anyone's eyes. It is rather a powerful and intentional literary device, which we can only presume would have been well known at the time, the purpose of which is to establish the worthiness of the author's subsequent observations. He is not lying, but getting his point across — that all is absurd — by adopting a royal persona. It is, after all, the king — particularly Solomon the wise — who would have all the resources at his disposal to embark on a thorough investigation of what makes life worth all the labor. The king has no shortage of time, money, power, or influence to pull it off. This is not the quest of a common worker musing on the meaning of life. He is Israel's wisest king on a deliberate, expansive, even exhaustive ("under the sun") search. And if anyone can pull it off, he can. If he cannot, no one else can. The frame narrator's evaluation in 12:8-14 echoes this sentiment: do not add to Qohelet's words (12:12), nothing else remains to be said (12:13). The readers are warned they can do no better than Qohelet and they should not try.

The seriousness of Qohelet's quest is already indicated in v. 13. He says, "I

---

1. See Seow, *Ecclesiastes,* 119; Fox, *Time to Tear Down,* 170-71; Longman, *Ecclesiastes,* 76.

gave my heart" (וְנָתַתִּי אֶת-לִבִּי/*wĕnātattî 'et-libbî*), which is a phrase that recurs throughout the book (1:17; 7:2, 21; 8:9, 16; 9:1), and connotes a sincere, heartfelt commitment.[2] His energies are geared toward investigating (דרשׁ/ *drš*) and searching out (תור/*tûr*) by wisdom (בַּחָכְמָה/*baḥokmâ*) everything (כָּל/*kol*) done "under the heavens" (תַּחַת הַשָּׁמָיִם/*taḥat haššāmāyim*).[3] To put it more succinctly, he gave it everything he had, and his search was a wise one.[4] And what does he find? This is stated at the end of v. 13, which is a terse and jarring summary of Qohelet's entire investigation (a summary within the summary, so to speak), and gives a clear signal as to what the reader is to expect for the remainder of the book. As the NIV has it, "What a heavy burden God has laid on man." This translation works, but there is more that can be said by looking at the Hebrew. "Heavy burden" is a translation of עִנְיָן רָע/*'inyan rā'*. One may be tempted to translate this "evil burden," but the NIV is certainly correct in giving *rā'* its less moralistic interpretation here and elsewhere in Ecclesiastes. The term *'inyan* is better translated as "task/business," or perhaps "preoccupation."[5] One might translate the adjective as "grievous/burdensome/heavy" and the noun as "task/preoccupation/business." More to the point, however, is Qohelet's comment that it is God who is responsible for laying this business on humanity. And what is that business? This is already stated in the first half of v. 13: investigating all that is done under the heavens.

Although I want to avoid overinterpreting this one phrase so early in our reading of Ecclesiastes, we should nevertheless pause and allow the force of this statement to come through. Qohelet is saying that the very search for meaning is a *heavy burden* that *God* has imposed on man in order to "occupy him" (see the end of the verse and the use of the cognate verb לַעֲנוֹת/*la'ănôt*).

---

2. Elsewhere Qohelet refers to speaking (אמר/*'mr* or דבר/*dbr*) "in his heart" (e.g., 1:16; 2:1).

3. This occurs also in 2:3 and 3:1, and its meaning is synonymous with the more common "under the sun." It "simply means everywhere in the world, a spatial description" (Seow, *Ecclesiastes*, 121).

4. It is possible to understand Qohelet's appeal to wisdom as ironic, as Bartholomew has argued (*Reading Ecclesiastes*, 229-37). In other words, even though Qohelet appeals to wisdom, his subsequent search indicates that he is in fact not wise. Hence he is not really being guided by wisdom. This option is worthy of serious consideration, but at the end of the day I am not convinced, as it would create too much tension with the frame narrator's own evaluation. On a related matter, it is important to note that Qohelet's search is *by* wisdom and not *for* wisdom. Wisdom is his tool (Carasik, "Qohelet's Twists and Turns," 202-3).

5. For the former see Fox, *Time to Tear Down*, 171. For the latter see Seow, *Ecclesiastes*, 121. Seow adds that the word occurs in the OT only in Ecclesiastes (1:13; 2:23, 26; 3:10; 4:8; 5:2, 13 [Eng. 3, 14]; 8:16). In Postbiblical Hebrew it carries the connotation of "subject, business, case," and sometimes has the nuance of causing anxiety.

His issue is with God and what *he* has done in putting humanity through this grievous task of searching out what it is about life that makes it worth the effort. One might say that Qohelet is angry with God, and keeping this important element of the book in mind will help us keep our focus on its theological message. It is helpful, again, to think of Ecclesiastes as being analogous to lament psalms, where the psalmist bears the burden of seeing the grave disjunction between what he as an Israelite is to expect about God and his world, and what he experiences living in the day-to-day struggles and tensions of life (a good example is Psalm 73). In other words, Ecclesiastes is not a philosophical mind experiment about "the meaning of life." It is written by a profoundly religious — indeed, wise (see 12:9) — Israelite, one who is not outside of the covenant but inside; one who is looking at Yahweh not from the outside in, but as an insider who is deeply perplexed, confused, perhaps even teetering on the brink of total skepticism, and this struggle finally comes to expression in such statements as we find in 1:13 and elsewhere in Ecclesiastes (esp. in v. 15 below).

Verse 14 is parallel to v. 13. In vv. 13a and 14a we have Qohelet's announcement concerning the nature of the search (citing TNIV):

> v. 13a: *I applied my mind* to study and to explore by wisdom *all that is done under the heavens.*
> v. 14a: *I have seen all the things that are done under the sun.*

In the second half of both verses we see Qohelet's conclusion:

> v. 13b: What a heavy burden God has laid on the human race.
> v. 14b: all of them are meaningless, a chasing after the wind.[6]

In both cases Qohelet's observations yield an unflinchingly negative evaluation and highlight the blame he places on God: the meaninglessness of it all (v. 14b) is the heavy burden God has laid on humanity (v. 13b). Here, in Qohelet's own words, we are provided with a preview of things to come, and the words of Qohelet from here and throughout the book to 12:7 must be understood in this light. It should also be pointed out that Qohelet's own words in v. 14b have already been faithfully adumbrated by the frame narrator in 1:2-

---

6. Here is the first instance of the recurring phrase רְעוּת רוּחַ/*rĕʿût rûaḥ* (see also 2:11, 17, 26; 4:4, 6; 6:9), describing the senselessness of what Qohelet is observing. The related phrase רוּחַ רַעְיוֹן/*raʿyôn rûaḥ* is found first in 1:17. Searching for subtle differences between the two forms is itself futile.

3: everything done[7] under the sun is absurd. Both the frame narrator's introduction and that of Qohelet himself are making clear that Qohelet has searched and found the predicament to be dire. And, as 1:13a only begins to address, this is God's doing.

This sentiment comes to an even greater crescendo in v. 15. Here, in the opinion of some, Qohelet seems to be quoting a proverbial saying of some sort,[8] but settling this issue is not the main focus of our attention. What is more to the point theologically is what is said, not where Qohelet got it from. Qohelet is expressing a view that can fairly be described as complete resignation to the way things are, and that they cannot be changed. He will return to this theme repeatedly in the book, albeit with different words and from different angles. Here he puts it this way: Crooked things are just crooked, and cannot be straightened; something that is lacking cannot be counted.

So, beginning in v. 13, Qohelet says that he searched everything that is done (עשׂה/'śh) under the heavens, and that task is a grievous burden. In v. 14 he makes the very similar point that he has "seen" (ראה/r'h, in the sense "observed" or perhaps "experienced") everything done ('śh) under the sun, and concluded that everything is הֶבֶל/hebel. Verse 15 adds that this is simply the way it is, and the passive verb מְעֻוָּת/mě'uwwāt (Pual participle, "what is [made] crooked") could be an ever so slightly veiled reference to God, the one who made things crooked to begin with. In other words, v. 15 and v. 13b are parallel. Both express a frustration not simply with the way things are, but with what God did to make them so. This should give us pause to consider what is fairly obvious in the larger scope but can be lost when struggling to interpret individual passages here and there. When modern readers read Ecclesiastes, we are confronted with the words of an Israelite, a deeply religious man, to be sure, with significant struggles. He is not someone who "does not know God" and is trying to make sense of life apart from him. He knows how things are supposed to be, yet his experience does not mesh with the ideal. This is not to suggest that the purpose of the book is for readers today, or for ancient Israelites, to try to emulate such deep struggle. But it is to impress upon us that, in an effort to apply Ecclesiastes to our lives today, we should not be so eager to soft-peddle the many jarring statements he makes. As mentioned earlier, it is for us to understand the words before us as best as we can

---

7. The frame narrator uses the verb עמל/'ml, whereas Qohelet uses עשׂה/'śh. This is not a significant distinction, and the subtle differences between these words in these contexts should certainly not be pressed.

8. That this notion is virtually repeated in 7:13 may lend some credence to this view. Fox says that this saying "has the ring of a traditional proverb" (*Time to Tear Down*, 172). Crenshaw refers to it as "an ancient aphorism" (*Ecclesiastes*, 73).

and only then to struggle ourselves with how to bring Qohelet's words into conversation with the theology of the OT and the gospel.

1:16–2:11: Pursuit of Meaning by Kingly Means

The note of pessimism with which we leave the previous section is quickly countered by Qohelet's robust assertion of his own kingly stature — at least, this appears to be the case at the outset. His litany of self-praise and accomplishments is quickly tempered by his own recognition of the futility of it all. And any lingering hint of value to his pursuit is neutralized in his emphatic and blunt conclusion in 2:11.

Qohelet's comments in this section are in keeping with the documented ancient Near Eastern genre of "royal testament." Not surprisingly, kings like to tell their subjects and neighboring nations just how accomplished, powerful, and beneficent they are, to leave a legacy and thus achieve some measure not only of fame but immortality. Qohelet's opening words reflect similar boasts. He is greater and wiser than any king before him (1:16).[1] He devoted himself (וָאֶתְּנָה לִבִּי/*wā'ettĕnâ libbî*, lit. "I gave my heart") to knowing not only "wisdom and knowledge" but also "madness and folly." Qohelet is covering all the bases. He will avoid no issue: he will explore the depths not only of wisdom but of depravity as well.

With such a start one would expect a more positive line of argumentation than what we see at the end of v. 17. Having just told us how much wiser he is than any of his predecessors, and how thorough his investigation will be — in other words, having set the reader up for the expectation of something good to come of all this — Qohelet drops another bomb: "I know that this, too, is a chasing after the wind."[2] What is the "this" he is referring to? It is not wisdom itself but the entire quest outlined in vv. 16-17. To paraphrase Qohelet's words, "Since I am more wise than any king as there ever was in Jerusalem, I will apply myself to the quest of knowing wisdom and folly, and the difference between them. But, even for me, this is a futile quest."

---

1. Seow suggests that "all who were before me" is a stock phrase of ancient royal inscriptions (*Ecclesiastes*, 124). In an earlier article, Seow cites the inscription of the Assyrian king Idrimi, "Nobody understood the things I understood" ("Qohelet's Autobiography," 281). See also Fox, *Time to Tear Down*, 173.

2. The phrase רַעְיוֹן רוּחַ/*ra'yôn rûaḥ* is found elsewhere in Ecclesiastes in 4:16, as well as 5 times in the Aramaic portions of Daniel. It is related to the more common phrase in Ecclesiastes רְעוּת רוּחַ/*rĕ'ût rûaḥ* (occurring 7 times; see 1:14). The two phrases should be understood identically.

As startling as that may be, Qohelet does not leave us in the dark. He explains himself in v. 18. The reason why even his royal wisdom quest is futile is that the more you know, the worse off you are. It is futile not because of what he cannot find out, but because of what he does find out. As he puts it, wisdom is accompanied by *sorrow,* knowledge by *pain.*[3] Or as we might put it today, ignorance is bliss. The burden he bears as the paradigm of a wise king is a heavy one, and others not so well endowed by wisdom save themselves a lot of grief. In fact, he will later caution his readers in 7:16, "Do not be overrighteous, neither be overwise — why destroy yourself?" As we will see in the next section, wisdom for Qohelet is a relative good (see 2:13: "wisdom is better than folly, just as light is better than darkness"), but it can be pressed too far. Verse 18 is the first instance of such a tempered appreciation of wisdom, which is a far cry from declarations such as we find in Prov 4:7: "Wisdom is supreme; therefore get wisdom. Though it cost you all you have, get understanding."

Qohelet began this section with self-praise, which is quickly countered by the recognition of the futility of all his accomplishments. One would expect the one who wrote these words to cease and desist from recording such a hopeless quest. Yet, when we turn to 2:1ff., we seem to see Qohelet recounting his investigation having already admitted its futility. He assigns himself the task of testing himself with pleasure (שִׂמְחָה/*śimḥâ*) to see what is good (טוֹב/*ṭôb*).[4] Pleasure is clearly tied to those things that produce laughter (2:2), such as wine (2:3), but the word does not seem to be restricted to such things. His list of accomplishments in 2:4-9 is also, at least broadly speaking, in the same category, as the summative use of *śimḥâ* in 2:10 suggests. His topic from 2:1 through 2:9 is "pleasure" and it takes various forms, including wine and going about kingly business. A preferable translation for *śimḥâ*, therefore, is "joy" since it is more neutral with respect to its moral connotations.[5]

Still, as we have seen in the previous verses, Qohelet does not send his readers on a wild goose chase. Even in 2:1, where he seems to be on the verge of sidestepping his sober reflections of 1:17-18 by applying himself to the test, he immediately reminds his readers that he is under no delusions concerning its final outcome: "It is also absurd (הֶבֶל/*hebel*)." As in 1:17 where "this" (זֶה/*zeh*) refers to the activity of *seeking* wisdom (not wisdom itself), here "it"

---

3. "Sorrow" (כַּעַס/*ka'as*) may be better translated as "anger" or "vexation" (see also 2:23; 5:16 [Eng. 17]; 7:3, 9: 11:10). "Pain" (מַכְאֹב/*mak'ōb*) can be understood as "irritation" (2:23). The idea of this verse is not so much of sadness or hurt as anger and vexed annoyance, again seemingly directed at God.

4. As mentioned in the introduction (at n. 16), *ṭôb* is not a moral category, but concerns the experience of joy.

5. See Longman, *Ecclesiastes,* 88.

(הוּא/*hû'*) refers to the *testing* of joy (not joy itself). Already at the end of 2:1, Qohelet announces that the verses to follow, despite the superficial impression that they may be of some lasting value, will amount to nothing that would counter Qohelet's grand observation, the theme of the book itself, that everything is absurd. And he underscores this point in 2:2: laughter is madness, and joy *(śimḥâ)* is worthless.[6]

The first item by which Qohelet tests himself is wine (2:3). We read he "turned his heart" (תַּרְתִּי בְלִבִּי/*tartî bĕlibbî*), a phrase we saw in 1:13 and will see again in 7:25. It is similar to his other "heart" expressions scattered throughout the book, and connotes determination and focus. Of course, this tells us little of what precisely he is after with respect to wine. He affirms that he is even here guided by wisdom, but does this mean that he kept the drinking under control or, conversely, that he goes all out to see just what wine has to offer. I am not sure how important it is to arrive at a definitive conclusion here, but I suggest that the latter is more consistent with the context. He makes clear in this same verse that he is "grabbing hold of folly" (לֶאֱחֹז בְּסִכְלוּת/*le'ĕḥōz bĕsiklût*) to see what good it will bring. This does not suggest a cautious, tempered investigation. This interpretation is further supported by 1:17, where Qohelet tells us that his intention is to understand wisdom and knowledge, on the one hand, and madness and folly, on the other. Also, 2:10 makes clear that he did not withhold from himself anything he saw, nor did he keep his heart from any sort of joy. His plan seems to be to leave no stone unturned rather than holding back in his quest.

Another important point is highlighted in 2:3. His purpose for investigating the effects of wine is to see "what is worthwhile for men to do under heaven during the [few] days of their lives."[7] What was already hinted in 1:11 is now made a bit more explicit. The specter of death begins to loom as Qohelet's potent adversary. It is death that casts a shadow over every allegedly profitable activity that humanity can engage in. As with the other hints dropped throughout this section, the reader is alerted that, whatever is to follow, one should not expect too much from it.

---

6. Laughter as "madness" is a disputed translation for מְהוֹלָל/*mĕhôlāl*. It is considered by some to be a Poal participle of הלל/*hll*, and thus a form of the same root as הוֹלֵלוֹת/*hôlēlôt* in 1:17 (Longman, *Ecclesiastes*, 86; apparently Fox, *Time to Tear Down*, 174). Seow argues that this is problematic, and emends the text to read, "what does it boast," מֶה הוֹלֵל/*meh hôlēl* (*Ecclesiastes*, 126). Concerning joy, Qohelet states emphatically מַה-זֹּה עֹשָׂה/*mah-zzōh 'ōśâ*, i.e., "what (in the world) does this do?!" On the emphatic function of *mah-zzōh* and similar forms, see *IBHS* §17.4.3.c.

7. "Few" certainly communicates what Qohelet is after, but it is not explicitly reflected in the Hebrew (מִסְפַּר יְמֵי חַיֵּיהֶם/*mispar yĕmê ḥayyêhem*).

With this in mind we can properly appreciate the purpose for which Qohelet recounts his royal accomplishments (2:4-8). Although these verses reflect other ancient Near Eastern texts aimed at self-promotion, that is not Qohelet's aim. If we are correct that Qohelet is not a king of Israel but a theologian employing the royal persona to make his point, it becomes clear that there is much more to this than a list of accomplishments to impress his readers. Indeed, his aim is to do precisely the opposite. In the ancient Near East, listing one's royal activities no doubt demonstrates the quality of a king's rule, but such lists do more. These "deeds of permanence" are a means of achieving "immortality." The point is clearly illustrated in the well-known ancient story of Gilgamesh.[8] He was ruler of Uruk around 2600 B.C. and, as the story goes, became obsessed with the notion of dying after losing his best friend. He goes on a quest to find Utnapishtim, the Noah figure of the story, who gained eternal life by saving humanity from a flood. Unfortunately, Gilgamesh finds out that the gift of immortality is for Utnapishtim only, because of his great deed. The only recourse Gilgamesh has is to return to Uruk and achieve an alternate immortality: building city walls that stand for all time.

Qohelet mimics this ancient Near Eastern royal testament genre only to deconstruct it.[9] He lists his activities in 2:4-8, which include (1) buildings (2:4), (2) various horticultural projects (2:4-6), (3) amassing of servants and cattle (2:7), and (4) amassing wealth, luxuries, and concubines (2:8).[10] But these significant public works do not achieve anything of lasting quality. He seems to be asking (rhetorically), "What can *I*, the superwise king, do so that I will be remembered, something to give lasting meaning to these fleeting days spent on earth?" (2:3). The answer given to his readers in 2:10-11, and consistent with what he has already announced in 1:11, is "nothing." He will not be remembered, and nothing even *he* does here to try to counter that will achieve the desired results. To put it plainly, Qohelet's royal voice is used to undercut any attempt to escape the finality of death — and the resulting absurdity of knowing that all human achievements will one day lie in ruin.

The final declaration of 2:10-11 is quite emphatic and contains elements that are very important for understanding the theology of Ecclesiastes. Indeed,

8. See Provan, *Ecclesiastes*, 38-39.

9. For a different point of view, that Qohelet is not only posing as a king "but even — for a moment — as God," see Verheij, "Paradise Retired," 113. I would add, however, that the role of any ancient Near Eastern king already had quasi-divine status.

10. On the last item mentioned, there is some debate concerning exactly what שִׁדָּה וְשִׁדּוֹת/ *šiddâ wĕšiddôt* refers to, but "a good number of concubines" seems to be the most defensible translation (see Fox, *Time to Tear Down*, 180; Longman, *Ecclesiastes*, 92). Seow argues for the alternate, "chests" or "coffers" (*Ecclesiastes*, 131-32).

they form a mini-summary of the book thus far, and as such act as a guidepost as we continue our study of the theology of Ecclesiastes. In v. 10 Qohelet says that he did not withhold "anything my eyes asked" (וְכֹל אֲשֶׁר שָׁאֲלוּ עֵינַי/ *wĕkōl ’ăšer šā’ălû ‘ênay*) nor did he "keep from my heart any sort of joy" (לֹא-מָנַעְתִּי אֶת-לִבִּי מִכָּל-שִׂמְחָה/ *lō’-māna‘tî ’et-libbî mikkol-śimḥâ*). Indeed, he took pleasure in all his "labor" (עמל/ *‘ml*). This is a very common root in Ecclesiastes and means more than just "work" in the contemporary sense of the word. It refers to any sort of labor or activity in which humans engage. Qohelet is saying here that his "work" is a source of joy *(śimḥâ)* for him, but — and this is crucial for understanding Qohelet's message — the benefit that comes from work in no way lessens or counters the impact of the inevitability of death to make all such work ultimately absurd. As he says in v. 11, everything (כֹּל/ *kōl*) is still absurd (הֶבֶל/ *hebel*), and every human activity is ultimately without profit (יִתְרוֹן/ *yitrôn*) because of the inevitability of death. But whereas our labors yield no ultimate, lasting benefit, they do yield some temporary benefit. To use Qohelet's words, our labors might not yield true *yitrôn*, but finding joy in them here and now is our portion, our lot (חֵלֶק/ *ḥēleq*).

Unfortunately, for someone as wise as Qohelet, he cannot help but ask, "But what real meaning is there in *that*, in finding joy here and now, knowing that death brings all such temporary joy to naught?" Qohelet is ultimately not satisfied or comforted by temporary joy, since what plagues him is not the absence of temporary meaning, but the absence of lasting meaning. To put it another way, what bothers him is that, at the end of the day, all our labor can *only* yield *ḥēleq*, not *yitrôn*. This is why wisdom is a burden that causes anguish (1:18) and why you are better off not having too much of it (7:16). Better to know less and just enjoy what you have and what you do. Or, as Qohelet puts it in the following chapter, "I know there is nothing better for men than to be happy and do good while they live" (3:12).

So, for Qohelet, having a "portion" is something to which one must be resigned. He makes this point in no uncertain terms in the closing verse of this section. In a retrospective glance, he surveys what he has done (root עשה/ *‘śh*) and that at which he had labored (root עמל/ *‘ml*) and concludes with a very emphatic pronouncement: וְהִנֵּה הַכֹּל הֶבֶל וּרְעוּת רוּחַ וְאֵין יִתְרוֹן תַּחַת הַשָּׁמֶשׁ/ *wĕhinnēh hakkōl hebel ûrĕ‘ût rûaḥ wĕ’ên yitrôn taḥat haššāmeš*, "Look, *everything* is absurd, a chasing of the wind. There is *no* payoff anywhere on earth." Once again, Qohelet underscores the driving theme of the book, announced in the introduction and to be reiterated at crucial junctures throughout the book. But already here we have reached a preliminary climax to the argument, for if even the king, who is wise beyond all others and has at his disposal all earthly resources, can arrive at only such a conclusion, then nothing more can be expected from commoners. Indeed, the epilogue warns us not to add anything to what has been said (12:12). In the next section (2:12-26) he develops even further that wisdom, folly, and labor have no payoff.

2:12-26: Wisdom, Folly, and Labor Have No Payoff

In 2:12 Qohelet picks up on a notion that he mentioned previously in 1:17: his consideration of wisdom (חָכְמָה/*ḥokmâ*), madness (הוֹלֵלוֹת/*hôlēlôt*), and folly (סִכְלוּת/*siklût*).[1] His reference to "the king" is not entirely clear, likewise the syntax of the second half of this verse.[2] Nonetheless, it seems safest to conclude that Qohelet's reference to royalty is to himself, and that his act of turning (פנה/*pnh*) to consider (ראה/*r'h*) wisdom, madness, and folly is one that others are in no position to duplicate. He is the king, and his search for meaning is, as he claims, qualitatively different from that of any other, even those who would succeed him.

What is more to the point here is what this search yields. He quickly asserts (v. 13) that wisdom has more profit (יִתְרוֹן/*yitrôn*) than folly, as light has more profit than darkness. Such a statement, however reassuring and orthodox it may appear, is in serious tension with his announcement in 1:18 that much wisdom brings much anger. It is also in tension with one of the driving concepts of the book, that there is really no profit in anything regardless of appearances (e.g., 1:3; 2:11; 3:9; 5:16-17). But wisdom seems to have partially escaped Qohelet's absolute sentence of futility. It is worth noting that nowhere does Qohelet say that wisdom is without *any* profit. Indeed, he begins his wisdom quest with the declaration that wisdom is his guide (1:13; 2:3). He continues in 2:14 to support the assertion by saying that a wise man's eyes are "in his head" while a foolish man walks about in darkness. He does not explain precisely what he means, but it is certainly a statement of at least the relative worth of wisdom over folly, if not an unqualified distinction between them.

---

1. The term for "folly" is spelled שִׂכְלוּת/*śiklût* in 1:17 and סִכְלוּת/*siklût* in 2:12 (as it is in all its other occurrences in Ecclesiastes: 2:3, 12, 13; 7:25; 10:1, 13). The variation is likely not significant, although it has been suggested that שׂכל/*śkl* in 1:17 may mean "prudent" (as it is understood in LXX, Peshitta, and Targums) and perhaps is meant by the author of Ecclesiastes to be understood ironically. See Seow, *Ecclesiastes*, 125.

2. The phrase מֶה הָאָדָם שֶׁ-/*meh hā'ādām še-* is difficult. The similar phrase מֶה שֶׁ-/*meh še-* is more common (1:9; 3:15, 22; 6:10; 7:24; 8:7; 10:14) and typically means "whatever." Also, the phrase "after the king" (אַחֲרֵי הַמֶּלֶךְ/*'aḥărê hammelek*) is awkward in that it is followed by a direct object, which leads Fox to pose an emendation, "after me who will rule" (אַחֲרַי הַמֹּלֵךְ/*'aḥăray hammōlēk*; see the use of *'aḥăray* in 2:18; Fox, *Time to Tear Down*, 182; Seow, *Ecclesiastes*, 134). Longman sees no need to emend the text (*Ecclesiastes*, 96-97).

But Qohelet does not leave us to ponder for long how to understand the implications of this comment. As we have already seen in 1:12-18, the momentary possibility of a positive move forward is quickly neutralized. Whatever profit there might be to wisdom over folly is leveled by the stark realization that "one fate fates both of them [the wise and the fool]."[3] It is, in other words, the specter of death that relativizes any profit to be found in this life. Wisdom truly has benefits over folly — so much so that the advantage can be spoken of as "profit." But any advantage of wisdom over folly is good only for this life and will come to an abrupt end when one dies, and this causes Qohelet serious consternation. Wisdom, in other words, has only relative profit, not absolute.

Beginning here and through v. 17 is Qohelet's first explicit reference to death's role as driving the breakdown of meaning, hinted at in 1:11. As such, it forms a handy summary of the book as a whole: *whatever haggling we do about what is of meaning, importance, and value in this life must face the fact that it is only for this life that such a discussion has any significance.* The universality of death ultimately and incontestably renders all things naught. Note that in v. 15 his fate is no different from that of the fool, an idea that stands in contrast to the thought expressed in the previous verse. Indeed, this observation leads Qohelet to question the value of being too wise (a thought he will revisit in 7:16). The reason death neutralizes the benefits of wisdom is expressed in v. 16. Neither the wise nor the fool is ever (לְעוֹלָם/*lĕʿôlām*) remembered, a theme introduced in 1:11, and that certainly appears to be in considerable tension with, for example, Prov 10:7.[4] Quickly[5] both are forgotten; there is ultimately no distinction between the two. In death the wise and the fool are on equal footing.

It is this situation that Qohelet refers to as הֶבֶל/*hebel* (v. 15). We see here quite clearly why *hebel* cannot mean something like "ephemeral" or "vacuous." The situation Qohelet is describing is not so much "empty" of meaning but nothing less than absurd, a maddening affront to reason where even such a basic principle as wisdom versus foolishness is turned on its head. Indeed, Qohelet's moral universe has become destabilized, and the inevitability of

---

3. "Fate" (מִקְרֶה/*miqreh*) occurs 7 times in Ecclesiastes (2:14, 15; 3:19 [3 times]; 9:2, 3) and always refers to death, so too the verbal form קרה/*qrh* (2:14, 15; 9:11). This wooden translation of 2:14b is meant to convey the rhythm of the Hebrew: מִקְרֶה אֶחָד יִקְרֶה אֶת-כֻּלָּם/*miqreh ʾeḥād yiqreh ʾet-kullām*. On the role of fate in Ecclesiastes see Machinist, "Fate, *miqreh*, and Reason."

4. "The memory of the righteous will be a blessing, but the name of the wicked will rot."

5. The Hebrew phrase הַיָּמִים הַבָּאִים/*hayyāmîm habbāʾim* is translated "all too soon" (Seow, *Ecclesiastes,* 136) or "only too soon" (Longman, *Ecclesiastes,* 99), and refers to the near future (Fox, *Time to Tear Down,* 184).

47

death is to blame. And this leads him to declare that he hates life itself (v. 17; הַחַיִּים/*haḥayyîm*, understood as "life," not "living people").[6] Qohelet's contention is not with people but with the entire state of affairs, as can be seen in what immediately follows: he is distressed (lit. "it is grievous to me" [רַע עָלַי/ *ra' 'ālay*]) by "the things done" under the sun. In other words, because the inevitability of death — and the speed with which the dead are forgotten — cancels out whatever advantage there might be to wisdom, life and all that is done under the sun are distressing. And this sentiment is underscored at the end of the verse: *everything* is *hebel* and a chasing of the wind.

But perhaps not all is as it seems, as Qohelet reasons in 2:18-23. Perhaps there is a way after all of infusing this situation with something positive. Perhaps one way to beat death is to leave the fruit of one's labor to your descendants. There is strong precedent in the OT for this line of thinking. The patriarchs, for example, found evidence of God's continued covenant faithfulness in seeing their offspring multiply and thrive in the land. Indeed, it is through one's *offspring* that God demonstrates favor to the *ancestor*. To put it another way, it is through the offspring that the ancestor continues to live, even after his own death.[7] And there is never any pessimism attached to earthly wealth, as it too is a sign of God's blessing. For Qohelet, however, the thought of finding such solace in those who come after is *hebel* (2:18-19). Why is this such a problem for Qohelet? He tells us in v. 19: there is no guarantee that the one to come after him, the one who will be in charge of the things Qohelet worked for, will be foolish or wise.

This point should not be passed over too quickly. What is absurd for Qohelet is that there is no way of knowing what kind of person will inherit the things he has worked so hard and so wisely to attain. Why is this absurd? Because, should the man be a fool, he would benefit from that for which he has not labored, a potential situation that further throws out of kilter the notion that wisdom brings blessing but foolishness brings negative consequences (e.g., Psalm 1). Qohelet's concern here is not so much the 50/50 possi-

---

6. See also Fox, *Time to Tear Down*, 181; Longman, *Ecclesiastes*, 100; Seow, *Ecclesiastes*, 118.

7. This holds well enough for the point being made here, but the matter is much more involved than how I have stated it. Brichto has argued, in painstaking detail, that in biblical Israel the dead experience some sort of nonmaterial consciousness, and that they do not simply live on through their descendants in the land, but: "They remain very much concerned about the fortunes of their descendants, for they are dependent on them, on their continued existence on the family land [i.e., to maintain their proper burial], on their performance of memorial rites, for a felicitous condition in the afterlife" ("Kin, Cult," 48). Whether or not one is immediately persuaded by Brichto's argument, the point remains that Qohelet would see little value in either explanation.

bility of a fool inheriting the fruit of his labor. It is the unpredictability of it all — it *should not* be left to chance like this. Yet this is how it is, and it causes him to despair.[8] After all, the one (i.e., Qohelet) who labored by wisdom, knowledge, and skill will wind up giving his portion to someone who did not work for that very portion (v. 21). In other words, the strict deed-consequence relationship, so often touted in Proverbs and in the law, comes to naught by simple virtue of the fact of death. Leaving one's goods to one's descendant is not the solution to the problem of death but the very thing that makes death's sting so harsh.

Moreover, Qohelet continues (vv. 22-23) that one's efforts in this life not only have no benefit in the face of death, but even now cause pain and grief. More specifically, he says, "all his days are מַכְאֹבִים/mak'ōbîm, and his עִנְיָן/ 'inyān is כַּעַס/ka'as." This is language we have seen already in chapter 1. In 1:13 it is God who has given humanity a grievous task (עִנְיָן רָע/'inyan rā'), and in 1:18 Qohelet complains that "much wisdom brings much *ka'as* [anger], and adding knowledge adds *mak'ôbîm* [irritation]." It should not escape our notice that Qohelet's complaint in 2:22-23 is in keeping with what he says in 1:13, 18: "There is no way out of this situation, and I do not like what *God* is doing here. You work your whole life and leave it to someone who did not work for it. To boot, all the effort exerted, which includes sleepless nights (v. 23b), is nothing more than pain and grief. This is absurd (הֶבֶל/hebel)."

It is with this in mind that we come to our first so-called carpe diem passage in Ecclesiastes: 2:24-26.[9] We should not think of what Qohelet utters here as a brief moment of clarity where he comes to a suitable resolution to his anguish expressed above — much less to a "positive" statement[10] more suitable for a sermon topic. He is not admonishing his readers to "seize the day" or "grab for the gusto" while they have a chance. Rather, Qohelet strikes a tone of deep resignation. To see this we need only glance down to the end of v. 26, where he repeats his *hebel* refrain: what he is about to say will further enforce the general tone of absurdity struck above. Also, this is the first of sev-

---

8. Fox argues that the root יאשׁ/y'š here suggests not simply despair but disillusionment, as it does in Rabbinic Hebrew (*Time to Tear Down*, 188).

9. Fischer offers the inviting thesis that Qohelet's "call for joy" passages have been indirectly influenced in numerous ways by the "'heretic' Harpers' Songs of Egypt," which "agree not only in the content and reasoning for joy, but also in the use of idioms, phrases and themes, which occur not just in key texts but elsewhere in Qohelet" ("Qohelet and 'Heretic' Harpers' Songs," 105, 117).

10. Cf. Paulson's view, "I do not read these as words of despair but as words of wisdom. This is the wisdom of one who understands God, not the human, is the center of all that is, the center of being and knowing and doing" ("Use of Qoheleth in Bonhoeffer's *Ethics*," 309).

eral **אֵין-טוֹב**/*'ên ṭôb* ("there is nothing better than") sayings in Ecclesiastes.[11] Whatever "good" there is in this life is provisional, that is, the best we can do. There is nothing better for people, in view of the inevitable and leveling effect of death, than to eat, drink, and enjoy themselves[12] in their labor. Why? Because, as Qohelet tells us, "it is from the hand of God" (**מִיַּד הָאֱלֹהִים**/*mîyyad hā'ĕlōhîm*). But this should not be understood as a note of thanks to God for his gracious provision. It is, as we have seen in 1:13, 18, and will see again later, a concession that all this *hebel* is God's doing. After all, Qohelet tells us, "who eats and who frets (**יָחוּשׁ**/*yāḥûš*) apart from him (**מִמֶּנּוּ**/*mimmennû*)?"[13] God is in control; he determines the good and the bad. This is not a comfort for Qohelet but the very reason for his consternation. Keeping this in mind will help us understand Qohelet's meaning in 3:1-9 below, a passage that is often misunderstood in popular expositions.

Qohelet's final note of resignation is in v. 26. He might appear to be saying, "God gives a reward to saints, but punishes sinners." A more careful reading, however, will reveal the opposite. We must remember that Qohelet's argument thus far has been anything but "God's rewards are just." Rather he has been questioning that very notion. The phrase in question, "to the man who is good before him [God]," does not mean "the one who behaves well toward God [and is therefore 'good' before him]," or something like that. To be "good before God" (**טוֹב לְפָנָיו**/*ṭôb lĕpānāyw*) means to be pleasing to God, or better, to be one God favors. In other words, being pleasing to God is not, for Qohelet, a result of what we do, but a result of what God feels like doing. So God gives wisdom, knowledge, and joy to whomever he pleases. Likewise, the word **חוֹטֵא**/*ḥôṭe'*, elsewhere translated (correctly) as "sinner," here has a different nuance. Rather than signifying a transgression of a moral code, it means "one who is offensive to God," or as Seow adds, "the offender."[14] His offense seems to be nothing in particular — or at least Qohelet does not specify — and so suggests that he is simply one on whom God's favor does not

11. Or perhaps better, "there is nothing good except." See also 3:12, 22; 8:15. See Ogden, "The 'Better'-Proverb."

12. See Seow, *Ecclesiastes*, 139. The Hebrew reads: **וְהֶרְאָה אֶת-נַפְשׁוֹ טוֹב**/*wĕher'â 'et-napšô ṭôb*, "cause him to see/experience good."

13. We encounter a couple of problems in the Hebrew text. The root **יחשׁ**/*yḥš* can mean to hasten or enjoy, but it is understood by Seow (*Ecclesiastes*, 139-40; "glean"), Longman (*Ecclesiastes*, 108-9; "worry"), and Fox (*Time to Tear Down*, 189; "fret") as standing in some sense as antithetical to "eat" in the first half of the verse (note a similar antithesis between two opposites in v. 26). The final word is about as clear a case of textual corruption as one finds in Ecclesiastes. As the MT stands, it reads "apart from me" (**מִמֶּנִּי**/*mimmennî*) but should certainly be understood as "apart from him" (**מִמֶּנּוּ**/*mimmennû*), and commentators are in routine agreement with such an emendation.

14. Seow, *Ecclesiastes*, 141-42.

rest, a "tough-luck guy."[15] It is to this sort of person that God has given the task (עִנְיָן/*'inyān*) of working for the benefit of the one he favors.

This very set of circumstances, which occurs at God's discretion, is judged by Qohelet as absurd. God does as he pleases, even if it is an affront to reason, and explains himself to no one. This same theme is developed further in the following passage.

3:1-15: All Things Have Their Place

This section concludes with Qohelet's second carpe diem passage and includes the first of four instances of the phrase כָּל-הָאָדָם/*kol-hā'ādām* (v. 13). The latter issue in particular has already been treated in the introduction as it pertains to the epilogue and the meaning of Ecclesiastes as a whole, and so I will not dwell on it in this passage.

When we come to the opening verses of this passage, it is important that we resist playing in our minds the catchy tune written by Pete Seeger and made more popular by the Byrds in the 1960s ("Turn, Turn, Turn"). The harmonies are nice, but this passage is anything but harmonious. Rather, we must read this passage in light of what we have seen this far and what we see later.

First, in v. 1 Qohelet says that for "everything" there is a "season" (לַכֹּל זְמָן/*lakkol zĕmān*). Both the words and the context indicate that a specific, perhaps even appointed, time is in view. In English, "season" can have the unfortunate connotation of a rather pleasing passage of time, or at least a passage of time that may simply fade into another season. But we should not make such an assumption in the case of Qohelet. He has not yet defined what he means by "season," but he will make things clearer as we go along. The same holds true for the next phrase, "and a time for every 'pleasure/purpose'" (וְעֵת לְכָל-חֵפֶץ/*wě'ēt lĕkol-ḥēpeṣ*). The word *ḥēpeṣ* normally refers to some something pleasurable or delightful, but, as Qohelet's subsequent remarks make clear, there is little delightful about it. It may be that Qohelet is being ironical here, perhaps even a bit sarcastic: "My, all these things I am about to list are so *wonderful*, aren't they?"

The nuances of v. 1 can only be explained on the basis of what follows, but one last comment on this introductory verse is in order, and it concerns the familiar phrase "under the sun." Qohelet's scope here is to describe what is

---

15. But see Fox, who argues that some offense is in view, namely the offense of endless toiling (*Time to Tear Down*, 190).

going on across the expanse of the human drama (see 1:3). He is not just casually kicking around some concepts, but making a comprehensive statement of some sort. And, if we have learned anything about Qohelet's outlook thus far, we should expect that statement to have a rather pessimistic slant, perhaps even a further airing out of his grievances toward the one who is ultimately responsible for setting "times" and "seasons."

Qohelet's famous list of activities in 3:2-8 exhibits a pattern. Each verse is composed of two pairs of opposing concepts, each prefaced with "a time for."[1] One observation is that the reference to opposite extremes may be an example of merism, a poetic device whereby extremes are used to describe not only the extremes but everything in between (e.g., birth and death referring to the whole of one's life). One cannot be dogmatic on this point, but there is some value in at least entertaining this notion, for it seems that Qohelet's scope is sweeping, not only in his use of "under the sun" in v. 1, but in the very list of activities to follow. With each pair, Qohelet is saying something that is intended to speak to *all* of life, not merely parts of it. Precisely how very despondent Qohelet is will be made clearer in vv. 9-11, but even here at the outset we see clues that what is to come may be a bit more challenging than we often allow.

To come more directly to the point, these "times" enumerated in vv. 2-8 are things that happen *to* us. We do not choose them. Again, this will be clearer below, but even here we see that Qohelet does not say something like, "Sometimes we are born, sometimes we die." He is saying, "There *is a time* for being born and a time for dying." There is a distinction between these two ways of understanding Qohelet. The former allows for the effectiveness of human will, to choose one or the other. Such a conclusion is hard to square with what we have seen thus far (and, again, will see in a few verses). If anything, Qohelet is about the absurd inevitability of what "life" brings us — or, more pointedly, what God brings us. Think here again of passages like 1:13 and 1:15, where Qohelet, very early on in his opening remarks, clues the readers in that it is with God that he takes issue. Indeed, it is profitable for us to think of this list in 3:2-8 as a reiteration of what was declared earlier in the opening chapter, 1:5-8. Qohelet's list of human activities in 3:2-8 parallels his list of natural activities in 1:5-8. Both are inevitable, frustrating, absurd — and the way in which God himself set things up. This is not to say, for example, that God dictates the precise moments in which certain activities happen. Rather, he is making a case that our activities fit into a grand design,

---

1. The Hebrew is either עֵת/'ēt followed by the preposition ל/l, or simply עֵת/'ēt (vv. 4b and 8b). There is no subtlety to be distinguished between these forms.

where everything, from birth and death, to war and peace, to silence and speaking, is affected.[2]

Before we flesh this out a bit further, we should take a closer look at the list itself. It covers a wide gambit of human activities, even though some of what Qohelet refers to eludes our understanding. It does not seem that there is anything special about the ordering of the list, although the fact that the first pair, "a time to be born[3] and a time to die," is a fittingly comprehensive way to begin. There is a "time" (appointed by God) for when we begin and end life. In a manner of speaking, this is a grand merism that envelops the merisms of the subsequent verses. And it is perhaps no accident that the life cycle of helpless, nonvolitional plants is outlined in the very next pair: planting and uprooting. At first glance one might suggest that these describe human activities of farming, and hence are descriptive of human life, as are many of the pairs that follow. That may be the case, but it could also be understood as an unnerving illustration of his declaration of human frailty on the previous pair. Either way, the inevitability of these activities is not affected: one does not sow whenever one wishes, nor uproot what was planted when it is convenient. God has appointed these times (in this case, corresponding to our word "seasons") when such things are possible.

What follows in v. 3 is killing/healing and tearing down/building up. Again, it is tempting to understand the second pair as an illustration of the first. I am fairly convinced this is the case, but one must also observe that this pairing of human and nonhuman elements is quickly abandoned in vv. 4ff. It could be that vv. 2 and 3 serve as a broad introduction of sorts to the entire list, but little is gained by insisting on the point. What is more important for understanding the overall message of vv. 2-8 is not trying to delineate the precise meanings and relationships within and among the pairs,[4]

---

2. See Fox, *Time to Tear Down*, 197-98.

3. The Hebrew infinitive is active (לָלֶדֶת/*lāledet*), which has led some commentators to translate the phrase "a time to bear, and time to die" or perhaps better "birthing" and "dying" (Seow, *Ecclesiastes*, 160). The matter affects only the precise translation of the phrase, and not the merismatic contrast between the two events. Blenkinsopp argues that the term must be transitive and so likewise לָמוּת/*lāmût* does not mean a time of "death" but "to put an end to one's life," i.e., suicide ("Ecclesiastes 3.1-15," 57). This, Blenkinsopp continues, is consistent with early Stoic philosophy, and therefore suggests that the entire poem of vv. 2-8 is not original to Qohelet but only appropriated by him.

4. For example, the meaning of v. 5a is not clear (casting and gathering stones). On the basis of v. 5b, some have suggested a possible sexual connotation, whereas others suggest it refers to caring for one's flock. See Fox (*Time to Tear Down*, 207-8), Longman (*Ecclesiastes*, 116), and Seow (*Ecclesiastes*, 161-62) for succinct discussions on the matter. Also worth noting is the use of the preposition לְ/*l* throughout these pairs except for v. 8b, where the nouns "war" and "peace" are used.

but keeping in mind the broad picture and seeing where Qohelet is leading these observations.

In addition to the hints we have already seen to this point, whatever notions one might still have that 3:1-8 are serene words of comfort begin to dissolve completely when we come to v. 9. Here we see a phrase that includes three words that should already be familiar to us. Translated somewhat literally, "What profit (יִתְרוֹן/*yitrôn*) is there for the doer (הָעוֹשֶׂה/*hāʿôśeh*) in which he toils (עָמֵל/*ʿāmēl*)?" This sentiment concludes the list of activities we have seen in vv. 2-8 and asks the rhetorical question: "All this toiling; what payoff is there for the one engaged in all these things?" In other words, the list of activities in 3:2-8 illustrates there is no payoff, no surplus for life's "times." Moreover, in v. 10 he makes his point more clearly, where he repeats 1:13, virtually verbatim, "I have seen the preoccupation that God has given humanity with which to occupy him." This wooden translation clarifies that, as in 1:13, it is God who has given humanity a "task" or "preoccupation" for the simple purpose, it seems, of keeping people occupied. Perhaps the most important difference between 3:10 and 1:13 is that in the latter Qohelet refers to this task as a "grievous task," an עִנְיָן רָע/*ʿinyan rāʿ*. Still, the point remains that this cycle of life serves no ultimate purpose, and it is by God's doing. In other words, 3:2-8 are without profit, and these tasks of planting, uprooting; living, dying; dancing, mourning, and so on, are God's fault. What Qohelet mentioned at the outset, perhaps somewhat unexpectedly, is here repeated, and so drives home what may be one of the most important themes for understanding Ecclesiastes, a theme that casts a dark shadow over much of the book: *Qohelet is at least disillusioned with God, if not out-and-out angry with him, for the way things are.*

Verse 11 must be read in the same vein. When he says, "He [God] has made everything יָפֶה/*yāpeh* in its time (בְעִתּוֹ/*bĕʿittô*)," Qohelet does not mean that everything is "beautiful" (a common translation of *yāpeh*). This is hardly the place for an aesthetic comment, which would be wholly out of accord with the persistent point Qohelet is making here. Rather, God has made everything "appropriate" or perhaps better "well-ordered" in its *time* (the word עֵת/*ʿēt*, which we have seen throughout 3:1-8). In other words, Qohelet is simply reiterating the note of despondency we have seen beginning at 3:1: God ordains the times and seasons, and humanity pretty much goes along for the ride.

For Qohelet, however, it is worse than this. As if to frustrate humanity further, God has also set עֹלָם/*ʿōlām* into their hearts (v. 11). We must resist reading foreign notions of "eternity" into *ʿōlām* (see 1:4, 10; 2:16). Qohelet is not saying that, despite this sorry state of affairs, God reminds us that there is an afterlife awaiting us, where all these questions will be answered. Rather,

God has put in our hearts, that is, made us aware of, the *expanse of time,* both backward and forward.[5] We, as human beings, are unfortunately conscious of the passage of time, and we can extrapolate on and on, both back in time and forward in time. This is precisely what Qohelet is doing, for example, in 1:9-10. He is able to say that, regardless of outward appearances, there really is nothing new — ever. Whatever is, "already was לְעֹלָמִים/*lĕ'ōlāmîm*" (1:10). To put it another way, *'ōlām* is a companion concept to "under the sun." They reflect the great expanse of human existence, and it is this very awareness, that time goes on and on, both into the past and future, that God has placed in our hearts. And to clinch it Qohelet himself provides the reason in the second half of 3:11 for why God has done this: "so that[6] man is not able to comprehend that which God has done from the beginning to the end." God is no friend to humanity, as Qohelet sees it. God orders and appoints times, from which there is no escape, and laboring, which brings no profit. This is just the way God wants it, and to top it all off, he gives humanity the ability to comprehend the futility of it all.

Qohelet's flourish here sets a tone of discouragement, to say the least. But in vv. 12-13, as discussed in the introduction, Qohelet finds a way forward, however provisional and ultimately unsatisfying for him. In view of this depressing state of affairs, he proclaims that there is "nothing better than" to enjoy and do "good" (again, not a moral concept but referring to experiencing good things) in one's life (v. 12). He continues in v. 13 by saying that our existence is summed up (כָּל-הָאָדָם/*kol-hā'ādām*) by "eating, drinking, experiencing good in all of our labors." *That* is the "gift" God has given us.

As if Qohelet even delights in driving home a difficult point, vv. 14-15 bring even further clarity to the general point he has been making throughout

---

5. See also Provan, *Ecclesiastes,* 90; Shields, *End of Wisdom,* 142; Bartholomew, *Reading Ecclesiastes,* 243. The entire matter is summarized well by Gault, "Reexamination of 'Eternity.'" After assessing the options, Gault argues for revocalizing עֹלָם/*'ōlām* to the hapax legomenon עֶלֶם/*'elem* (darkness). Hence God has placed darkness in the heart of humanity so that they would enjoy what they have, trust his sovereignty, and not try to discover his divine program (57).

6. The Hebrew phrase I translate "so that" is a bit cumbersome; it is unique in the OT: מִבְּלִי אֲשֶׁר לֹא/*mibbĕlî 'ăšer lō'*. It could be understood either as indicating purpose, as I have done (see also Seow, *Ecclesiastes,* 163), or result (i.e., the result of God making everything fitting is that he has put עוֹלָם/*'ōlām* into our hearts). Fox translates this phrase "without" (*Ecclesiastes,* 23; *Qohelet and His Contradictions,* 191), which renders a different sense: God has put *'ōlām* into our hearts (which Fox emends to עָמָל/*'āmāl,* "toil," but that is beside the point here), but without giving man the added benefit of being able to discern just what God is doing. Longman finds here a double negative, "but still, no one. . . ." (*Ecclesiastes,* 112). I find the "purpose" option to be most convincing, but again, the more basic point of this passage is not affected: what God is doing is being seriously questioned, even challenged, by Qohelet.

this passage. He knows that *everything* God has done, he has done לְעוֹלָם/
lĕʿôlām. "Everything" certainly refers to the activities of God mentioned thus
far, not least the profitless cycle of life situations outlined in 3:2-8. This is what
God has done and it will last, rest assured. Qohelet himself clarifies this in the
following clause in a manner somewhat reminiscent of 1:15: there is no adding
to it or taking from it. There is, in other words, nothing we as people can do
other than the meager "there is nothing better than" advice given in v. 12. And
God does this, to close out v. 14, so that "they will fear him." To put it rather
starkly, Qohelet here considers God to be no friend of his, no source of comfort.[7] And the final verse of this passage reintroduces an idea first uttered in
1:9-11, and thus helps clarify how the frame narrator was intent on summarizing Qohelet's outlook: "What is, already was; what will be, already was." Again,
this is just the way things are, and there is nothing any of us can do about it.

What is difficult to discern in this closing verse is the meaning of the final clause. It appears to be disjunctive (ו/*w* followed by the noun הָאֱלֹהִים/
hāʾĕlōhîm). Literally it can be rendered: "*But* God seeks that which is pur-
sued," a combination of words that sparks much discussion among commentators. The general notion is certainly one of futility, and commentators
widely agree on that point. Seow suggests, for example, that God seeks "all
those matters that are beyond human grasp."[8] Or, one might suggest, in keeping with the previous clause, that God seeks that which has already happened.[9] Along these lines, Crenshaw's explanation, cited approvingly by Fox,
is worth citing here as well.[10] He also ties 3:15 to 1:9 and writes, "There is nothing new. Why? Because God ensures that events which have just transpired do
not vanish into thin air. God brings them back once more, so that the past circles into the present."[11] Ecclesiastes 3:1-15 is a passage that argues in greater
detail what has been addressed more briefly earlier in the book, both by
Qohelet himself and the frame narrator. He gives us here his blunt, even unsettling, observations on what he thinks God is doing. And this is no passing
thought, for, as we shall see, he returns to similar articulations elsewhere. At
this point, our objective is to see as best as we can precisely where Qohelet is
taking us and why. This passage is a significant signpost on that journey.

---

7. I disagree with views, such as that proposed by Parsons, that 3:14 is one example (along
with 5:7; 7:18; 8:12-13) that the fear of God, understood in the more traditional sense (e.g., Prov
1:7), "is not an afterthought but is a theme woven into the fabric of the book" ("Guidelines, Part
1," 164).

8. Seow, *Ecclesiastes*, 174.

9. See brief discussion by Longman, *Ecclesiastes*, 124-25; Fox, *Time to Tear Down*, 213-14.

10. Fox, *Time to Tear Down*, 213-14.

11. Crenshaw, *Ecclesiastes*, 100.

3:16–4:3: Everything Dies

This is a relatively brief section (ten verses), but it is marked off by an "I saw" (רָאִיתִי/*rā'îtî*) clause in 3:16 and then another in 4:4. It seems, therefore, that 3:16–4:3 is a unit that, although not self-contained (nothing in Ecclesiastes is self-contained), is nevertheless a portion of the book that adds its own distinct contribution to the flow of Qohelet's argument.

Qohelet begins with a complaint about the lack of justice in the world (3:16-17). No matter where he looks under the sun, justice and guilt, right behavior and guilt, are flip-flopped. In v. 17 he considers the fact that God will judge the one in the right and the perpetrator, but that is at best a temporary and shallow consolation, if not an outright taunt, for v. 17 closes with words familiar to us from the previous section: "There is a time (עֵת/*'ēt*) for every matter (חֵפֶץ/*ḥēpeṣ*) and for every deed there."[1] The flip-floppings of justice and injustice are likewise times under God's complete control and direction. God's order of life's events goes beyond times of birthing and dying, sowing and reaping, sewing and tearing as in 3:1-8. It includes the very notion of justice, an observation of Qohelet that clearly puts him in some tension with his own Israelite heritage, but such is the level of frustration and despondency he is experiencing. It is, as he has already put it twice, a "task" or "grievous task" that God has laid upon humanity (1:13; 3:10). One begins to sense that Qohelet is beginning to let his hair down.

This tone of despondency continues with vigor in the verses that follow, although we are faced here with an interpretive difficulty. Verse 18 begins, "I thought[2] concerning humanity . . . ," but the following phrase is not clear.[3] Specifically, the problem word is לְבָרָם/*lĕbārām*, followed by "God" (הָאֱלֹהִים/*hā'ĕlōhîm*). Various attempts have been made to make sense of *lĕbārām*, but none is universally convincing. There is no question, given the immediate context, that, whatever the word means, it is not intended to be an encouragement.[4]

---

1. "There," Heb. שָׁם/*šām*, seems to echo שָׁמָּה/*šāmmāh* in v. 16 (with the locative ה/*h*). It ultimately refers, I think, to "under the sun" at the beginning of this section. Hence an acceptable translation for the last line in v. 17 is, "For there is a time for every matter, and concerning every deed there/under the sun."

2. Lit. "I said in my heart," which is to be understood as a cognitive act. Qohelet is here, as he is throughout the book, engaged in a thought experiment based on his own broad experiences and observations. For an important distillation of Qohelet's epistemology, see Fox, *Time to Tear Down*, 71-86.

3. See Buhlman, "Difficulty."

4. The preposition ל/*l* seems to be followed by a verbal root ברר/*brr* I (to purge, sort, choose) followed by the plural masculine suffix. Fox, however, leaves the word untranslated,

Whether we render the verb "test" or "choose," it is Qohelet's observation that God wants to see[5] that "they are like animals." We have here one of the more beautiful examples of alliteration in the entire book: שֶׁהֶם-בְּהֵמָה הֵמָּה לָהֶם/ *šĕhem bĕhēmâ hēmmâ lāhem*. Seow suggests that *hēmmâ* is redundant and should therefore be omitted.[6] Fox suggests the same for *lāhem*.[7] But, as we have seen already, as early as 1:7, alliteration is a tool of Qohelet that audibly communicates what he is saying conceptually — what goes around comes around, and there is nothing at all that humanity can do about it. Here Qohelet is making that point by saying that humanity, in clear tension with Genesis 1, is no better off than animals. In God's eyes nothing separates the two.

Qohelet apparently just cannot wait to explain in precisely what way humans are no different from animals. In somewhat repetitive fashion, he states in v. 19 that both humanity and animals share one fate (מִקְרֶה/*miqreh*). One may recall a similar sentiment expressed in 2:14, 15, where Qohelet tells us that the wise and foolish share the same fate. There is no ultimate advantage of the wise over the fool, since both die. Death nullifies any possibility of "profit" (יִתְרוֹן/*yitrôn*). Here it is even worse. Death even levels the playing field between humanity and animals. As v. 19 makes clear, both share the same fate, one dies like the other, both have "one breath,"[8] there is no advantage[9] for humans over animals, for (predictably) "everything is absurd" (הַכֹּל הָבֶל/*hakkōl hābel*).

Qohelet is clearly quite consumed with this observation, for he continues his relentless description through v. 21. We see in v. 20 that everyone (הַכֹּל/*hakkōl;* or perhaps better, "everything") goes[10] to one place; everything

---

noting that a finite verb seems to be missing (*Time to Tear Down*, 214, 216). Seow reads the *lamed* as an asseverative "*surely* God has chosen them" (*Ecclesiastes*, 167). Longman translates the verb "test," akin to "choose" or "sort," based on broader contextual factors (*Ecclesiastes*, 128). Like Seow, Longman takes the *lamed* as an asseverative and the verb as a finite verb (Qal perfect), noting the awkwardness of having "God" as the subject of an infinitive. As Longman explains, however, and I agree, the general sense of the passage is clear.

5. The verb here is a Qal infinitive construct of ראה/*r'h*, although commentators routinely suggest a revocalization to a Hiphil. This is not an issue, however, that need detain us. Whether God himself wants to see (Qal) or he wants to show (Hiphil), the result is the same: people are like animals.

6. *Ecclesiastes*, 168.

7. *Time to Tear Down*, 216.

8. Here, as in v. 21, breath symbolizes life.

9. The Hebrew word here is מוֹתַר/*môtar*, which is from the same root יתר/*ytr* that gives us the more common word in Ecclesiastes, יִתְרוֹן/*yitrôn* (profit).

10. The verbal root here is הלך/*hlk*, which, as we have seen as early as 1:4, often, though not exclusively, carries connotations of death in Ecclesiastes.

comes from dust and returns to dust. That is what awaits every living creature. And do not bother trying to provide solace for Qohelet with some notion of the afterlife: he rejects it, or at least any way of knowing for sure. It is worth mentioning that some notion of the afterlife in Israelite thought must have been current for such a denunciation to have made sense (although there are hardly enough details here to suggest a full picture for us). As Qohelet argues in v. 21, however, no one knows one way or the other whether the "breath" of a human goes up or whether the "breath" of animals goes down.

The word picture Qohelet is painting here is clear, if also out of accord with the overall biblical witness. Still, Qohelet leaves us no safety net here, no escape into the mainstream of orthodoxy. He is almost taunting his readers: "I dare you, make a case for how we differ from animals in terms of our ultimate end! Any case you make, I can thwart with simple observation: we do not know — period. What we do know is that we will all die, and it is this ever-present threat that renders any activity, and labor in which we engage, wholly pointless, without profit."

Qohelet puts the final stamp on his observation by reiterating in v. 22, albeit in a more abbreviated fashion, his conclusion in the previous section (3:12-14). This state of affairs leads Qohelet to the lamentable conclusion that there is "nothing better than"[11] to enjoy one's work, because that is our portion. As we have seen above in 2:24-26 and 3:12-14, these carpe diem moments are anything but a resolution to the problems he articulates. They actually underscore the severity of the problem. In other words, in view of what he has been saying through v. 21, the *best* we can do, our "portion" (חֵלֶק/*ḥēleq;* see 2:21), is to enjoy what we do (i.e., day to day). Live in the now, for, as v. 22 ends, "Who can bring him to see what will happen after him?" "Him" refers to humanity, and "after him" could refer to after one's death, which would be in keeping with the theme of the (unknown) afterlife mentioned just above. The point would be that no one knows what will happen to him/her after death. On the other hand, "after him" could also refer to what will happen on earth after one is gone. Some have also understood the word simply to mean "afterward," that is, in the course of one's life. Commentators are somewhat divided over this issue,[12] and I will not try to resolve the matter here. What is important to focus on is that death is what renders life absurd (v. 19), and the best

---

11. The Hebrew phrase here, אֵין טוֹב מֵאֲשֶׁר/*’ên ṭôb mē’ăšer,* is repeated in some form at various junctures throughout Ecclesiastes (e.g., 2:24; 3:12).

12. See Longman, *Ecclesiastes,* 131; Fox, *Time to Tear Down,* 217. Seow argues that the phrase must mean after one's death (*Ecclesiastes,* 168).

one can do is provide for provisional meaning for oneself, to live in the moment, because the future is not known to anyone. And going back to 3:11, it is precisely this knowledge that God has enabled humanity to ponder. Qohelet's struggle here, not only with death but with a God who allows this absurdity to continue, is evident.

It may appear as if a new section begins at 4:1, and such a demarcation is quite defensible (note the language of "turning" and "seeing"), but I have chosen to address 4:1-3 in this context because of Qohelet's continued focus on death. Moreover, I see a more major transition at 4:4 with the repetition of רָאִיתִי/*rā'îtî* (I saw), as we saw in 3:16.

In 4:1 Qohelet laments the injustice of oppression, that it simply continues and there is no comfort. Although not stated explicitly, we see perhaps not too far below the surface the question lurking, "And why doesn't God do something about it?" Qohelet's solution in v. 2 is to find some solace, no doubt ironically, in death. The "dead who have already died" are to be praised more than "the living who were still alive" (note Qohelet's redundancy in both clauses). And as if to drive the stake further in, he completes his thought in v. 3 by echoing words reminiscent of Job (see Job 3:1-26): "Better than both of these is the one who has not yet been, who has not seen the רָע/*rā'* deed which is done under the sun." That which raised in Qohelet an angry rebuttal in 3:19-22, the inevitability of death, now turns out to be a welcome solace in view of the inevitability and invincibility of oppression. Indeed, nonexistence is preferable to looking upon such a state of affairs.

At this point, we have moved through only roughly a quarter of the book, and the picture painted by Qohelet is one of utter exasperation with what he sees all around him, without any attempt at making the best of a bad situation, with the inevitability of death, and its ability to render all human effort without profit, and the fact that God does not simply stand there and do nothing, but is actually overseeing the entire process. One might breathe a sigh of relief that the book is not nearly over: perhaps Qohelet can redeem himself. But he has not finished twisting the dagger. He will move on from here to address other issues, although he does not leave behind the themes developed in the first three-plus chapters. Relief is not in sight for us. That is not Qohelet's intention.

4:4-16: Hard Work, Ambition, Advancement Have No Payoff

Having ended on the rather despondent note of 4:3, that it is better not to have been born at all rather than to experience the harsh realities of life under

the sun, Qohelet continues his note of despair. In the following verses he focuses on themes such as hard work, ambition, and advancement, all of which
one might think can bring meaning to life, but that in reality provide no solution to the dilemma Qohelet is laying out for his readers.

Qohelet introduces a new concept in 4:4 (as seen by the repetition of
רָאִיתִי/rā'îtî; see 3:16). With respect to one's toil and skillful deeds, he declares
that it all boils down to a matter of jealousy (קִנְאָה/qin'â). It is not entirely
clear from the syntax of v. 4 whether one's labor causes such jealousy or
whether jealousy is what drives humanity to do such "skilled work," although
many commentators seem to prefer the latter.[1] I agree with this general consensus, and this underscores Qohelet's recurring evaluation that "this too is
absurd and a chasing after the wind." The very thing by which humanity can
have some solace, to experience the "good" in one's labor (e.g., 3:13), is here at
least relativized, if not swept into the dustbin. One's labor, indeed, even the
successful, skilled work we might achieve, is driven by human jealousy. In one
respect, this observation comes out of nowhere in Ecclesiastes, but its universal and timeless dimensions are not difficult to see: people want more than
the next guy; we keep up with the Joneses; we covet.

But what then would Qohelet have us do in view of this insight? Should
we abandon all work, lest we give in to jealous desires? He "clarifies" the matter
in vv. 5-6 by posing two scenarios on opposite extremes. Verse 5: The fool folds
his hands (i.e., does not work) and so "consumes his flesh" (וְאֹכֵל אֶת-בְּשָׂרוֹ/
wě'ōkēl 'et-běśārô).[2] Laziness is one extreme that Qohelet quickly mentions, as
if to say to his readers, "I do not mean to go *there*." On the other hand, laboring
in the sense of chasing the wind, as mentioned in v. 4, is not the answer either.
Rather, the proper perspective is to find the mean amid the extremes. As v. 6
puts it, it is better to have one hand full with a bit of peace of mind (lit. "rest")[3]
than to have two handfuls and be on a fruitless quest (chasing the wind). This
principle of "moderation amid extremes" is one Qohelet will return to later
(e.g., 7:15-18), and it seems to be a coping technique of Qohelet for addressing
the absurdity of life. As he has argued before, too much wisdom can get in the
way. It is better just to lie low, accept what you have as a gift from God (2:24;

---

1. The Hebrew phrase כִּשְׁרוֹן הַמַּעֲשֶׂה/kišrôn hamma'ăśeh implies some sort of well-done
piece of work, hence "skilled work" (Fox, *Time to Tear Down*, 220); "success in work" (Longman,
Ecclesiastes, 136); "achievement" (Seow, *Ecclesiastes*, 177). Seow and Longman understand jealousy to be the cause of our attempts at achievement, whereas Fox's translation leaves the matter
unclear: "all toil and skilled work are [merely] one man's envy of another."

2. As Seow puts it, "Qohelet is using the grotesque imagery of self-cannibalism to speak
of self-destruction" (*Ecclesiastes*, 187).

3. As Fox puts it, "earned calmly" (*Time to Tear Down*, 220).

3:13), not ask too many questions, and try not to let wisdom drive you crazy (1:18; 3:10-11).

In the following verses, Qohelet presses the matter even further, arguing that being alone especially makes one's labor worthless. There is perhaps a sense of irony here. He began this section by saying how one's labor is a result of the jealousy of one for another. Here he laments the lack of companionship in one's labor. One gets a mental picture of Qohelet on a lonely walk, talking to himself, trying to make sense of it all, seeing how true something is on the one hand, yet how utterly true and devastating the opposite is too. Or more appropriate might be the picture of poor Gollum (of Tolkien's *Lord of the Rings* series), whose inward struggles between two extremes are laid bare for the reader to see ("nasty hobbitses" vs. "no, master is good to Smeagol"). So here too, as we have seen, Qohelet ends with at least some sort of resolution in v. 6 (work but do not let it consume you) only to follow with another discouraging observation, which, to remove any doubt, he labels as another example of absurdity under the sun (v. 7).

What is his problem now? He imagines someone alone in the world, with no "second," no son or brother. Still, there is no end to all his labor, and he never seems to get enough (v. 8). The last phrase may be more woodenly rendered: "his eyes are not sated of wealth." What is interesting is that he follows this third person observation with a first person comment: "For whom am I laboring and depriving myself of what is good?" The move to first person may reveal Qohelet's inner struggle, that labor, as unavoidable as it is, is of no value when done solely for oneself. Or, the first person may give some concreteness to the observation. Either way, it is, once again, absurd, and a "grievous task" (עִנְיַן רָע/'*inyan rāʿ*), a phrase already encountered in 1:13 and 3:10. But recall that Qohelet's point in those two verses is to lay the blame at God's feet for why things are the way they are. There is no reason to assume the same line of thought is not being carried forward here. There is something deeply wrong in what he is describing, and God is at the root of it.

His mind keeps running forward, and he observes that, rather than laboring alone, two are better than one because they will receive a good wage for their labor together. It is hard to see the logical flow of how, in the span of a few verses, we can move from Qohelet saying, on the one hand, it is better never to have been born than to live, that any good labor is a result of jealousy, one is better off not to grasp for *too much*, to, on the other hand, laboring alone is absurd because with a partner you can earn *more*. Perhaps Qohelet is thinking that, if left to oneself to amass some wealth, the task is too great and creates too much stress, and so it is better to have a partnership. But if this is the case, he does not explain how any *one* person can really profit if one would, presumably, need to share the proceeds with the partner. He offers a metaphorical explanation in vv. 10-11: "If either of them falls, his partner can pick him up; but woe to him who falls alone and there is no one to pick him up!" The context seems to suggest that a financial "stumbling" is in view.

Verses 11-12 continue this line of thought, likewise employing metaphorical language. Two are better than one, because together they can keep "warm." Two are better than one, because, if "attacked," together they can resist. Qohelet concludes with what is almost certainly a well-known proverb: a threefold cord is not easily broken. The metaphor of a *three*-ply braided cord represents the advantage that *two* have over *one*.[4] Commentators routinely, and correctly, make note of an ancient Near Eastern analogue to this idea found in a Sumerian text *(Gilgamesh and Huwawa)*, where Gilgamesh is reminding his friend Enkidu that there is strength in numbers.[5] As Longman describes it:

> Enkidu is about to give up a mission, and Gilgamesh tells him (in Shaffer's translation): "Stop, Enkidu! The second man will not die. The boat-in-tow will not sink. No man will cut the three-ply cord." He [i.e., Shaffer] further showed connections between this Sumerian text and the entirety of Ecclesiastes 4:9-12. . . . Schaffer's [*sic*] work shows that Qohelet is likely alluding to a well-known ancient Near Eastern proverb concerning the benefits of friendship.[6]

I agree with the conclusion Longman and others have reached. It raises the issue of whether proverbs are present elsewhere in Ecclesiastes, which may be of interest, although not so much to see whether Qohelet "borrowed" from the literature of his world. After all, no author weaves his/her words in isolation from their world. It may be more a matter of interest, however, to see how Qohelet uses such well-known material. It may be no more than our saying "a stitch in time saves nine" or "easy come, easy go." Or perhaps it is more akin to citing some famous author such as Shakespeare, "My kingdom for a [fill in the blank]."

In my opinion, there is nothing particularly telling about Qohelet's use

---

4. Note the progression in v. 12 of "one . . . two . . . three." This is a good example of numerical heightening, a property of biblical poetry that communicates intensification.

5. Seow, *Ecclesiastes*, 189-90; Fox, *Time to Tear Down*, 223-24; Longman, *Ecclesiastes*, 143. Fox and Longman credit A. Shaffer for making the initial observation ("Mesopotamian Background"; idem, "New Information").

6. Longman, *Ecclesiastes*, 143.

of this proverb, that is, that he is using it ironically or polemically. We have seen Qohelet's polemical use of the "deeds of permanence" motif in 2:4-8, where the very things about which ancient Near Eastern kings boasted are declared by Qohelet to be absurd and without profit (2:11). Here, however, this proverb seems to maintain its expected sense. As such, this section of Ecclesiastes may be roughly analogous to Qohelet's notion of carpe diem we have seen before and will see again. To paraphrase vv. 4-12: "Ah, work. It is never enough and it has its roots in competition. Better to have less and no headache than more and be stressed out. What makes it better is if you have someone who shares your labor, who works alongside you. That is a tough combination to beat. It can stand up against any challenge."

Having ended on a relatively positive tone, now Qohelet turns to consider a matter that might seem altogether unrelated. On one level this perception is correct, but what connects vv. 13-16 to what precedes is the notion of wealth. The connection may be no more than simply Qohelet's stream of consciousness, a pacing, irritable tiger, pen in hand, eyes darting back and forth.

Unfortunately, the final verses in this section are fraught with a number of interpretive difficulties, but one thing seems clear enough: it is here that we find Qohelet's first overt, if also oblique, criticism of kingship. I would suggest a paraphrase of this passage along the lines of the following: "Age and wealth do not translate to success for a king, if he cannot listen to advice. It is better to have a young king, born of poor circumstances, indeed even coming from prison. But in the end, this does not amount to much. While that king rules, another, of likewise humble circumstances, is born and will one day take his place. And it just keeps going. There is no end to this succession, and to top it all off, people's loyalties change. This is absurd."

One can perhaps hear echoes of 1:11, the last verse of the frame narrator's introduction: people come and go, the dead are forgotten, and those who have to be born will likewise be forgotten once they die. In 4:13-16, however, the focus is on the king specifically, and that, one has to admit, seems to come out of the clear blue. Of course, the royal persona dominates the entire book, being announced in 1:1, 12, and developed in chapter 2. In those cases, however, it is Qohelet who is identified as king and it is his kingly stature that gives weight to his quest. But in 4:13-16, after drawing a banal conclusion that more is better, we find ourselves talking about royal succession, humble beginnings, and fickle loyalties of the people. Where does this come from?

As mentioned above, one factor that carries over from the previous section is wealth. There is little else, however, that provides logical connection between vv. 4-12 and vv. 13-16, and it seems unwise to press points dogmatically. There are also numerous syntactical difficulties in this section that leave its basic content somewhat hard to define. For example, who is the subject of the verbs in v. 14? The king? The youth? Who is the "second" in v. 15? Dominic Rudman has provided a reading of vv. 13-16, in particular juxtaposing 4:13-16 to 9:13-16, that helps bring some order and theological vitality to this passage.[7] The poor wise man of the latter passage is described the same way as the youth in 4:13-16: מִסְכֵּן וְחָכָם/*miskēn wĕḥākām* (although without *wĕ* in 9:15). What the two have in common is their poverty. Rudman comments, "Because they are poor, yet dare to become conspicuous by their own efforts, they will always be the target of detractors." "For Qohelet," therefore, "wisdom is indeed better than strength (4:13; 9:16) or weapons of war (9:18), but poverty nullifies its advantages in the long term (4:16; 9:16). This bleak message of the power of poverty and the powerlessness of the poor begins and ends Ecclesiastes 4."[8] In this respect v. 16 can be seen as a concluding statement that echoes 1:11 and is summarized well by Longman.

> The sense of the verse, in my opinion, leads to the following interpretation. Countless people followed the "next youth" of v. 15, who replaced the wise young man of vv. 13 and 14, who came to the throne from humble origins to replace the old, foolish king of v. 13. Yet not even the final king mentioned, the popular one, continued to enjoy the people's favor. In the end, people did not like even him.[9]

And all this Qohelet pronounces as הֶבֶל/*hebel* and a chasing/shepherding of the wind. This is the final occurrence of the latter phrase in the book.

5:1-7 (MT 4:17–5:6): Watch Your Mouth with God

Having thus ended his discursive thought on the perils of kingly succession, Qohelet moves to another authority to be dealt with, God himself. Thus one might say that the theme since 4:13 has been leadership, and we will see another transition to this general theme in 5:8. But much of what occupies Qohelet's thoughts here and in the following verses concerns watching one's mouth with respect to God, and this makes good sense in view of Qohelet's occasional oblique accusations toward God (e.g., 1:15). It is also worth noting here how Qohelet begins using a string of imperatives, something missing

7. Rudman, "Contextual Reading."
8. Ibid., 73.
9. Longman, *Ecclesiastes*, 147.

thus far.[1] So he begins by warning his readers to watch their step as they draw near to God's house, which is explained in the next clause: "Draw near to hear rather than offering a sacrifice of fools, for they do not know that they are doing wrong." This sentence has two major difficulties: how to handle the infinitive absolute קָרוֹב/*qārôb* (here translated as an imperative),[2] and what to do with the tricky syntax מִתֵּת הַכְּסִילִים זָבַח/*mittēt hakkĕsîlîm zābaḥ* ("rather than offering a sacrifice of fools").[3]

These precise details, however, are not of ultimate importance, for the point is clear enough. When you approach God (and here "house of God" likely refers to the temple), be circumspect. Listen! That is better than sacrificing like a fool. In the context, this seems to suggest accompanying a sacrifice with excessive talk, which is one characteristic of the fool (Prov 13:3). One might also hear an echo (albeit distant) of Eccl 3:7, where there is a time to speak and a time to keep silent. On the other hand, the nature of the sacrifice that makes it "wrong" (רָע/*rāʿ*) may simply be that it is a fool who is giving it, with no indictment of wordiness. This is possible, but the admonition to "listen" in 5:2, plus the topic of the verses to follow, favor the former interpretation. Also, Longman hits the mark when he points out that Qohelet's advice here should not be understood as particularly pious, since he has been anything but pious up to this point.[4] Rather, as we shall see, Qohelet's comments here are just another expression of the sense of distance and even indifference he feels with respect to God.

In 5:2 Qohelet warns his readers neither to be "hasty" with one's mouth, nor to be in a hurry to bring a matter before God. Both actions seem to pertain to speaking in God's presence, as one might do in the temple. But what sort of a portrait is Qohelet painting here? On the one hand, a bit of irony cannot escape us, for, after all, what has Qohelet been doing for the past four chapters but speaking up, indeed quite stridently, about what in the world God is doing? Or is he, perhaps, being a bit sarcastic here? *Why* is it that one should not be too quick to approach God? He tells us in the second half of v. 2: "because God is in heaven but you are on earth, therefore let your words

---

1. As Seow notes, "The language of reflection in 4:1-16 gives way to the language of instruction in 5:1-7 (Heb 4:17–5:6). Qohelet moves now from the first block of materials (1:2–4:16), to the second block (5:1–6:9 [Heb 4:17–6:9]) — from reflection to ethics" (*Ecclesiastes*, 197). This observation is valid, although "ethics" may suggest a much more positive tone than what we will encounter in the coming verses.

2. Longman, *Ecclesiastes*, 149. Seow treats it adjectivally, "It is better . . ." (*Ecclesiastes*, 194).

3. The problem is that the last two words should likely be reversed. (Note that זָבַח/*zābaḥ* is the pausal form of זֶבַח/*zebaḥ*.)

4. Longman, *Ecclesiastes*, 151.

be few." This is not a note of comfort or even awe, but, as we have seen, exasperation. Thus far in this section, Qohelet seems to be saying, "Watch yourself when you approach God. Save your words. They will not do any good. He is far off."

Qohelet supports his point in v. 3, although it is not exactly clear what he is getting at. "For a dream comes with much עִנְיָן/'*inyān*, and the voice of a fool with many words." It seems clear that Qohelet is following up on his previous cautions concerning excessive speech. Verse 3 also supports the notion that in 5:1b, the reference to fools' sacrifice concerns speech. Yet the reference to dreams bringing about '*inyān* ("task," or as elsewhere, "preoccupation") here is not transparent. It does seem, however, that the two halves of 5:3 are meant to support each other in some way, and so Longman's observation may be correct, "that those who are so foolish as to think their words have any appreciable effect on God are also living in a fantasy world."[5]

Verses 4 and 5 move from the topic of words to that of fulfilling one's vow before God. Still, the general topic remains one's conduct in God's presence. Vows were one way of expressing service to God, along with prayer or sacrifice, and the taking of a vow was a solemn act of cultic commitment. When one makes a vow before God, therefore, one should not dawdle to see it through, to fulfill (שַׁלֵּם/*šallēm*) it. One should go about it quickly. Such a directive is fully in keeping with standard wisdom teaching (e.g., Deut 23:22-24; Prov 20:25; Num 30:3; Ps 50:14b; Sir 18:22). It is not stated explicitly just what a fool would do in this context, but the swift fulfilling of the vow is contrasted to fools in whom "there is no delight." The implication is that God does not delight in the tardy fulfillment of vows, which is what fools do. (Note here another example of Qohelet's passive, i.e., indirect, reference to God; cf. Eccl 1:15.)

To avoid the whole problem, as Qohelet says in v. 5, you are better off not making a vow in the first place than making a vow and not seeing it through.[6] Also at work here is Qohelet's recurring use of the "better than" saying, found also in 4:3, 6, 9, 13, and in various places in subsequent sections. This should not be passed over too quickly, as if merely a stylistic convention of Qohelet. Remember that Qohelet has declared everything to be absurd, that there is no profit to be had in any area of life, in large part because death is the end of everyone (see 7:2). Moreover, as we have seen elsewhere, it is God

---

5. Ibid., 152.

6. Seow comments that the use of אֲשֶׁר/'*ăšer* as "that" along with the same use of the particle שֶׁ/*še* in the second half of the verse attests to the late dating of the Hebrew of Ecclesiastes (*Ecclesiastes*, 195-96).

whom Qohelet holds responsible for such a state of affairs, sometimes directly, other times with a degree of reticence. There is no reason not to understand this "better than" statement here in the larger context of Qohelet's other "better than" statements, especially like those in 3:12. In other words, I do not think that Qohelet's statement here is one of reverence toward God any more than 5:2c is. God's place in heaven creates distance between him and the one approaching him in the temple. The warning here to avoid vows altogether rather than leave a vow unfulfilled is not to motivate his readers to heartfelt, authentic worship. It is warning that God is not to be messed with. I suggest, therefore, that the emphasis in v. 5 is not: "you really ought to make sure you follow through with your vow." Rather it is, "You know, you are really better off not vowing at all. It is not worth the risk." In other words, the "better than" statement, here as elsewhere in Ecclesiastes, is a statement of resignation.

This interpretation of v. 5 brings us back to the sentiment expressed at the outset of the passage: "Keep your mouth shut when you approach God. Who knows, you might wind up giving a fool's sacrifice by saying something you cannot take back and that would oblige you to follow through. Better to keep your mouth shut from the beginning and avoid the problem." Qohelet drives the point home in v. 6: "Do not let what comes out of your mouth cause your whole being to fall into sin."[7] What you say has consequences, and again, we should not assume that Qohelet here is referring to a "just" consequence of one's rash words. One gets the impression that, for Qohelet, God is waiting for the worshiper to trip up with his words. And one should not try the excuse: "it [the vow] was an accident" (v. 6b).[8] All that will do is anger God even further. Or, as v. 6c puts it, "Why should God become angry because of your *voice*?" The Hebrew (MT v. 5c) is קוֹל/*qôl*, which is used elsewhere in this passage in v. 3 (MT 2) to describe the speech of the fool. Hence making a vow, not fulfilling it, and then trying to make an excuse for it is a foolish act that will anger God. That anger will result in — what in the abstract one might consider a disproportionate punishment — the destruction of the "work of your hands" (v. 6d).

Defining just what Qohelet means by the "work of your hands" may

---

7. This is a slight paraphrase of the Hebrew, which reads more literally, "Do not allow your mouth to make your flesh/body sin."

8. Verse 6 (MT 5) is a bit ambiguous in that the identity of the "messenger" (מַלְאָךְ/*mal'āk*) is not clear. It likely refers to a priest whose role it was to ensure that vows were fulfilled. See Longman, *Ecclesiastes*, 154; and in more detail, Seow, *Ecclesiastes*, 196. Some have thought that the "messenger" is either an oblique reference to God or to an avenging divine messenger (see, e.g., LXX, Targum), but Qohelet's explicit references to God in 5:1, 2, and 4 make it unlikely that he is pulling back here.

lead us to focus more on the trees than the forest. We should not get lost in this one detail. The overall picture Qohelet is portraying is clear enough: "God is to be feared. Be careful how you approach him. Best to keep silent. But if you make a vow, by all means, hurry to fulfill it. Come to think of it, it is really best not even to go down that road, because once you do, you are obligated, and there are no excuses. God is watching, and if you fail to follow through, you are in for a lot of grief." Hence I understand Qohelet's pessimistic, frustrated tone in these verses to be quite consistent with what he has been arguing thus far. He has also prepared us for the final verse of this passage.

In v. 7 (MT 6) Qohelet returns to the notion of dreams mentioned in v. 3 (MT 2), and these dreams are now defined as הֶבֶל/*hebel*, "absurd."[9] The syntax of this verse is very difficult, but, as is often the case in Ecclesiastes, the gist is clear. There are "absurd dreams" and "many words" aplenty. Clearly, his intention is to help keep his readers from doing the very things he has just been describing and that could result in God's punitive response. It is in this sense that we understand the last portion of v. 7. His exhortation to "fear God" is not to be understood in the productive sense as one finds it in Proverbs (see also 3:14). If anything, he is taking a jab at such a notion (if it is on his mind at all). This is a different kind of fear, one that concerns a God, as we have seen throughout Ecclesiastes thus far, whose inscrutable acts produce pain, anxiety, frustration — fear.

It would be wrong to read this section as simply encouraging worshipers to make sure they approach God with proper decorum and respect. He is saying, in effect, when you approach God, you are taking a risk. "Be careful," he says at the beginning of 5:1. "Just listen. It is fools who use words. And if you make a vow, keep it brief, knowing that God is distant, unless, of course, you are too wordy or fail to keep the vow in a timely manner. In that case, he will come swooping down and destroy the 'work of your hand.' So be afraid, Israel."

In this respect, and in closing, it is important to make a brief comment on the nature of fear here and how the epilogist returns to this theme in 12:13. Simply put, the epilogist uses the phrase in its more traditional sense, and no pressure need be exerted to align 5:7 and 12:13. The broad impact of the epilogue for understanding the words of Qohelet has already been touched on in the introduction and will be revisited later when we look more closely at the final section of the book.

---

9. The two words "dream" and "absurd" are connected by a ו/*waw*, which in this case forms a hendiadys (one idea described by two words connected with "and"). See Seow, *Ecclesiastes*, 197.

5:8(MT 7)–6:9: Death Comes to Both the Greedy and Those Who Are Just Trying to Get Along

This section begins with a somewhat cryptic and out-of-the-blue comment about injustice toward the poor and just by a corrupt system. Hence it seems to begin a new section, which focuses on both greed and the everyday fruit of one's labor, and how, once again, death is the leveler.

Unfortunately, the first two verses of this section are difficult to translate, and various attempts have been proposed. Concerning v. 8, the first half is clear enough (do not be surprised when the poor and just suffer corruption), but the meaning of the second half suffers a bit from the ambiguity of the root גבה/*gbh*. James Kugel argues that it refers to taking payment, whereas Seow understands the root as referring to arrogance.[1] I am not sure that the two views are mutually exclusive. The poor and righteous are being oppressed by those in positions of power, who feel, by virtue of their position, that they cannot be touched. That the remainder of this section is so focused on wealth makes perfect sense with either of the options mentioned here. Verse 9 woodenly reads: "The profit [produce] of the land is for all; the king for a cultivated field." The ambiguities have led both Seow and Fox to suggest a redivision of the words.[2] These suggestions are worthy of consideration, to be sure, but the overall meaning of these verses, particularly in light of this section as a whole, seems to be discernible. Further, if we understand v. 9 to follow the sense of v. 10 (as Longman does),[3] a general picture presents itself that will carry over nicely to the following verses: "Corruption abounds. The poor are helpless. Even the king seems to be involved in taking advantage of the laborers in the fields."

This sense of corruption continues in the following verses. If you love money or wealth, you never have enough. This is a rather horrid situation when one stops to think about it, and Qohelet wastes no time proclaiming it as absurd (v. 10). Furthermore, when one has much "good" (הַטּוֹבָה/*haṭṭôbâ*, which we should certainly understand as something like "property" or "possessions"), all you get is others wanting to come in and consume (from the

---

1. Kugel, "Qohelet and Money," 35-38; Seow, *Ecclesiastes*, 203. Seow's argument against Kugel is that his reading requires an unattested alteration of the consonantal text, which Seow argues is unnecessary. Fox renders the term "highly placed" (*Time to Tear Down*, 233-34). See too the judicious summary of the difficulties in this verse in Longman, *Ecclesiastes*, 158-59.

2. Fox has: "And the advantage of a land in all regards is *every worked field[?]*" (*Time to Tear Down*, 233). Seow reads, "But the advantage of the land is in its provision, that is, if the field is cultivated for provision" (*Ecclesiastes*, 201, 204).

3. Longman, *Ecclesiastes*, 158-59.

root אכל/*'kl*) it right out from under you. So, in the end, the only advantage[4] the owner has — one detects a bit of sarcasm or at least disgust here — is to gaze at it (one might think of a Silas Marner secretly counting his coins). Just who these consumers of the property are is not made explicit but surely they are identified in the previous two verses: those in positions to take what they wish regardless of ownership rights. "Owners" really do not own anything, and they can only stare helplessly and watch corruption happen.[5]

As always, once Qohelet gets on a roll, the matter continues to get worse (v. 12). The poor, even though they are oppressed in v. 8, are still pretty well off. Whether they eat much or little, at least they can get some sleep. But those who are wealthy are robbed of sleep. These wealthy may be those who own property that is seized by others in authority, and so their sleep is fitful. Or it might describe those who consume the wealth of others and still are not sated. When you get down to it, Qohelet says, wealth is not what gives meaning to an absurd existence. Here Seow's understanding of the socioeconomic context of Ecclesiastes is helpful in rounding out the theological thrust of passages such as this.[6] The introduction of currency (daric, by the Persian king Darius I, 549-486 B.C.) restructured the ancient Near Eastern economy. Qohelet's words here seem to be addressed to an audience "facing a new world of money and finance," and his message to them is that money will not afford the protection they seek. Seow adds that the pressure to be competitive might have tempted Jews to violate the Sabbath, and so Qohelet employs the very economic categories with which they have become enamored in order to make his appeal.

Qohelet continues in v. 13 (MT 12) by referring to the hoarding of wealth as a "sickening evil" (רָעָה חוֹלָה/*rā'â ḥôlâ*), another thing he has observed "under the sun" (see the same phrase below in 5:16 [MT 15], and a virtual mirror of this verse in 6:1). Again, it is probably best not to think of "evil" here in categories familiar to Christian readers (as is also the case with words like "righteous"). Seow handles this well by translating the phrase "sickening tragedy."[7] Qohelet sees that hoarding wealth (rather than simply the "enjoy-

---

4. The Hebrew term is כִּשְׁרוֹן/*kišrôn* (elsewhere in Ecclesiastes only in 2:21; 4:4), meaning "benefit"; as Seow suggests, it is essentially equal to the more common term in Ecclesiastes, "profit" (יִתְרוֹן/*yitrôn*) (*Ecclesiastes*, 205).

5. To revisit the issue of authorship discussed in the introduction, it is passages such as this that suggest that a king, whether Solomon or someone else, is not responsible for writing this book. Qohelet is highly critical of power structures, including kings, and it seems most likely to the vast majority of scholars that this was not written by a king.

6. Seow, *Ecclesiastes*, 21-23.

7. Ibid., 201.

ment" of what one has) brings nothing but harm to the owner. How exactly does the hoarding of wealth harm the owner? It may go well temporarily, but the time will come when the wealth is lost by a "grievous task" (עֲנְיַן רָע/ *'inyan rāʿ*, v. 14 [MT 13]), a phrase we have seen already in 1:13 and 4:8. In both these instances it is implied that *God* is the one responsible for the unfortunate circumstance being described. Here too the owner loses his wealth by a "grievous task," or perhaps better here, a grievous situation that God has either directly engineered (as in, e.g., 1:15) or that happens simply by virtue of how God has set up the world (e.g., 3:1-8).

Hence one hoards wealth, but, in an echo of 2:18-23, leaving it to the next generation is no profit. In 2:18-23 the issue is that one does not know whether the one who comes after will be wise — not to mention that this one did not work for the wealth. Here the issue is that, because of the loss of hoarded wealth, there is nothing to leave the son. The contradictory observation made between these two passages is evident: in the first, it is lamentable that one's wealth is left to an offspring who does not deserve it (either by being unwise, or simply because he did not labor for it); in the second, what is lamented is that the father may have nothing to leave the son. No matter. Qohelet is not presenting a systematic theology of wealth, but scanning his gaze to every corner of the world ("under the sun") and addressing each circumstance as it comes to his mind. Here his train of thought has taken him from the oppression of the poor by the powerful to the ultimate futility of hoarding wealth. In a word, God can take it in an instant and leave you and your offspring with nothing.

Unfair, you might say? No, it is not. You came into this world with nothing, and that is just how you are going to leave it (5:15). This verse is commonly used in funerals, but the dilemma Qohelet is portraying is often missed. There is no sense of the laudatory "circle of life," let alone a word of comfort. Qohelet, rather, is reiterating the theme that has occupied his thoughts from the outset: you work, and whether or not you have something to leave your son (if that is even desirable; see 2:18-23), you are going to die and take nothing with you. There is, in other words, no profit for our toil (1:3). Death is the leveler. And this final point Qohelet makes powerfully clear in 5:16 (MT 15). The עֲנְיַן רָע/*'inyan rāʿ* mentioned in v. 14 (MT 13) is here defined more precisely: death leaves you with nothing and so all your toil is for naught.

And this is God's doing. One wonders at this juncture whether Qohelet already has God somewhat in mind when speaking of the arrogant ones in 5:8 and the king in 5:9. People in authority are all the same. And at the end of the day, God is just like them. People work, and he takes it away, not by consuming the wealth but by consuming *them.* And their days on earth, in case his readers need reminding, are not filled with laughter and satisfaction (v. 17). All their days they eat in darkness[8] and great anger[9] and sickness and frustration.[10]

This brings us to a pivotal point in Qohelet's argument in 5:18-20 (MT 17-19), similar to what he has uttered in 2:24-26, 3:12-15, and 3:22. In view of what he has just observed, Qohelet concludes what he considers to be "good" (טוֹב/*ṭôb*): it is "fitting" (יָפֶה/*yāpeh*, not "beautiful"; elsewhere only in 3:11) to eat, drink, and experience the good in one's labor under the sun. But Qohelet drives the dagger a bit deeper this time, leaving little doubt that these so-called carpe diem passages are anything but a word of comfort to his weary readers. Humanity is to plod along in such activities "the number of the days of their lives." The same expression was seen in 2:3 and will be seen again just below in 6:12. There is without question a deep note of resignation here, for this is what *God* has given him. It is, as Qohelet summarizes at the end of v. 18 (MT 17), his "portion," his חֵלֶק/*ḥēleq*. This is one of the pivotal words we have encountered already in 2:10, 21, and 3:22. This "portion" that God has given is not a sigh of relief but the very thing that concerns Qohelet so much. To repeat the general flow of Qohelet's thinking (see the introduction): all one's labor amounts to nothing (no profit) because at the end of the day all die. The best that one has is the here-and-now portion that God has given.

The point is driven home more directly in v. 19: "everyone to whom God has given riches and wealth and gives them the ability to 'eat' of it and to accept his portion and rejoice in his labor, *this* is the gift of God." This verse, as part of the larger passage of vv. 18-20, is pivotal for understanding Qohelet's theology, and as remarked in the introduction, mirrors well 3:12-15. The phrase "everyone" (כָּל-הָאָדָם/*kol-hā'ādām*) appears in 3:13, 7:2, and then in the climactic comment in 12:13. As in 3:13, the notion of "everyone" is associated with the procurement of some satisfaction in life, while in 7:2 it refers to the inevitability of death. The use of the phrase in 12:13 brings to an end such talk (without dismissing Qohelet's observation) by pointing humanity to what is truly for "everyone": fearing God and keeping his commandments.

Second, the meaning of this verse is not that God gives wealth, and so on, to everyone; rather, it is: "everyone *to whom* God gives" wealth, and so on. There is, in other words, a significant note of despair here, for it is for *God* to

---

8. Kugel emends חשׁך/*ḥšk* to חסך/*ḥsk,* meaning "restraint," hence to "eat sparingly" ("Qohelet and Money," 38-40).

9. Or frustration. See the use of כעס/*k's* in 1:18; 2:23; 7:3, 9; 11:10.

10. Or anger. See the use of קצף/*qṣp* in 5:5 (Eng. 6).

determine not only who will and who will not have wealth, but who will have the ability[11] to partake[12] of it! Qohelet restates the point unequivocally in the last part of v. 19: "to accept one's portion, to enjoy one's labor, *this* is the gift of God." One cannot help but be reminded not only of the similar sentiment found in 3:13 ("gift," מַתַּת/*mattat*, is used there as well), but of a theme that has been announced since 1:15: you cannot straighten this out; it is crooked by God's doing. To stress the point once again, these so-called carpe diem passages are anything but. "Seizing the day" ultimately gets you nowhere except to give the gnawing, hounding notion that you are a pawn in a cruel game.

Third, as if the previous thoughts were not enough to drive one to despair, in 5:20 Qohelet undermines his own point about one's ability to partake in one's daily labors: you do not remember much about your life anyway. It is all a blur, because God keeps you so busy[13] "with the pleasure of his heart." One can only take this last clause as sarcasm. It is not a last-ditch effort to put a smiling face on a dreadful situation, that is, God will keep you busy and you will love every minute of it. The "pleasure" (שִׂמְחָה/*śimḥâ*) of which he speaks, which is embedded in one's heart, is a fleeting pleasure. It is a chasing of the wind. It is absurd. It is nullified by death, and even in this life God keeps us so busy with these "pleasures" that we do not even remember them. One wonders what keeps Qohelet putting one foot in front of the other, day after day.

One is perhaps weary by now of Qohelet's less than optimistic view of life. I think that is the very goal he desires to achieve. But even now there is no rest from his bold assault on superficial optimism. He begins in 6:1 by alerting the reader to another observation: "There is a tragedy[14] I have seen under the sun, and it is great upon humanity." What is this observation? It is more or less what he just said, but he elaborates on it in 6:2. He says again that God may give some wealth, possessions, and honor (כָּבוֹד/*kābôd*), but not the ability to partake of them. What is worse is that someone else, a "stranger," gets to partake of them. We should not lose sight here that this is all God's doing. He

---

11. This is a Hiphil of שׁלט/*šlṭ*, i.e., to exercise proprietorship. See 2:19 and Seow, *Ecclesiastes*, 136-37.

12. The Hebrew is אכל/*'kl*, "to eat," and I see no reason not to take it figuratively in this context. One does not eat wealth or possessions, although food would certainly be accounted among one's belongings. The root is also used in this passage in 5:10 (Eng. 11) figuratively as well as in 6:2.

13. The Hebrew is a Hiphil masculine singular participle of ענה/*'nh*. It means "occupy," or perhaps "preoccupy," or "keep busy." It almost certainly does not mean "afflict" in this context, though Seow suggests an intentional ambiguity (*Ecclesiastes*, 209-10).

14. As elsewhere, I prefer a less morally charged translation for the root ער(ה)/*r'(h)* rather than "evil."

is the one who keeps them busy (5:19). He is the one who gives wealth, but then in a perverse trick lets a stranger enjoy it rather than the rightful possessor (6:2-3). This situation Qohelet pronounces in one of his strongest, if not the strongest, remark in the book: "This is absurd; it is a sick tragedy (חֳלִי רָע/*ḥŏlî rāʿ*)."

One cannot find solace from this tragedy by appealing to many offspring and long life (v. 3). The echo of patriarchal blessing of children and long life is unmistakable, and Qohelet simply sweeps it aside. The syntax of the clause וְרַב שֶׁיִּהְיוּ יְמֵי-שָׁנָיו/*wĕrab šeyyihyû yĕmê-šānāyw* is considered awkward by most commentators, and is usually translated "However many are the days of his life."[15] The general point is that neither children nor long life (regardless of how long) is necessarily beneficial. If this good (הַטּוֹבָה/*haṭṭôbâ*) does not satisfy, and if one does not even get a burial[16] at the end, well — a stillborn baby is better off. These are harsh words, especially considering that Qohelet has been arguing that one can never get real satisfaction in anything anyway, since death always intrudes. One wonders, also, why in the world a burial would have made any difference in this despairing portrait Qohelet is painting for us. We are certainly in the midst of one of the more depressing sections of the book. God controls who has wealth and who enjoys it; there are no guarantees. All we have is our portion. Nothing can counter this situation, certainly not offspring and long life, for such things do not bring satisfaction. One might pause here and ask whether the contrary is a possibility: if one were to find satisfaction, would one be better off than a stillborn? The answer is no, and I maintain this is fully in keeping with where Qohelet has been leading. Satisfaction is never a guarantee, because whether one is satisfied is in God's hands, not ours.

This leads to Qohelet's final thoughts in this section, in which he elaborates on the benefits of the stillborn. Man is born, first of all, "in הֶבֶל/*hebel*," or as Fox puts it, "into absurdity."[17] I agree with Fox's general flow of thought here, that v. 4 describes the unfortunate persons of vv. 2-3: they are born into absurdity, they "walk"[18] in darkness, and in darkness their reputation (lit. "name") is covered. One thinks here of 1:11, where death eventually erases the memory of those who die. In v. 5 the reference is to the stillborn, who, by contrast, has more rest than the unfortunate man, even though the stillborn has

---

15. Longman, *Ecclesiastes*, 163; Fox, *Time to Tear Down*, 241, 243. For an alternate view see Seow, *Ecclesiastes*, 211.

16. The Hebrew simply reads קְבוּרָה/*qĕbûrâ*, "burial" or "burial place." "Decent" or "proper" is normally inferred, although I see no reason why the Hebrew cannot be left as it is.

17. See Fox, *Time to Tear Down*, 241.

18. We may recall how the root הלך/*hlk* is often used in the sense of "death" (e.g., 1:4, 6, 7).

never seen the sun. This is in keeping with 4:2-3, where Qohelet argues that the one not yet born is better off than the living or the dead.

The point is further emphasized in v. 6: you can live two thousand years, but such a long life will be of no avail for the one who does not experience "the good." After all, Qohelet concludes, everyone goes (הלך/*hlk*) to the same place (see 3:18-20). Once again, the question to be asked is whether experiencing the good is a viable option in Qohelet's mind or whether he assumes its impossibility. The latter is consistent with the larger sentiment of the book as a whole, but it is still possible that Qohelet, who is far from a systematic thinker, is simply following a particular, momentary train of thought, and concluding that length of life without quality is useless because death comes to all. Of course, the larger point he has been making is that death comes to everyone, regardless of quality of life, and so death is what yields any sort of life as absurd and without profit.

Qohelet concludes his thoughts here with what appear to be three comments with no apparent coherence. In v. 7 he comments on how humans toil but their efforts do not satisfy the appetite. In v. 8 he remarks that the wise has no advantage over the fool (see 2:13-14), and questions whether the afflicted (or poor) have anything to gain by knowing how to "go along with life."[19] It is far from Qohelet's concern here about the afflicted getting along with "the living," as some commentators suggest. The point, rather, is that there is no sense in the afflicted even making the effort to negotiate the ups and downs of life. The central point here is that no one has an upper hand in making it through life victorious. We all come to the same end.

Verse 9 has another problematic phrase in Hebrew. Qohelet says that the "sight of the eyes" is better than מֵהֲלָךְ-נָפֶשׁ/*mēhălāk-nāpeš*. This phrase is more commonly translated as the "roving of the appetite," but a much more natural translation is "death" or "passing of life" (remembering the use of הלך/*hlk* earlier and elsewhere).[20] In other words, in a stark about-face, Qohelet concludes (at least momentarily) that living is better than dying. As we have already seen, however, it is part of Qohelet's frustrating rhetoric to give with one hand and take with the other, for he concludes this entire section with the familiar refrain, "This too is absurd, a chasing of the wind." As elsewhere, I take this concluding comment to refer to the entirety of Qohelet's argument in this section, not simply to this one verse. Death comes to all, the

---

19. This is Seow's translation of the somewhat difficult לַהֲלֹךְ נֶגֶד הַחַיִּים/*lahălōk neged haḥayyîm* (*Ecclesiastes*, 214).

20. See Seow, *Ecclesiastes*, 214-15, although see Longman's argument to the contrary (*Ecclesiastes*, 174).

greedy and those just trying to get along. Neither has the advantage. This is absurd.

6:10–7:14: The "Advantage"(?) of Wisdom in the Face of Certain Death

There is little doubt that this section, particularly its opening verses, connects well to the previous section. Death is still very much on Qohelet's mind, and this theme will continue through 7:14. The הֶבֶל/*hebel* saying in 6:9, however, justifies some sort of break, or at least pause, between these sections, but I do not wish to suggest that the two should be held in isolation.

Qohelet begins with a phrase we have already seen similarly expressed in 1:9-10 and 1:15. The gist of 6:10-12 is basically, "nothing changes and you cannot do anything about it." Compare 6:10 to 1:9-10. Both argue that what happens is old news. The second half of 6:10 brings God into the picture once again: you cannot contend (דּין/*dyn*) with someone stronger than you. You can argue (with God) all you want, says Qohelet in 6:11, but those many words are nothing but *hebel* and offer no profit[1] to humanity. Then, to drive the point home, in v. 12 he laments, "Who knows what is good for humanity in life during the number of the days [see also 2:3 and 7:15] of his *hebel* life." The phrase is a bit awkward when translated so woodenly, but the point is certainly clear. Life is absurd, and who knows what, if anything, is worth all the hassle. Indeed, Qohelet continues, "He makes them like a shadow." The subject "he" certainly refers to God, who is, once again, responsible for what humanity must endure. The object "them" could refer either to humanity (although Heb. אָדָם/*'ādām* is singular) or to the days of one's life. Either way, the point is the same. One's life or one's days are like a shadow: little substance, coming and going quickly. Finally, no one knows what will happen under the sun after one is gone (6:12b). The theme is familiar by now: life is absurd, you die anyway, and God is to blame.

This section forms a bridge between the previous section and 7:1-14, although in the latter the imagery and literary form change. Still, one can see how Qohelet's obsession with death remains his central concern.

What predominates in the opening verses of chapter 7 is the "better-than" pattern (seen first in 4:3), which is a stylistic device used by Qohelet to contrast one thing with another.[2] He begins with a somewhat cryptic saying,

---

1. The Hebrew here is יֹתֵר/*yōtēr*, which we have already seen in 2:15 and 6:8, and is a variation on יִתְרוֹן/*yitrôn* (first seen in 1:3). The meaning is the same.

2. See the important work of Ogden, "The 'Better'-Proverb."

"Better a name [i.e., reputation] than fine oil."[3] So far so good: a reputation is better than fine oil, because, presumably, fine oil can spoil in some way whereas a reputation lasts. The second half of the verse, however, adds an unexpected dimension: "the day of death is better than the day of one's birth." The analogy is quickly apparent: one's reputation *as well as one's death* are to be preferred over fine oil and one's birth. What started out as "words to live by" quickly plunge us back into Qohelet's despair. After we allow the dust to settle, what he is saying here is quite plain. Oil can spoil, as can one's life. Things start out fine for both, but after just a little time things get rotten. Not so with a reputation: that stays intact, as does death. Both are impervious, in contrast to their counterparts.

One point worth raising here is why Qohelet would favor a reputation over fine oil, since one of his recurring themes is that everyone dies and no one is remembered (i.e., a reputation is precarious in this life and evaporates after death). But that is precisely the point Qohelet is making. The potential benefit promised in v. 1a (which echoes such proverbial sayings as Prov 22:1) is swiftly undermined in v. 1b. This is not the first time Qohelet has given with one hand and taken with the other. His exasperation (shall we go so far as to say sarcasm?) is evident.

The thought is continued in v. 2, where Qohelet declares that it is better to walk (הלך/*hlk*) to the house of mourning than to walk to the house of feasting, because[4] "it is the end of everyone, and the living should take it to heart." As discussed in the introduction, 7:2 is one of three verses in Qohelet's monologue that employ the phrase כָּל-הָאָדָם/*kol-hā'ādām*. The other two appear in 3:13 and 5:18 (Eng. 19), and the epilogue uses the phrase in the climactic assessment of Qohelet's words in 12:13. To repeat, 3:13 and 5:18 remind the readers that it is for "everyone" to enjoy what one has. Here in 7:2 we are reminded that "everyone" dies. Making do and then dying are dominant themes for Qohelet, but the epilogue places these themes in a larger context: despite the observations Qohelet makes, what is finally the case for "everyone" is: "Fear God and keep the commandments" (12:13). And just as the epilogue does not dismiss Qohelet's observations as foolish or impulsive, neither should we. So here, in this extended discussion of death, we should resist the temptation to find fault with Qohelet and try to enter his train of thought

---

3. The alliteration and wordplay are exquisite: טוֹב שֵׁם מִשֶּׁמֶן טוֹב/*ṭôb šēm miššemen ṭôb*.

4. Just how one should handle בַּאֲשֶׁר/*ba'ăšer* is debated. Longman understands it causally (*Ecclesiastes*, 180), as I do, although Seow translates it "since," and begins a new sentence (*Ecclesiastes*, 229). Similarly, see Fox's translation "inasmuch" (*Time to Tear Down*, 249). The precise Hebrew phrase is found elsewhere in Qohelet only in 3:9 and 8:4. It seems to be causal in 8:4, although in 3:9 the meaning is the more transparent "in which."

and allow him to lead. After all, should not the living take to heart that they, like everyone else, will one day depart this life?

Qohelet continues this theme in v. 4, but not before making a rather cryptic comment in v. 3. We have here the third "better-than" saying: "anger is better than laughter." "Anger" (כַּעַס/*ka'as*) is first seen in 1:18, and recurs in 2:23, 5:16 (Eng. 17), 7:9, and 11:10. In all three previous uses, the word refers to a sorry, lamentable situation to which humanity is subjected, but is that the case here? It would seem not, since here anger is *better* than laughter, presumably because it comports more with the reality of life.[5] This is true, but it is precisely here where the previous uses of *ka'as* come into play. This lamentable situation of anger (or frustration, perhaps) toward God and his world is to be preferred over laughter exactly *because* this is the true nature of things. Why waste your time with laughing when what God has in store for you are things you cannot control or "straighten" (1:15; 7:13)?

Qohelet plays out this notion further in vv. 5-6. Listening to a wise rebuke is better than someone who listens to a "song of fools." I do not think it is straining matters at all to suggest that the song (שִׁיר/*šîr*) of fools is to be connected with the laughter (שְׂחֹק/*śḥq*) mentioned above in v. 3 as well as the feasting (שְׁתֵה/*šth*) in v. 2. All three are variations on the same theme: things not worth doing. Hence I do not think Qohelet, by saying "song of fools," is making a distinction between some songs that fools sing and some that the wise may sing. Rather, the genitive is subjective: fools sing. They also laugh and feast. Such an interpretation is supported by the phrase "laughter of the fool" in v. 6. "Laughter" is not qualified in v. 3, and v. 6 simply expresses more pointedly the foolishness of *any* laughter for Qohelet. It is, as v. 6a puts it, "like the sound of thorns[6] crackling under the pot." The sound is itself a demonstration of the absurdity of existence: you make a little noise and then you are gone. Or perhaps better: the very noise you make is an indication that you are on the way out.

In this broader context, the second half of v. 3 makes sense: "in the sadness of the countenance the heart will be made well." This means that, as one faces head-on the stark reality of death, it is reflected in our expression ("scowl," as Fox puts it).[7] In doing so, one is better off. Qohelet's point in 7:1-6 is clear: death, anger, mourning, and rebuke are better than feasting, laughing, rejoicing, and singing. This may be a hard lesson to hear, but it is what

5. Longman, *Ecclesiastes*, 183.

6. I do not think there is anything significant about saying "thorns" (הַסִּירִים/*hassîrîm*) as opposed to "twigs," etc. The word choice seems driven by the homonym סִיר/*sîr* (pot), and thus provides a pleasing wordplay.

7. Fox, *Time to Tear Down*, 249.

Qohelet is clearly saying. And he is not quite finished. His final blow comes at the end of v. 6: "this too is absurd." As we have already seen (e.g., 2:15, 23), Qohelet's use of "this" (הַזֶּה/*zeh*) refers to the situation he has just described, not simply the immediate antecedent, "the laughter of fools." The very fact that death, and so on, is to be preferred over life, and so on, is what is absurd. The truth is better than fantasy, but it does not set you free — it leads to despair.

Verses 7ff. seem to interrupt the flow of Qohelet's argument as a miscellany of sayings, but I do not think this is the case.[8] I am not interested in offering some forced interpretation of vv. 7ff. to make the connection with the previous emphasis on death, but I do think that, at least in Qohelet's mind, v. 7 follows on v. 6 in some sense. One strong argument is כִּי/*kî*, which begins this verse as well as v. 6, although one must admit that it can be functioning here as an asseverative ("indeed") rather than the conjunction "for." At any rate, I am interested in seeing how these verses contribute to the theme thus far, whether directly or indirectly.

If we look at vv. 7-14 as a whole, we observe several points of contact with what comes before. First, in v. 8, that the "end of a matter is better than its beginning" certainly echoes much of vv. 1-6. Note too that it is a "better-than" saying as we find in vv. 1, 2, 3, and 5. Second, it is foolishness to think of the "former days" as better than today. The rationale is not given, but presumably it is for the very same reason we have seen throughout this section: later is better than earlier, end is better than beginning. Third, we see once again Qohelet's observation that what is crooked cannot be straightened. We have seen similar language in 1:15 and how that was reflected in 6:10. Finally, the ending verse of this section is a compact carpe diem passage, where Qohelet advises his readers to enjoy the good as well as the bad, since God has made them both and no one can know what will come. Although death is not explicit in v. 14, Qohelet's dismal view of what lies before us is thoroughly consistent with his argument thus far. It seems to me, therefore, that, although Qohelet is branching out in vv. 7-14 to address other topics, the manner in which those topics are addressed is certainly influenced by the overall tone set in this section.

So, with respect to v. 7, we note that v. 6 ends with an observation concerning foolishness. Verse 7 counters that wisdom is no guarantee by which

---

8. Fox states that v. 7 "has little connection with the preceding" (*Time to Tear Down*, 253). See also Longman, who entitles the entire section 7:1-14 as "Miscellaneous Advice" (*Ecclesiastes*, 179). Seow points out that scholars have been puzzled as to the connection between vv. 6 and 7, although Seow does not seem to be overly concerned (*Ecclesiastes*, 237).

one may extricate oneself from the facts related in vv. 1-6. One might think wisdom will come to save the day, but it is easily derailed by extortion or a simple bribe. It can hardly be counted on. We have already seen that the first half of v. 8 echoes Qohelet's previous concerns. Verse 8b supports this view in that patience for, perhaps even a resignation concerning, the end leaves one in a much better place than a prideful spirit that thinks it can make something of life that God himself seems determined to undermine. Moreover, do not get angry too quickly (about all this). That is for fools who do not understand the way of things (v. 9). This is not pious advice coming from Qohelet, as if he is suddenly spurred on to make a new quest for wisdom (e.g., Prov 29:8; 30:33). He is, rather, advising his readers not to let this הֶבֶל/*hebel* situation carry them away — although one must also point out that Qohelet does not always follow his own advice!

This interpretation fits well with v. 10. Neither get angry nor wish for the good old days, as if they were better than today. Such nostalgia is useless, and is born out of lack of wisdom. Of course, wisdom often counts for little, if anything, with Qohelet, so one wonders why he should chide nostalgia as a lack of wisdom. The answer is that Qohelet has shown throughout what one might call a love-hate, or at least ambivalent, view toward wisdom. Qohelet appeals to wisdom with one hand and dismisses it with the other, and this is precisely part of his rhetoric (see, e.g., 2:13-16). So do not be a fool by asking for the good old days, because anyone with eyes to see can tell you that there is no substantive difference between the two. There is no profit; all is *hebel*.

Verses 11-12 continue this (perhaps unexpected) support of wisdom, and by doing so Qohelet is demonstrating his confusion over what he sees in the world around him, or, to be reminded of Fox's position discussed above in the introduction, Qohelet is *observing* the contradictory nature of reality. Sometimes wisdom works (at least for now), sometimes it does not. The larger point is that wisdom cannot be counted on. Qohelet's words here simply underscore that point. So he remarks that both money and wisdom offer some "protection,"[9] and that knowledge has some profit in that wisdom pre-

---

9. The noun צֵל/*ṣēl* occurs in 6:12 and 8:13, both with negative overtones. Here "shade" or "shadow" offers protection. Seow argues that the transient meaning of the word in 6:12 and 8:13 carries over to 7:12, and so both money and wisdom are indicted. Likewise, in 7:11 wisdom is as "good" as an inheritance ("Theology"). Although our points are diametrically opposite on this matter, either position is consistent with Qohelet's overall skepticism about the ultimate advantage of wisdom or anything else in the face of death. The only question is whether Qohelet here has that ultimate perspective in mind (as Seow argues) or whether we have here simply another weak attempt to resuscitate wisdom despite his own ultimate declaration that all is *hebel*. What is so fascinating and frustrating about Qohelet's theology is that either option makes sense.

serves the life of the one who possesses it. But, as vv. 13-14 remind us, the previous discussion is ultimately for naught, regardless of where it might go. "Look at what God is doing! Can you really change it?! Whether things happen to go well or badly for you right now, God is responsible for both, so nothing you do will have any effect." In making this observation, Qohelet has brought us back not only to a recurring theme in the book, but to the beginning of this section: whatever happens has already been named by God, and no amount of struggling will change it.[10] This is not a pious acknowledgment that all of Israel's circumstances are in God's hands (e.g., Lam 3:37-39, where similar language is used). And, as we will see in the next section, Qohelet's frantic grasp for wisdom to provide some sense to it all is not over, although there too the frustration is palpable.

7:15-29: A Frantic Grasp for Wisdom

This section provides some of the more startling glimpses into Qohelet's thinking. Verse 15 clearly introduces a train of thought that Qohelet considers absurd. Along the way, he will comment on the wisdom of not having too much wisdom, while at the same time acknowledging that wisdom is worth more than the bigwigs in the city. Further, righteousness is not at all an easy commodity to grasp, a fact Qohelet discovers by, of all things, pursuing wisdom. He seems to conclude with a renewed determination to seek wisdom, but quickly lands in a familiar place — and along the way seems to take a pretty hard swipe against women. Quite a busy section, and not an easy one to untangle.

Qohelet begins by making an observation, introduced by the commonly recurring root רָאָה/*r'h* (see, e.g., 1:14; 2:13; 3:16). That his observation is one of despair is already signaled in 7:15 by saying that this is what he has seen "in my הֶבֶל/*hebel* days." Whatever follows is not going to be good. What is it that he has seen? הַכֹּל/*hakkōl*, which is somewhat ambiguous. It could be translated "both," since the text that follows juxtaposes the righteous and the guilty (see also v. 18, where it clearly means "both"). On the other hand, it could mean "everything" in the sense, "I have seen it all in my absurd life." Either way, what follows is a state of affairs Qohelet looks on as something to be grieved: a righteous one perishes in his righteousness, but a guilty one lives long in his "badness." The terms צַדִּיק/*ṣaddîq*, צֶדֶק/*ṣedeq*, רָשָׁע/*rāšāʿ*, and רַע/

---

10. Seow points out the lexical similarities between 6:10-12 and 7:10-14, and concludes that this section is a coherent unit (*Ecclesiastes*, 241).

ra' are translated here "righteous," "righteousness," "guilty," and "bad," respectively, but we must remember that Qohelet is not concerned with abstract moral categories, but with very practical ones. He sees people doing the right things and perishing, while those in the wrong live long. As we will see in a moment, this is by no means a universal state of affairs, but the very fact that it happens at all is highly disturbing to Qohelet and calls into question whether there is anything one can count on in life (including God).

Now, one must notice that this observation is in some tension, not only with, say, 7:1 (where death is better), but Qohelet's overall observation on the absurdity of life, since death brings to naught all attempts at achieving some profit. But here Qohelet seems to be interested in describing a relative good (as in the so-called carpe diem passages), not making a general and final pronouncement as he does elsewhere. He is trying to strike a path through this life that acknowledges the absurdity while also giving the reader the best shot at some sense of order amid the chaos. So given the unfairness of life, Qohelet advises that one be neither abundantly righteous nor show oneself excessively wise.[1] One cannot imagine such words to be found in Proverbs, for example, where wisdom is supreme and is to be sought after as more precious than anything (Prov 3:13-18; 8:10). But for Qohelet the categories "too wise" and "too righteous" exist, and they lead to being "confounded."[2] The sentiment expressed here has already been seen in 1:17-18 and 2:14-16, at least with respect to wisdom: too much of it will drive you to anger and despair. Qohelet advises that you keep an even tone, stay centered, and do not get carried away. Since righteousness and wisdom do not guarantee a beneficial outcome, one would be "wise" to find the happy medium. If you expect righteousness and wisdom to pay off consistently, you will be confounded. Qohelet's point is not that righteousness and wisdom never pay off, only that they do so inconsistently.

This is why he counters quickly in v. 17 that one should neither be too "in the wrong" (רָשָׁע/*rāšā'*) nor be a fool, since these lead to premature death. Oddly enough, Qohelet indicates here that a timely death (prolonged life) is desirable, a thought that takes us very far from, say, 7:1ff. Moreover, being a fool means that one will die before one's *time* (עֵת/*'ēt*). One may recall the use of this word elsewhere in Ecclesiastes, especially in 3:1-8, where God directs *every* time, that is, there is no "time" that is not under God's control. Here, however, one's actions do indeed seem to have an effect on outcomes. It seems

---

1. On the Hithpael of חכם/*ḥkm*, meaning "show oneself wise" or "deal wisely," see Exod 1:10.

2. The verb is the Hithpolel of שמם/*šmm* (to be confounded, astounded, or appalled). The word occurs in Ecclesiastes only here.

clear that, once again, Qohelet is here not thinking of the big picture but a relative one. In the here-and-now, good things happen to bad people and bad things to good people. Hence do not get caught up in trying to be too good; of course, do not just cash it all in and be a fool. That has consequences of its own. Better to stay in the middle and avoid all extremes. Or as v. 18 puts it, "It is good to lay hold of the one and not let go of the other. The one who fears God will follow both of them (כֻּלָּם/*kullām*)."[3] To paraphrase, if you are moderately wise, you will not let life burn you. Your expectations are moderate, centered; you will not be frustrated or appalled at what you see. This is what it means for Qohelet to "fear God": not a healthy, covenantal fear, as we see elsewhere in the OT, but something dysfunctional, born out of frustration. God is not to be trusted, so keep out of his way.

This train of thought evidently leads Qohelet down another, yet related, path, where he continues discussing the relative benefits of wisdom. As we read in v. 19, "Wisdom gives strength/power (עזז/*ʿzz*) to the wise, more than ten city leaders."[4] Wisdom makes a wise man stronger than ten city leaders, simply meaning that the benefits of wisdom are tenfold better than whatever gives these city leaders their status (it is unclear whether their status is governmental or socioeconomic).[5] It is not entirely clear just what Qohelet is getting at in this verse, apart from a simple continuation of the "benefits of wisdom" theme. But why, of all things, make a disjointed remark about the benefits of wisdom over city leaders? This disjointedness has led Fox and others to suggest that sometime during the history of transmission v. 19 was erroneously transposed from its original position after v. 12. I often wonder in

---

3. Note the use of כֹּל/*kōl*, here meaning "both," as mentioned above.

4. Verse 19 poses issues that have occupied interpreters for some time. (1) Fox argues that this verse is out of place and should come after v. 12, and so continue, "the teaching of wisdom's superiority to wealth" (*Time to Tear Down*, 256-57). I agree that vv. 19 and 12 share a similar topic, but I do not think one needs to argue for an alternate original location for v. 19. (2) Another issue concerns the root עזז/*ʿzz*. It typically refers to strength, but Seow argues that such a meaning is out of place here: "Why would wisdom be stronger *for the wise* than for anyone else?" (*Ecclesiastes*, 256). He then goes on to argue, on the basis of biblical and postbiblical usage, for a broader meaning of the root, which leads to his translation, "Wisdom is dearer to the wise" (252). Here I follow the more conventional translation, as does Longman (*Ecclesiastes*, 193, 197). I collapse the relative clause at the end of the verse, "who are in the city," and treat it adjectivally for purposes of translation, i.e., city leaders. (3) The translation of שַׁלִּיט/*šallîṭ* is uncertain; it may mean "citizens" (Longman), "magnates" (Fox), or "proprietors" (Seow). I feel it means more than simply citizens, more likely those in positions of status or authority. The related problem, however, is how to handle עֲשָׂרָה/*ʿăśārâ*. The word means "ten," but both Seow and Fox consider this problematic and redivide and repoint the phrase to read "wealth of the שַׁלִּיטִים/*šallîṭîm*." My understanding differs, as can be seen above.

5. Seow, *Ecclesiastes*, 257.

hearing such suggestions, however persuasive they are in certain instances, why it is that the erroneous transposition was not immediately corrected by a subsequent copyist, given its problematic nature. I am not suggesting that textual emendations, on either the word or verse level, are to be avoided at all costs, only that posing them can sometimes introduce a problem at another level. It is my opinion, therefore, that even though this one verse does not seem to fit well into this context, it is there, nevertheless, intentionally. Its apparent misplacement would in this case reflect the author's own discursive, roving gaze — a quality not lacking elsewhere in the book. It causes me no interpretive difficulty, in other words, to see our author jumping around a bit, allowing his train(s) of thought to take him in multiple directions.

In v. 20 Qohelet returns to the topic of righteousness and declares, in a manner reminiscent of Pss 14:1-3 and 53:1-3 (see Rom 3:10-12), that, at the end of the day, no one is righteous, in that no one does good (טוֹב/*ṭôb*) and does not sin (חטא/*ḥṭ'*). One syntactical difficulty is the opening word, כִּי/*kî*. If it is causal, this verse would be seen as a result of the preceding verse, but one must admit there is little causal about this relationship. If it were asseverative (emphatic), however, it would be translated "surely" or "indeed." The latter seems to make much more sense because, even given Qohelet's penchant for discursive thought, wisdom is the topic of v. 19 and righteousness is the topic here. Still, Seow's suggestion is most helpful: *kî* is adversative, "but."[6] Seow's reading creates a contrast between wisdom, which is available as a relative good in v. 19, and righteousness, which in v. 20 is not available.

This raises the question, however, of what Qohelet means here by "good," "sinning," and "righteous." We have seen all three Hebrew roots elsewhere in Ecclesiastes, most often "good" and "righteous," but *ḥṭ'* (to sin) as well (2:26; see also 5:5 [Eng. 6]; 7:26; 8:12; 9:2, 18; 10:4). In 2:26 the root refers not to someone who has done wrong but to someone who is at the short end of the stick with respect to God's dealings. Elsewhere, however, it has a more traditional overtone: that of one behaving in at least a flawed way, which is the case here. What is worth noting is that nothing mentioned in v. 20 offends God, although contemporary readers think of "sinning" as such an offense. I do not think Qohelet is particularly concerned with breaking God's law, for example. He is more of the mind to point out that, as Fox puts it, "To be human is to be flawed. . . . Do not expect much righteousness from anyone, including yourself."[7]

6. See Seow's brief defense of this view (*Ecclesiastes*, 258). Fox translates it "for," connecting vv. 20 to 18, having placed v. 19 after v. 12.

7. Fox, *Time to Tear Down*, 262. Seow translates the root as "err," which is consistent with Fox's translation (*Ecclesiastes*, 258).

Verse 21 follows upon v. 20 in that the flawed human condition means that one should not "let it get to you" (lit. "take to heart" what people say), otherwise you might hear your servant cursing you. This is a potentially telling comment by Qohelet. It seems that Qohelet has a more upper-class audience in view here, since servants are mentioned (and see 2:7: Qohelet acquired servants). Moreover, since no one is free from wrongdoing, you know that you yourself are guilty of cursing others. One wonders whether this is perhaps a veiled reference to Qohelet's own "cursing" of God throughout the book.

I take v. 23 to reflect both on what preceded and what follows, which is a standard conclusion reached by other commentators. Qohelet is reflecting on his observation in this section and, again, giving credence to wisdom: "All this I have tested by wisdom" (see the similar expression נסה/*nsh* plus "wisdom" in 2:1). But note the immediate tone of resignation in this verse and in v. 24, as he exclaims that, although he has been wise,[8] it is "far from him," and all that happens is "inaccessible" and "utterly unfathomable,"[9] so much so that he asks, "who can find it?"

This passage concludes with what one might call a small subsection, vv. 25-29. The language of v. 25 is similar to 1:13 and almost gives the impression that Qohelet is starting a new wisdom quest. It is worth noting that, once again, Qohelet's assertion here to "seek wisdom" is in some tension with what he says above in v. 23, but such is his rhetoric.[10] We also see introduced here the word חֶשְׁבּוֹן/*ḥešbôn*, which recurs in 7:27, 29; 9:10. The word's basic meaning is something like "calculation," and so Longman offers "sum of things" while Fox suggests "solution."[11] Seow's translation is a bit more specific, "accounting," and reflects his understanding of the root as being a Persian-era economic term (ledger, inventory).[12]

Qohelet also wants to understand רֶשַׁע כֶּסֶל וְהַסִּכְלוּת הוֹלֵלוֹת/*reša' kesel wĕhassiklût hôlēlôt*. There is some disagreement just how to translate

8. Seow translates the imperfect in v. 23 as "I would be wise," thus making explicit Qohelet's failure to attain wisdom (*Ecclesiastes*, 252, 259).

9. The translation here is Seow's (*Ecclesiastes*, 259-60). More literally it means "far off" (רָחוֹק/*rāḥôq*) and "very deep" (עָמֹק עָמֹק/*'āmōq 'āmōq*).

10. Rudman argues that the repetition of the verbs בקש/*bqš* and מצא/*mṣ'* indicates that vv. 23-24 are to be taken together with vv. 25-29 ("Woman as Divine Agent"). By connecting Qohelet's language of entrapment here with 9:12 and the determinism of 3:1-15, Rudman argues that the woman of vv. 25-29 is "the agent of a deterministic force. . . . an instrument of divine judgment on humanity. . . . Possibly she is a symbol of the arbitrary nature of the deity's intervention in life" (418-20).

11. Longman, *Ecclesiastes*, 202-3; Fox, *Time to Tear Down*, 268.

12. Seow, *Ecclesiastes*, 260-61.

these terms, although it is worth keeping in mind that we have already seen the last two in 1:17 (note the variant spelling there of סכל/skl: שׂכל/śkl) and 2:12. They describe part of the purview of Qohelet's wisdom quest. Although different translations are proposed, it seems most natural to understand these as two pairs of terms, "evil of foolishness" and "folly of madness."[13] These terms contrast to "wisdom and accounting" in the previous clause. As we have seen earlier in the book, Qohelet is stating that his wisdom quest explores the breadth of existence: the good, the bad, and the ugly.

Would that Qohelet had simply stopped there, but he goes on to what is considered one of the more controversial topics, at least for contemporary readers, in a book already filled to the brim with challenges. Concerning v. 26, Fox comments, "There is both bathos and wit in these words: the result of his inquiries in the abstruse realms of intellect comes down to this: woman is dangerous."[14] That "woman" is preceded by the definite article (הָאִשָּׁה/hā'iššâ) does not delimit the reference to one specific woman, particularly in view of v. 28, which says that not a single woman could be found among a thousand. Seow argues at length, however, that "the woman" of v. 26 is an allusion to personified Folly, mentioned in v. 25 and well known from Proverbs 1–9. This requires Seow to conclude that v. 28, which clearly speaks of male and female in general, is a gloss. He supports his point by arguing that the vocabulary of v. 28 is uncharacteristic of Qohelet: the forty-eight other occurrences of אָדָם/'ādām in Ecclesiastes refer to humanity, not a male. Also, 'ādām is used in the very next verse to refer to humanity, not males.[15]

We have in this passage, therefore, certain ambiguities that do not find a clear solution. For Qohelet to speak of only one woman in v. 26 is in tension with v. 28, but v. 28 seems like a gloss, at least according to Seow. Let me try to put all these pieces together in as succinct a manner as I can.

Qohelet seems to argue in v. 26 that the woman "who is nets (מְצוֹדִים/mĕṣôdîm), whose heart is snares, and whose hands are bonds," is more bitter than death. Hence he is referring to a particular *type* of woman, delimited by the relative clause (אֲשֶׁר/'ăšer). The one God favors (טוֹב לִפְנֵי הָאֱלֹהִים/ṭôb lipnê hā'ĕlōhîm; see the similar language in 2:26) will escape from such a woman, although the one God does not favor (the חוֹטֵא/ḥôṭē'; see 2:26; contrast 7:20) will be caught by her. We have, therefore, an allusion to the metaphors used in Proverbs 1–9 (and described positively in Prov 31:10-31). In this sense I agree with Seow (although the woman of v. 26 is for me a type of

13. See Longman, *Ecclesiastes*, 203.
14. Fox, *Time to Tear Down*, 268.
15. Seow's argument is found in *Ecclesiastes*, 264-65.

woman, not a specific woman). Why Qohelet turns to this topic is beyond me, but we will have to leave that question to the side. Qohelet then declares that, after careful examination,[16] he has not actually found such a woman (vv. 27-28a). Rather than understand the rest of v. 28 as a gloss, it seems equally plausible to suggest it is a proverbial saying of some sort, which could account for the unusual use of vocabulary. In this respect, it could be understood simply as underscoring what we began seeing in v. 26: a (type of) woman (who is *not* a snare, etc.) is truly hard to find.

Qohelet has also "found" (v. 29) that God has made humanity (his more conventional use of *'ādām*) "straight" (יָשָׁר/*yāšār*) but they have sought out "great devices" (חִשְּׁבֹנוֹת רַבִּים/*hiššĕbōnôt rabbîm*). Qohelet argues that humanity's efforts to "calculate" (חֶשְׁבּוֹן/*ḥešbôn*) is undesirable.[17] We have, therefore, an ironic situation: the very act of seeking and finding solutions, which is portrayed positively in vv. 25 and 27, is in v. 29 portrayed as being in tension with God's design to make humanity "straight." In other words, the preferred state is one where one does not try to figure things out (see 1:18; 2:13-17). I take this passage, therefore, as a swipe against so-called traditional wisdom — a point strengthened by allowing "the woman" of v. 26 to allude to Proverbs 1–9 — more than against women in general (not that I would put misogyny beyond the scope of someone who thinks nothing of leveling some pretty serious criticisms against God himself).[18]

The remaining issue to be addressed in this section is the curious reference to Qohelet in the third person in v. 27, "says Qohelet." There are two problems: (1) Why is Qohelet referred to in the third person in the midst of his first person monologue? (2) Why is the verb feminine where elsewhere it is masculine (e.g., 1:2)? As to the first question, it seems fairly self-evident that the frame narrator "is making his presence known,"[19] but the question remains why. Perhaps there is no reason other than it seemed like the right moment. As for the second question, commentators typically redivide the Hebrew phrase אָמְרָה קֹהֶלֶת/*'āmĕrâ qōhelet* as אָמַר הַקֹּהֶלֶת/*'āmar haqqōhelet* on the basis of 12:8, that is, the proper name has the article and the verb is masculine. This seems the best solution to what is otherwise inexplicable.

In general, however, in this section we see Qohelet continuing his struggle to find some meaning in this life, which here includes a frantic grasp for

---

16. This is my translation of the phrase in v. 27, אַחַת לְאַחַת לִמְצֹא חֶשְׁבּוֹן/*'aḥat lĕ'aḥat limṣō' ḥešbôn*, lit. "one to one to find the solution [calculation]."

17. Longman refers the reader to Gen 6:5 for a similar use of the root (*Ecclesiastes*, 207).

18. On Qohelet reflecting the typical misogyny of his time, see Sneed, "(Dis)closure in Qohelet."

19. Longman, *Ecclesiastes*, 205. See also Seow, *Ecclesiastes*, 264.

wisdom, which he finds wanting, along with righteousness. The concluding section of this passage, 7:25-29, underscores this notion by Qohelet anticipating an interlocutor's appeal to Proverbs, which Qohelet deftly counters in a way we have seen throughout this book: "Show me, because I do not see it."

8:1-17: In the Hands of a Capricious King

It is not entirely clear whether 8:1 concludes the previous section or introduces this one. I am of the latter opinion. As I see it, this section begins and ends with a word about wisdom. Verse 1 is somewhat optimistic, in that it speaks of the benefit gained by an outlook characterized by wisdom. The question in the first part of v. 1 does not seem to be rhetorical but is answered in the second part: "Who is like the wise and who knows the interpretation of the matter? Man's wisdom brightens his face and changes his impudent[1] look." Verse 17, however, returns to Qohelet's generally pessimistic view of wisdom: God's works are incomprehensible, and even the wise are shielded from full comprehension. By now readers are certainly familiar with Qohelet's back-and-forth thoughts on the benefits of wisdom (e.g., 2:13-17). But what has happened here in 8:1-17 to cause this about-face? A capricious and unjust king — and an equally capricious and unjust God behind him.

Qohelet begins his observations here with a somewhat ominous tone: "As for me,[2] keep the king's command [lit. 'mouth'], and concerning an oath to God, do not hurry."[3] One can see an overlap in thinking here with 5:1. An oath toward God is not to be entered into lightly, nor is a king's command to be ignored. One cannot help but observe that both kings and God are being presented in a less than complimentary light here. If anything, this should alert us, as discussed in the introduction, that the kingly persona that Qohelet

---

1. I am following here Fox (*Time to Tear Down*, 273) and Seow (*Ecclesiastes*, 276) in translating עֹז/*'ōz* as "impudent," since the following verses pertain to one's conduct before the king.

2. Verse 2 begins abruptly simply with אֲנִי/*'ănî*. Both Seow and Fox argue for a textual problem here and so either delete it or emend it. I concur that it is unusual, but I understand the pronoun to be analogous to what we see, for example, in Gen 17:4, where it is translated, "As for me," or "For my part."

3. This translation reads the first two words of v. 3 with v. 2, to maintain the parallelism of the line. Seow argues that the idiom בהל/*bhl* (Niphal) plus מִפָּנָיו/*mippānāyw* is attested in Gen 45:3 and Job 23:15 to mean "be stupefied in his presence" (*Ecclesiastes*, 279-80). The net effect of Seow's reading is to underscore that the subject of the king should not stand there staring, but should leave as soon as possible, since the king will do as he pleases anyway. I am following, however, the more commonly chosen division, and the ultimate trajectory of this passage is not affected.

maintained at the outset has worn out its welcome. But why is it so important to obey the king and take care not to enter into an oath with God? Because, as v. 3 says, "Walk away from him[4] and do not stand [perhaps in the sense of 'persist'] in a harmful thing." The term used here for "harmful" is רַע/*ra'*, which, as elsewhere, should not be understood as "evil," but rather as something that is simply a bad idea. Qohelet is saying, "Make your point, to God or the king, and make yourself scarce as soon as you can, knowing that he will do as he pleases anyway."

After all, Qohelet continues in v. 4, the king's word has authority, and who can tell him what to do? The overlap between his description of the king here and his dismal appraisal of God in such places as 1:15 and 7:13 is unmistakable. Indeed, one can say that 8:3-4, where caution concerning the king is in view, parallels to some extent 5:1-7, where the reader is warned about God. It may be that Qohelet is aiming his arrows at both authority figures, or perhaps "king" here is code for "God." I do not think that this question can be (or needs to be) answered definitively, but the parallel is inviting in view of Qohelet's negative attitude toward both in various portions throughout Ecclesiastes.

In this respect, vv. 2-8 are of interest. Qohelet admonishes his readers that the one who keeps the king's command "knows" (i.e., experiences) nothing bad (רָע/*ra'*). Rather, someone who is wise will know time and custom. This phrase "time and custom" (עֵת וּמִשְׁפָּט/*'ēt ûmišpāṭ*) is not found elsewhere in Ecclesiastes, although both words are found in other contexts. We have seen *mišpāṭ* in 3:16 and 5:8 (MT 7) with respect to matters of due justice in the conventional sense of the word. Here, however, it seems to refer to custom, protocol, proper procedure vis-à-vis one's obedience to a king. With respect to *'ēt*, however, more important connections are forged. Verse 6 is an unmistakable echo of 3:1: "For, for every matter (חֵפֶץ/*hēpeṣ*) there is a time (*'ēt*) and a custom (*mišpāṭ*); for the trouble of man (רָעַת הָאָדָם/*rā'at hā'ādām*) is heavy upon him." As we have seen concerning God in 3:1-8, here too we see with kings: they do as they please, when they please. The "time" is theirs, and this weighs heavily on humanity. Qohelet continues this string of observations in v. 7: "For no one will know what will be, for who can tell you when it happens?" These themes are well known to readers by now (see 1:9; 2:18; 3:22; see also 6:12), although here they pertain to a king's actions: "He does as he pleases; this is a hardship (רָעָה/*rā'â*) for us; no one knows what he will do [or will happen]; no one can tell you what the future holds."

---

4. The focus here seems to be on the king, since he is mentioned again in v. 4, but the double referent should not be lost. Up to this point, Qohelet's ire has been directed at God. Here the king is brought into the picture, but with God still in view (v. 2).

To drive the point home, Qohelet comes right back to the theme that cancels out any chance of hope or "profit": death. "No one can control the 'wind' [רוּחַ/*rûaḥ*, i.e., life-breath],[5] to restrain the 'wind.' No one can control the day of death, there is no release for war, and guilty behavior (רֶשַׁע/*reša*ʿ) will not deliver the one who practices it." I take here the references to war and guilty behavior simply as further examples of things over which one has no control. One does not just walk away from battle, and the guilty will get theirs (although note the stark contrast here with 3:16).

These are the things that Qohelet has observed, indeed, he has "*devoted* himself to everything done under the sun — a time (עֵת/*ʿēt*) when man has power over another to his detriment" (v. 9). One must presume, in light of what has come before, that the first man mentioned who has power over the other is the king. With v. 10 we seem to shift topics somewhat, but it, along with vv. 11-17, are best understood in the context of what has just been said about the king. We revisit here the theme of doing wrong things and how, at the end, God lets it happen, and humanity is commended, once again, to enjoy what one has. As suggested above, king and God seem to be held guilty for the same type of unjust, even capricious, behavior.

In v. 10 Qohelet observes that the unjust (רְשָׁעִים/*rĕšāʿîm*) are brought to burial. These are the very ones who used to walk about the Holy Place. Those who acted justly, however, were neglected in the city.[6] This is absurd. Qohelet cannot abide the crass, public injustice of the guilty receiving a proper burial — those who had moved in and out of the Holy Place with impunity — while the just receive no such honor. This is something the ruler (king) allows, and the root of the problem is, as Qohelet remarks in v. 11, that the sentence (פִּתְגָם/*pitgām*) for a wrong deed is not carried out swiftly, which only encourages such behavior. It is the king's failure to keep order (v. 11) and his honoring of those who do wrong (v. 10) that sickens Qohelet.

Such a state of affairs leads Qohelet to offer a solution of sorts, one that we have already seen elsewhere: those who fear God will be better off (v. 12). This is one of those tensions in Qohelet's words that readers by now have

---

5. Seow, *Ecclesiastes*, 282. See also Fox, *Time to Tear Down*, 280-81.

6. Verse 10 is fraught with difficulties. Following Fox (*Time to Tear Down*, 282-85) and Seow (*Ecclesiastes*, 284-86), I read בָּאוּ/*bāʾû* as "were brought" (i.e., to burial) rather than "departed," since הלך/*hlk* is normally used for departure (death) in Ecclesiastes. Following Seow (*Ecclesiastes*, 285), I also take the phrase אֲשֶׁר כֵּן-עָשׂוּ/*ʾăšer kēn-ʿāsû* as the subject of the verb יִשְׁתַּכְּחוּ/*yištakkĕḥû*, and כֵּן/*kēn* as an adverb "justly," thus presenting a contrast between the guilty who are treated with honor and the just who are not. The verb *yištakkĕḥû* should not be emended to שׁבח/*šbḥ* (praise) as some translations (e.g., NRSV, NIV) do. I also understand the Hiphil of *hlk* as "walk about," as we see in 4:15.

come to expect, and so there is no need to reconcile his words here with his more pessimistic evaluations of the unreliability of God's justice elsewhere. Offenders[7] do what is wrong a hundred times over, but their lives are lengthened. It seems, especially in view of v. 13, that the lengthening of one's life is God's doing, but this presents a somewhat nasty logical problem. Verse 12 says that the offender may sin a hundred times over and his days are lengthened; yet "it will go well for those who fear God, because[8] they fear him." So far so good. This reads like standard wisdom teaching, at least in the sense that the one who fears God, despite appearances, is better off than the offender who lives a long life. But v. 13 comes right back and says something quite different. Here, as if he has forgotten what he just said, Qohelet announces that it will not go well for the guilty (רָשָׁע/*rāšāʿ*), that their lives will not be lengthened like a shadow, because they do not fear God. Which is it? Is Qohelet trying to hang on to some desperate hope that God's justice will triumph in the end? If so, it is perhaps an early glimpse of the very last verse of the book (12:14). But we must observe that the expression used twice in these verses ("fear him/ God") was seen already in 3:14, where the overtones are anything but comforting. Qohelet is clearly struggling here with a sense of not only royal justice but divine justice, and the role that the fear of God plays in that.

Even so, this glimmer of hope, if that is what it is, is short-lived, for in the very next verse (14) Qohelet reverses himself again, declaring what is in his mind "absurd": Those in the right get what the guilty deserve, and those in the wrong get what those in the right deserve. This situation Qohelet calls הֶבֶל/*hebel*, the word framing the verse itself. This is not an additional observation on his part, but a summary of the absurdity he has just described in the previous verses. The entire matter of human and divine justice is unpredictable, even if he holds out some hope for those who fear God. But even in that declaration, Qohelet ultimately, and quite emphatically, concludes that the injustice remains and it is absurd.

Qohelet concludes this section with another carpe diem passage of sorts. He commends pleasure, "because there is nothing good for man under the sun except eating, drinking, and having pleasure. This is what will accompany him the days of his life that God has given him under the sun." The note of resignation is clear, particularly in view of the fact that the specter of death

---

7. As in 2:26, I prefer to translate חֹטֶא (אֲשֶׁר)/(*ʾăšer) ḥōṭeʾ* as "offender" rather than "sinner" for no other reason than to help us think more of "sinner" in terms of concrete matters of justice, which Qohelet has in mind, rather than the ontological overtones, especially for Christian readers. I do not mean to suggest that the two terms are mutually exclusive.

8. I translate אֲשֶׁר/*ʾăšer* here and in v. 13 as "because," following Longman (*Ecclesiastes*, 217) and Fox (*Time to Tear Down*, 282).

raises its head once again. "Listen," Qohelet says, "life is not fair, so just enjoy yourself for the time God allows you to be here, however long or short that may be. Don't think that doing right will guarantee any longer life span than doing wrong. Just don't think about it." He finishes out this thought in vv. 16-17 with quite a flourish. It is as if he is taking a step back from the immediate dilemma and making a general observation about the wisdom quest he began in 1:12. He has devoted himself to knowing wisdom and seeing the "task" that has been done on the earth. Note that "task" is the word עִנְיָן/*'inyān*, which we have seen in 1:13; 2:23, 26; 3:10; 4:8; 5:2, 13 (Eng. 3, 14). I also take the passive "has been done" as circumlocution for an act of God (see 1:15). All this does is make you lose sleep.

That God is the ultimate purveyor of injustice is suggested again in v. 17. Qohelet has observed all the work of God and he concludes that no one is able to comprehend the work that is done (by God) under the sun, on account of which (בְּשֶׁל אֲשֶׁר/*běšel 'ăšer*) man toils to seek (בקשׁ/*bqš*) (i.e., understand why things are the way they are), but he cannot find. And this goes for a wise man too: he may claim to have comprehended the nature of things, but he has not. Qohelet, in other words, presents the problem of royal and divine injustice (that you can count on neither God nor ruler for justice), attempts some mediating position (vv. 12-13), but in the end not only does not follow his own advice, but calls the entire attempt to get one's arms around the matter futile. No amount of wisdom can solve this. Which is why, as he has opined throughout, wisdom brings anger and grief (1:18), and it is best to have wisdom only in a moderate amount, just enough to keep you from becoming a complete fool (2:16-18). In the following section, Qohelet proceeds with this line of thought and revisits another of his favorite topics, how death ultimately levels all playing fields.

9:1-12: Death Revisited

The previous section ends on a rather pessimistic note concerning even the ability of the wise to find knowledge. In 9:1-12 Qohelet continues such a dismal posture by revisiting the theme of death. It is not his final statement on the matter (see 11:1–12:7), but it is certainly a clear and climactic one: death comes to all, and it is, without question, the end. Other themes come and go with Qohelet, but the inevitable leveling effect of human mortality remains an active concept, directly or indirectly, in nearly all of his monologues. Moreover, in this section on death, Qohelet appeals, once again, to a provisional understanding of meaning in this life, the notion of carpe diem we have seen elsewhere. And because this meaning is provisional, it is quickly neutralized at the end of this section: carpe diem is subject to an unknown and unpredictable time of one's death.

Qohelet begins this section, as he has so many others, with a reminder that his observations are the product of a serious devotion, a dedication: "I have examined[1] the righteous and the wise and their works,[2] and they are all in God's hands." Now we must remember that being in God's hands is not a word of comfort from Qohelet. Rather, based on God's role in Qohelet's take on things, the reference here should signal that something rather uncomfortable is about to come up. To be in God's hands is to be subject to his actions, his timing (see 3:1-8), his will, which is neither consistent nor necessarily just (e.g., 2:18-26). "Love and hate," too, are in God's hands. Because all these things are under God's control, "no one knows anything in advance of what will happen."[3]

Not only is this so, but even if one could know anything of what will happen, the same fate awaits everyone anyway, and so any such knowledge would be cancelled out (v. 2). Indeed, the only thing we can know for certain is that all die; we do not know, however, when or how. And the inevitability of death, the "one fate" (מִקְרֶה אֶחָד/*miqreh 'eḥād*, 2:14-15; see also 3:19) will come home to everyone, regardless of whether they are in the right or in the wrong; to "the good,"[4] the clean and unclean; whether or not one sacrifices; whether one is good or an "offender" (חֹטֶא/*ḥōṭe'*; see 2:26); whether one swears or is afraid to take an oath.[5] These comments should not be taken lightly. In essence Qohelet is saying that being an obedient Israelite, at the end

---

1. The Hebrew root here is debated. It is either בור/*bwr* ("to explain"), which would be its only occurrence in Ecclesiastes, or ברר/*brr*, which we have seen in 3:18 ("to test"). The sense of the passage is not seriously affected either way.

2. The word here is Aramaic עֲבָד/*'ăbād*, rather than what has been used throughout, מַעֲשֶׂה/*ma'ăśeh*. See Fox, *Time to Tear Down*, 290-91; Seow, *Ecclesiastes*, 297-98.

3. The final portion of v. 1 has some difficulties, and my translation is closest to that of Seow (*Ecclesiastes*, 298-99). I do not think that the "not knowing" of humanity for Qohelet is limited to "love and hate," as Longman suggests (although not without discussion; see *Ecclesiastes*, 224). Fox's division is more involved and worthy of consideration, but not within the constraints of this commentary (see Fox, *Time to Tear Down*, 287, 291-92).

4. While the other words in the section are paired, טוֹב/*ṭôb* stands alone. Many commentators omit it, since it appears in a pair later in the verse, and may have simply been reproduced here by scribal error. Ancient versions (LXX, Syr., and Vulg.) add "and evil," thus completing the pair. At the end of the day, the question has bearing only on the text of Ecclesiastes, certainly not on the message of this section.

5. Seow points out, on the basis of an Akkadian parallel, that the contrast here is between one who swears falsely and one who respects the nature of making oaths (*Ecclesiastes*, 299). Otherwise, it may simply be a matter of contrasting those who do and do not swear oaths. As with other ambiguities in this passage, the general thrust is not in question.

of the day, amounts to nothing because death comes to all, a point he reaches quite clearly in v. 3. He says, "This is the עָר/*ra*ʿ in everything done under the sun." The use of the passive "done" is telling and echoes 1:15: it is a way of referring to God's activity, and here he refers to what God does as bad. More specifically, regardless of how one acts, "one fate" comes to all. In a manner of speaking, 9:1-3a is a summary of Qohelet's exasperation in the book: it really does not matter how faithful you are, God has it so that all die.

This is followed by a comment not on the state of God but on the state of humanity, that the heart of men is filled with עָר/*ra*ʿ and madness (הוֹלֵלוֹת/ *hôlēlôt*, 1:17; 2:12) throughout their lives and afterward "to death."[6] Nevertheless, despite these human failings, as long as one is alive, there is certitude (בִּטָּחוֹן/*biṭṭāḥôn*, v. 4), for a "live dog is better than a dead lion." Rather than understand this as an unqualified expression that life is better than death (which would be, for what it is worth, in serious tension with such passages as 4:2-3 and 7:1-6), Qohelet is really saying the opposite: the reason that the living have certitude is that they *know* that they will die. Qohelet's tongue is firmly pressed against his cheek here. This is not a word of comfort, but, as v. 5 goes on to explain, a blow to the stomach: the one thing the living have over the dead is that the living have certitude that they will one day join the ranks of the dead. The dead, being dead, have nothing. Moreover, the choice of animals is telling. Dogs were not pets, sitting under the shade of a porch, but animals of disrespect. Indeed, they were symbols of death and the underworld. Lions, on the other hand, were noble and admired animals. Yet a live dog is better off than a dead lion, regardless of the degrading quality of that life, because he at least knows *something*.[7] The dead, however, "have no 'reward,'"[8] and "their memory will be forgotten" (a clear echo of the frame narrator's comment in 1:11).

Also, as v. 6 continues, their love, hate, and jealousy have already per-

---

6. As with other portions of this passage, there is some syntactical ambiguity here. Seow considers the final phrase of v. 3 (וְאַחֲרָיו אֶל-הַמֵּתִים/*wĕ'aḥărāyw 'el-hammētîm*) to have been transposed from the end of v. 4. Neither Fox (*Time to Tear Down*, 287) nor Longman (*Ecclesiastes*, 225) takes this approach, but both read *wĕ'aḥărāyw* adverbially. I have followed their translation here, since the point Qohelet is making seems, quite plainly, to be that the heart of humanity is corrupt and then comes death.

7. On this see Seow, *Ecclesiastes*, 301; Longman, *Ecclesiastes*, 228. If the saying regarding live dogs and dead lions is a well-known proverb meant to exalt life over death, Qohelet's irony is more biting, although this is conjectural.

8. I put "reward" (שָׂכָר/*śkr*) in quotation marks to indicate that Qohelet surely does not mean some wage or reward (as he does in 4:9). He may be sarcastic or, as Longman notes, he may have chosen the word because of its assonance with "memory" (זֵכֶר/*zkr*) at the end of the verse (*Ecclesiastes*, 226).

ished. The next part of the verse is a bit clearer, that those who are dead will never again have a "portion" (חֵלֶק/*ḥēleq*) of what is done under the sun. This is self-evident, since one's portion is the daily enjoyment God allows humans in their labors (2:10; 3:22; 5:18-19). By definition, the dead have no portion. The choice of love, hate, and jealousy as those things that are lost to the dead is, however, a bit curious. Why these three? That is not clear, other than to say that these emotions may encompass the totality of life, although even here it is not clear why jealousy (קִנְאָה/*qinâ*) makes the list. Qohelet's comment in 4:4 is the only other occurrence of *qinâ* in Ecclesiastes, and it describes what is at the root of one's labor, which Qohelet quickly pronounces absurd. It may be, therefore, that love and hate, along with jealousy, represent for Qohelet the emotions of life, which, one might add, are not necessarily pleasant. As Longman puts it, "even unpleasurable emotions are better than no emotions at all."[9]

At this point Qohelet turns, as he has done so often, to a statement of resignation in the face of the stark reality he has just posited. Verses 7-10 are Qohelet's final advice to his readers to "seize the day," and it comes on the heels of one of the most, if not the most, despondent sections of the book. The wording is different from the other examples, but the idea is the same: seek enjoyment here because there is nothing after you die. The specifics Qohelet appeals to are interesting. Eating and drinking wine should be done with merriment, for God has already "approved" (רָצָה/*rāṣâ*) your actions. Just what this means is problematic for commentators, for it seems to suggest that God's approval is unqualified. I do not think, however, that this is what Qohelet is after. What God "approves" of is the enjoyment one has amid the absurdity of life. In other words, God's approval of eating and drinking with merriment is of the same tenor as when Qohelet says in 3:13 and 5:19 (MT 18) that enjoying the fruit of one's labor is the best one has, and God's "gift" (מַתַּת/*mattat*). Qohelet continues his advice (9:8) by telling his readers to wear white clothing at all times and pour oil on one's head liberally. Clearly Qohelet is sounding a note of festivity, as if to pour on his contempt for the way God has set things up.

One is also to "experience" (רָאֵה/*rě'ēh*) life with the woman[10] you love "all the days of your absurd life that he [God] has given you under the sun, all the days of your absurd life" (v. 9). Qohelet seems to have a bit of an edge about him here, as if he has had enough of all this, and wants to drive a dagger

---

9. Longman, *Ecclesiastes*, 229.

10. For a "syntactic-grammatical" analysis of 9:9 that argues that a married state is in view, see Pahk, "Syntactical and Contextual Consideration."

in his own heart and into that of his readers, while along the way taking a pretty strong swipe at God too. It is *God* who has made your days absurd. So have a good marriage. That is your "portion" in life and in your labor in which you are laboring under the sun (v. 9c). So whatever you do, do it with every ounce of strength you have, because in Sheol, where you are going, there is nothing, neither activity, nor thought,[11] nor knowledge, nor wisdom. Even though death levels every playing field, and all of our activity comes to naught, Qohelet still moves his readers to see, perhaps in an act of desperation, that living life with all our strength is our biggest protest against a fundamentally unjust and absurd circumstance that God has given us — like a soldier firing his pistol at a wave of bombers: "Do your worst, I'm going down fighting."

Qohelet concludes this section, however, with the sad — indeed crippling — realization that even this act of defiance will get you nowhere. Despite our best efforts — even as those efforts acknowledge that our end is inevitable — Qohelet says that we are all trapped, like fish in a net and birds in a snare (v. 12). As much as Qohelet tells his readers in the previous verse to grab hold of life with all one's power, he quickly acknowledges that speed and strength do not win out in the end (here Qohelet is clearly speaking metaphorically with respect to a race and a war). Moreover, neither wisdom nor understanding[12] nor knowledge (lit. "those who know"; יֹדֵעַ/*yd‘*) has even the most practical of payoffs (food, wealth, favor; v. 11).

Why is this the case? Once again it is because a "time" (עֵת/*‘ēt*) and a "mishap" (פֶּגַע/*pega‘*) happen (יִקְרֶה/*yiqreh*) to everyone (lit. "all of them," כֻּלָּם/*kullām*, v. 11d). The word choice here is not random. We have seen "time" before (3:1-8) as an expression of God's inscrutable control over what happens, a state of affairs that drives Qohelet to ask in 3:9, "What profit" is there in what we do? We have also seen the root *qrh*, referring to death (2:14-15). The root *pg‘* occurs elsewhere in the OT only in 1 Kgs 5:18 (Eng. 4). It seems to refer to an incident or accident that just "happens" to you.[13] Qohelet continues in v. 12 that no one knows his "time," of course, because every "time" is in God's hands. The implication here is not necessarily that of the time of one's

---

11. The word חֶשְׁבּוֹן/*ḥešbôn* occurs in 7:25 and 27 and means something like calculation. "Thought" seems to express well Qohelet's intention here. There is no doing or thinking in Sheol.

12. This is the only occurrence of the root בִּין/*byn* in Ecclesiastes. It is common, however, in Proverbs, where it is roughly synonymous with "wisdom" (חָכְמָה/*ḥokmâ*) and "knowledge" (דַּעַת/*da‘at*). Qohelet seems to be casting aspersions, as he has done throughout, on the benefits of wisdom.

13. Seow, *Ecclesiastes*, 308.

death. Rather, Qohelet seems to be referring to all the times of one's life that God holds firmly in his grasp, sometimes for good, sometimes for harm. This not-knowing is further explained as being trapped. Like helpless animals caught by men of prey, a "bad time" (עֵת רָעָה/ʿēt rāʿâ) will fall upon us suddenly by a God who — to carry through Qohelet's implicit analogy — is out to trap us.

In the following section, Qohelet tempers his comments somewhat, but here we see him in all his dismal and despondent glory. To summarize: everything is in God's hands, in his time. Nothing we do — regardless of how wise we are — can make a difference, because we will all die. The only advantage to the living over the dead is that they at least know that they will die, whereas that is too late for the dead. Living life with gusto is the best we have, but even those who know that this is a temporary pleasure are still subject to God's whim; they are trapped like dumb animals. When they least expect it, something bad will come to them without warning.

Of course, the book does not end here. There is more to be said, especially by the frame narrator (12:8-14), but the drama of the book will escape us if we do not allow Qohelet's words to sink in deep.

9:13–10:20: Wisdom Really Is Better Than Folly

What I have marked off as a section here is open for debate, to be sure. Seow's division goes from 9:11 through 10:15 and pertains to the matter of risk.[1] Fox and Longman are content to leave much of this section in smaller units.[2] One reason for keeping this large section (twenty-six verses) intact is that 11:1 clearly begins a new section. Also, interwoven in this section are the themes of wisdom, folly, and the role of the king. There is no linear, logical argument made here; as we reach the closing sections of Qohelet's words, we see a scattered, perhaps even frantic, effort to express himself. One might outline this passage as follows:

A. Wisdom has relative value over an attacking king: it works even though the wise man will be forgotten, despised, and unheeded (9:13-16).
B. Wisdom has value but it is *easily* spoiled (9:17–10:3).
C. Beware of the king's anger; respond gently, especially since I have seen society's rhythms turned over under his watch (10:4-11).

---

1. Seow, *Ecclesiastes*, 306.
2. Fox, *Time to Tear Down*, 297-311; Longman, *Ecclesiastes*, 233-53.

D. Once again, the relative value of wisdom is described (10:12-15).
E. A closing word about kings and wisdom (10:16-20).

This is the only section thus far where I have felt compelled to offer some sort of outline in an effort to give some sense to Qohelet's train of thought. What seems to provide coherence to this section is the notion of the value yet unreliability of wisdom and the role of power/leadership in securing (or not) the wise rhythms of life. This section is then followed by the final section of Qohelet's words, in which he speaks of human effort in view of the inevitability of death, a fitting final comment before we reach the epilogue and the frame narrator's evaluation.

As we have seen, Qohelet ended the previous section with a note of despair, remarking that everyone has his "time," and, like trapped animals, we — even those who are wise — are helpless to know when that time will be or to do anything about it. This section begins, however, with what appears to be a shift back to a positive assessment of wisdom. Qohelet remarks that he has seen wisdom under the sun, and it is something that he considers significant (lit. "great it was upon me," v. 13). A great king surrounds a small city with few people and builds huge siege works against it. But a poor but wise man comes to the rescue and delivers the city by his wisdom (vv. 14-15). In what echoes such previous passages as 1:11 and 9:5, however, that wise man who by his wisdom, though poor, overcame a powerful and hostile king is nevertheless forgotten — no one remembers (זכר/*zkr*) him.

As he has been throughout, Qohelet is clearly wrestling here with the relative merits of wisdom. Despite the fact that the poor wise man is not remembered, Qohelet affirms the relative good of wisdom: wisdom is better than strength, though the poor man was despised and his words ignored (v. 16). What is missing, however, from Qohelet's affirmation of wisdom is any reason why he would make such a declaration in the face of clear evidence to the contrary. It seems, simply put, that wisdom showed itself to surpass brute strength, but its advantage was only temporary. For whatever reason, no one remembers *(zkr)* that wise man, which in this context may indirectly refer to his death but likely refers to the scenario Qohelet depicts in v. 16: the poor wise man is despised and unheeded, presumably in situations subsequent to his heroic deeds described in v. 15.

What cancels out the wise man's words here seems to be the fickleness of the people who benefit from it one day and skip away the next. Qohelet pushes back against this, however, in vv. 17-18: "The words of a wise man uttered in calmness (בְּנַחַת/*běnaḥat*) are better heeded than the shouts of a leader of fools. Wisdom is better than instruments of war, but one offender can destroy much good." Here Qohelet seems to be lamenting the observation made in the previous verses. He again asserts the value of wisdom over foolishness and its superiority in times of war; but, unlike what we may gather from, say, Proverbs, wisdom is an unstable thing and can easily be toppled by a single person who means no good. Again, wisdom has value but it is a relative value, one that is inevitably and easily undone. One cannot count on wisdom to come through. One expects it to fail sooner or later, usually sooner.

Qohelet continues this observation in 10:1. It only takes a little folly to outweigh wisdom, just like dead flies can spoil a perfumer's oil. Wisdom has value that ought to be preserved, but it is easy to see it ruined. After all, the heart of the wise man is "to his right" while the heart of the fool is "to his left." It is not entirely certain what these idioms mean, although the general notion is apparent: "right" is something good, whereas "left" is not. Moreover, the contrast is obvious, as we see in 10:3: just by walking down the street the fool announces himself. Qohelet, at least at this point, is sounding a positive evaluation of wisdom, as he has done earlier in such passages as 2:13-14a and 8:1.

The following verses (vv. 4-7) bring us back to the topic of the ruler (מוֹשֵׁל/*môšēl*) mentioned in 9:17. Now Qohelet cautions his readers to appease such a ruler when his anger (temper, רוּחַ/*rûaḥ*) is roused, and so cover numerous offenses. This is good advice, of course, but one wonders what has happened, in just a few verses, to the alternate model Qohelet holds up, that of wisdom's superiority (even if only temporary) to a ruler's shout. The answer seems to be that the former ruler is an invader while this one is an insider. And, as Qohelet continues to explain in v. 5, the ruler (here referred to as הַשַּׁלִּיט/*haššallîṭ*) is responsible for something רָעָה/*rāʿâ*.[3] The concern he has with the ruler is a familiar one (see 3:16; 7:15). What one might consider to be the benefits of wisdom, that the rich and nobles are praised while the poor and slaves are at a lowly state, is reversed: slaves ride on horses and princes walk.[4] The rhythm of

---

3. The parallel between רָעָה/*rāʿâ* and שְׁגָגָה/*šĕgāgâ*, normally referring to an unintentional error (see 5:5 [Eng. 6], its only other occurrence in Ecclesiastes), is telling. If anything, it underscores the general meaning of the *rʿh* root in Ecclesiastes as referring to a category of deed, as something that is in the wrong, rather than an abstract concept. Throughout, Qohelet is very concerned about concrete actions, be it of kings, God, or others, that demonstrate the absurdity of life. But with respect to the use of *šĕgāgâ*, here to describe the king's actions, Qohelet may be putting into action his own advice from v. 4. By referring to the king's behavior as *rāʿâ*, and then as an "accident" or "error" (*šĕgāgâ*), he may be indicating his own reluctance to speak ill of the king.

4. Seow remarks that horses were marks of power and wealth and were reserved largely for military purposes and for bearing kings and nobles, never slaves (*Ecclesiastes*, 315).

society is being turned on its head; roles have been reversed. This is something Qohelet claims to have seen (רָאִיתִי/*rāʾîtî*; vv. 5 and 7), and it is further evidence that one cannot count on wisdom, and, more particularly, one cannot count on the king to make sure wisdom is upheld — even if only by accident.

Qohelet continues this line of thinking — in almost a stream of consciousness way — in vv. 8-11 by recounting other ways in which things do not work out as one assumes they ought. One who digs a pit may wind up falling into it. The pit is dug not for exercise but, as Seow notes, for hunting.[5] It is a good thing the digger is doing, yet, if he is not careful, he may be caught in his own trap. Fox remarks how falling into one's own pit is normally a sign of retribution (e.g., Pss 7:16-17 [Eng. 15-16]; 9:16-17 [Eng. 15-16]), but here this theme is given a twist: the digger is doing nothing other than what his daily duty called for. Hence there is no hint of retribution here but a declaration on the accidents that befall humanity.[6] Likewise, taking down a stone wall, a normal activity (perhaps for repair, since walls were meant to protect property), could result in being bitten by a snake hiding in a crack in the rocks. No one has done anything wrong. It is just something that may happen. So too (v. 9) quarrying stones and felling trees (presumably for building purposes) may result in injury, a "work-related accident." As for trees, the danger is increased if the ax is blunt and the worker needs to exert more effort, although wisdom (to know to keep the ax sharp) is the advantage of skill.[7] Verse 11 reinforces this idea. Just as a dull ax is about as advantageous as having no ax at all, so too is a charmer who does not charm the snake and so gets bitten.

What unites these incidents is that they describe situations that one would hope could be avoided. The difference, however, is that the first four (vv. 8-9) seem to be wholly out of the hands of the person involved. There is no mention of the skill or lack of wisdom in bringing about the injury. Rather, it is just "one of those things." The final two incidents, however, are different (vv. 10-11). There the trouble is caused by the individual's failure to access a basic level of wisdom for the work in which they are engaged. The reason for this shift seems to be to connect to the following verses where the

---

5. Seow, *Ecclesiastes*, 316. The word for "pit" (גּוּמָּץ/*gûmmāṣ*) occurs only here in the OT and is normally considered to be an Aramaic loanword.

6. Fox, *Time to Tear Down*, 305.

7. The last portion of 10:10 is very difficult. Fox repoints the Hiphil infinitive absolute הַכְשִׁיר/*hakšîr* (to succeed) to the noun הַכַּשִּׁיר/*hakkaššîr* (the skilled one) to smooth out the translation a bit (*Time to Tear Down*, 306). I am not sure if this is necessary. The Hebrew as it stands could simply be read "the advantage of skill: wisdom," meaning the experienced woodsman will know to sharpen his ax before going to work. The infinitive can be used in place of a noun (Seow, *Ecclesiastes*, 318, citing *IBHS* §36.2.1).

advantages of wisdom are once again addressed. Yes, things can happen that are out of our control, but at least here Qohelet wishes to maintain the position that wisdom has value over folly.

This is the explicit topic of vv. 12-15. If all one read from Qohelet were these verses, one might come away thinking that he has a very traditional view of wisdom over folly. In a certain restricted way, this seems to be the case, but again, in the overall context of Qohelet's words, wisdom will always come up short in the end. Death cancels out *any* advantage. But for now Qohelet's gaze is not as far ranging as in other portions of the book, and so he can settle, at least for the time being, on more immediate topics. One almost senses that Qohelet is demonstrating how, when one is not *too* wise, things look better (1:18; 7:16-18).

Qohelet's main focus in these verses is the words of the wise versus the words of the fool. The words of the wise are described as bringing favor (v. 12). Note the tension between Qohelet's comment here and what he has observed as recently as 9:11-12, 13-16, where his intention is to give a final pronouncement. The fool's words, however, are consumed by his lips (v. 12; see 4:5 for a similar expression); his words begin with folly and end in הוֹלֵלוּת רָעָה/*hôlēlût rāʿâ* ("terrible irrationality").[8] A fool also multiplies his words, which is already condemned by Qohelet in 5:1 (Eng. 2) and 6:11. In addition to the fool's words, Qohelet also remarks on his toil (עָמָל/ʿml), which wearies him, so much so that he no longer knows his way back to town.[9]

What is striking, however, is the meaning of v. 14b in this context. We have already seen near parallels to this verse in 6:12; 7:14; 8:7; 9:1, and 5. What is different here is that in these other passages ignorance of the future is not restricted to fools, whereas here it is. The point in 10:14b seems to be that all the words of the fool can be multiplied, but that will not gain him knowledge of what is to be. Of course, this is true, but the tension exists, nevertheless, with universal application of this theme in the other passages cited. It may be that Qohelet is here condemning the fool even further for not having heeded his sage advice offered earlier. This is possible, but such an explanation empties

---

8. Seow, *Ecclesiastes,* 307. See also Seow's notes to Eccl 2:12 (133-34), where he discusses הוֹלֵלוּת/*hôlēlût* in more detail.

9. Verse 15 receives a lot of attention among commentators. The feminine verb תְּיַגְּעֶנּוּ/*tĕyaggĕʿennû* does not agree with the masculine noun עָמָל/ʿāmal. Both Seow (*Ecclesiastes,* 319-20) and Longman (*Ecclesiastes,* 246-47) contend that this is simply a grammatical anomaly, a lack of concord well attested elsewhere in the OT. Also, not knowing one's way to town, according to Seow, suggests an urbanized society where the way to town would be common knowledge (*Ecclesiastes,* 320). The image, then, is that the fool's labor results in such weariness (perhaps reflecting 10:10?) that he is too disoriented to find his way to town.

these previous passages of their punch, for they are words of desperation, not "wise words to live by that only a fool would ignore." In other words, that we can know nothing of what will be is *not* a function of multiplying words, as Qohelet has it here in 10:14b. It is simply the way things are. It is not clear, therefore, what the force of Qohelet's particular disapproval of the fool is here. Furthermore, it is not clear why this particular criticism is leveled rather than any other, such as, "The fool multiplies words, but his end is just like any other. He too will die, and all his words will be הֶבֶל/*hebel.*"

Qohelet closes out this section, first by comparing the implications for the land of a young (immature, נָעַר/*nāʿar*) king/ruler versus a noble (-בֶּן חוֹרִים/*ben-ḥôrîm*) king/ruler (vv. 16-17). The former feasts in the morning while the latter feasts at the right time (בָּעֵת/*bāʿēt*), for strength, not for carousing. The role of the king has been much on Qohelet's mind in this section, and he will return to the topic one more time in v. 20. Here his intention seems to be simply to underscore that, even though one must be wary of the king's anger (10:4), and even if a king can be responsible for social upheaval (vv. 5-7), blessing awaits a land whose king is noble. Whether such a king actually exists, and whether, since everything is הֶבֶל/*hebel*, it matters anyway, are issues Qohelet does not raise here.

It does seem to me, however, that vv. 18-19 are in some way connected to Qohelet's comments on kingship, if anything because they are framed by remarks about kingship in vv. 16-17 and v. 20.[10] I understand the slothfulness and "slackness of hands" (שִׁפְלוּת יָדַיִם/*šiplût yādayim*) that result in a sagging and leaking roof to be a metaphor for what happens when an immature king is in charge. The making of "bread" (feasting) for laughter, wine to make life joyful, and money to keep everyone busy[11] are all activities that would be characterized by an immature, carousing ruler. One might think that such a king should arouse one's anger, but Qohelet warns that even in one's thoughts one should not curse the king, nor even in the privacy of one's bedroom curse the rich. Somehow, at some time, the king/the wealthy will find out (a little bird will tell him, v. 20).

In this section, Qohelet paints a somewhat confusing picture. He moves back and forth between wisdom's benefits over folly, and how a noble king can aid a country, and the disastrous effects of an immature king. At the end, one still is left with a rather dismal picture, where things are as they are, and even if

---

10. The relationship between these verses is much debated, and I do not wish to create a false impression of clarity. For a contrary view see Longman, *Ecclesiastes*, 251-52 (following Whybray, *Ecclesiastes*, 157).

11. Along with Seow (*Ecclesiastes*, 332-33) and Fox (*Time to Tear Down*, 310), I understand יַעֲנֶה/*yaʿăneh* to be a Hiphil of ענה/*ʿnh*, meaning "to occupy."

a corrupt king is to blame, one should surely keep his mouth tightly shut. One must not even think of cursing the king. As I see it, it is hard to escape the notion that Qohelet's view of kingship is similar to his view of God. Both have their moments when their presence offers some benefit. With God it is the "portion" that he "gives" us (5:19), with the king it is the potential for just rule. At the end of the day, however, neither can be counted on. What we can do, and this is how Qohelet concludes his monologue in the final section, is to do the best we can with what we have — but know that death awaits us all.

11:1–12:7: Do Your Best While You Can

This final section of Qohelet's monologue[1] presents some interpretive challenges, but the general message is quite clear. The opening verses, 11:1-6, are directed at the unpredictability and uncertainty of human behavior. The remainder of this section, 11:7–12:7, deals in varying ways with the concept of death that has so dominated Qohelet's thoughts throughout. Although the vocabulary differs, one might even think of this entire section as an extended carpe diem passage. What is perhaps most striking is the transition between how this section ends, with the utter despondency of death (12:7), and the affirmation of Qohelet's words, which are first summarized in 12:8 and then evaluated in 12:9-14.

The first verse of this section is well known, even in popular culture, though its meaning is not apparent. It has been understood as an encouragement toward foreign investment, thus interpreting "bread" as goods in general and "upon the waters" as maritime trade, but this interpretation is not without its difficulties. It is worth noting that the imagery is *upon* the waters, not "beyond" or "over." Also, if some sort of investment is intended, finding "it" after many days makes little sense, since one would expect a *return* on one's investment. A much more likely and commonly held interpretation has been that vv. 1-2 speak of charity, giving liberally to others, even to one's own risk, without expecting a reward. One releases bread[2] on the water and walks away. Give to seven, no, eight,[3] people: you do not know what bad thing could happen.

---

1. Although others see this section ending at 12:8, I am in agreement with Fredericks that this lengthy section begins at 11:1 and extends to the end of Qohelet's words at 12:7 ("Life's Storms and Structural Unity").

2. Seow remarks that flatbread, which floats, is meant, not a loaf, as we might assume (*Ecclesiastes*, 335).

3. A numerical expression in the OT "N, N+1," is a common way of expressing not literal numbers but "a lot."

I have left untranslated here the Hebrew word כִּי/*kî*. It could mean "because," in which sense liberality is encouraged *because* we do not know what danger may befall us. Seow suggests a concessive force, that one should give liberally *even though* one does not know what may befall us.[4] What is attractive about the latter, apart from its lengthy history of interpretation, is that it fits a bit better with the surrounding context than an offhand comment about trade practices. In view of the fundamental absurdity of life, and in view of the lengthy discussion of death that will occupy much of the remainder of this section, I think Qohelet is saying: "you cannot take it with you, so give liberally without thought to what may happen."

Indeed, what happens happens, and as we have seen at various junctures throughout the book, there is nothing we can do to effect any change. Clouds get full and it rains; trees fall and there they are (v. 3). Watching the wind and the clouds will not make a difference, other than to keep you from your work (v. 4). In the same way that you have no way of knowing[5] the way of the "life breath into the bones[6] in the womb," so too you do not know the action of God, who does everything. Once again, God's actions are brought to the forefront as the *reason* why we cannot know what will happen. God does what he does, when he does it (cf. 3:1-8). For this reason (v. 6), work long hours,[7] do not rest, for you have no way of knowing which of your deeds will succeed, whether "both" (הֲזֶה אוֹ-זֶה/*hăzeh 'ô-zeh*, meaning the morning or evening activity) will do equally well. A modern analogy comes to mind. It is like a caretaker of an estate of several hundred acres assigned to spread weed killer over the entire property. The project will take a week, and there is a possibility of rain at some point. The product, however, can only be spread profitably when no rain falls within a twenty-four-hour period. The one following Qohelet's advice will, rather than watching the weather, put in a long and hard day's work, day after day, until the task is completed. If it rains, it rains. You have no control over it anyway, so just keep working. All of your work may be successful, or some of it may be for naught. You do not know what God will do, so just keep at it.

---

4. Seow, *Ecclesiastes*, 336.

5. I understand the phrase אֵינְךָ יוֹדֵעַ/*'ênĕkā yôdēa'* in v. 5 to be particularly emphatic, as in v. 6 below.

6. Following Seow (*Ecclesiastes*, 337) and Fox (*Time to Tear Down*, 314-15), I read the preposition כ/*k* as ב/*b*, hence, "*into* the bones."

7. The reference to "morning" and "evening" is not literal but representative of either the long workday, or, as Fox suggests, being ready to work hard at any time. He also suggests that the reference could be to the early and later stages of life, which would mean that the subject of much of the remainder of the passage, age and youth, is being adumbrated here (*Time to Tear Down*, 315).

That Qohelet introduces here a note of resignation is, as the book has made clear, a common resting place for Qohelet's musings. It also leads nicely to the remaining portion of this section of the book. The section 11:7-9 is a warm-up for what will follow, and 12:7, Qohelet's final word to us, is a resounding restatement of the finality of death. It is the intervening verses, 12:1-6, that raise some interesting and important interpretive choices. But regardless of where one finally ends up, the general tone of the remainder of the passage is clear: all things come to the same end, and we do well to keep this in mind, even in our youth.

So, with respect to 11:7-9, Qohelet begins by acknowledging that the light is "sweet" and that it is good for the eyes to see the sun. Of course, this may just be a way of saying it is good to be alive. But is it? Hasn't Qohelet been driving home the very opposite message? Yes, but his struggles in this regard have been evident throughout the book, and, true to form, this somewhat positive statement is followed up immediately by a more sobering remark, which begins innocently enough: "*If*[8] someone should live many years, let him rejoice in all of them." But he then remarks that one should remember the "days of darkness, for they will be many." The force of v. 8 taken as a whole seems to be: rejoice in long life and remember along the way there will be many dark days. These days are probably an anticipation of the topic of 12:1-7, old age (not death), and so Qohelet is reminding his readers that a long life, however valued it might be, is not as much of a bargain as one might think. Much of it is spent in old age, with the specter of death hot on one's heels. So Qohelet concludes at the end of v. 8: "all that comes is הֶבֶל/*hebel*."

I do not think he is referring yet to death specifically, but to the days to come, the dark days. As we see in v. 9, Qohelet turns to the youth, who is exhorted to rejoice in his youth (i.e., while he is young); let his heart rejoice; walk in the ways of his heart and the sight of his eyes (i.e., follow your heart and enjoy life). This sudden introduction of youth is, in my view, an anticipation of the exhortation in the epilogue to "my son" (12:12). We are, in effect, winding down and approaching the conclusion of the book.

At this juncture, however, Qohelet's point is that the youth must also know that for all that he does, God will bring him to judgment. On this we should note first that Qohelet is certainly not speaking of some eschatological or afterlife punishment. Such a view would be completely out of step with the

---

8. The Hebrew is כִּי אִם/*kî 'im*, which Fox translates "even if" (*Time to Tear Down*, 316), Longman "Indeed, if" (*Ecclesiastes*, 258), and Seow simply "If" (*Ecclesiastes*, 348). Elsewhere in Ecclesiastes it is translated "except" (3:12; 5:10 [Eng. 11]; 8:15), but that makes no sense here. Both Longman and Seow understand *kî* here to have an asseverative force, although Seow leaves it untranslated as a "weakened asseverative."

entirety of the book thus far. Nor should we think that God will judge the youth's bad or wrongful actions only. That is not the point here. Qohelet is not saying, "Have a good time, but be good or God will punish you." He is saying, "Enjoy it while you can, but know that God's judgment is coming, that is, old age," and then, as our passage ends, eventually death. The meaning of "judgment" (מִשְׁפָּט/*mišpāṭ*) here is not in keeping with how it is used in 3:16 and 5:7 (Eng. 8), where it refers to human courts of appeal and the injustices done.[9] Here, in what seems to be a clear anticipation of 12:14, it is God who will judge. The "justice" in view here, however, is not necessarily "just." Rather, Qohelet is remarking once again on how the life we live is subject to God's direction, which in this passage is focused on the fact that youth will pass and old age will come.

So in v. 10 Qohelet encourages his readers to turn aside from כַּעַס/*kaʿas* and רָעָה/*rāʿâ*. The former word we have encountered in numerous contexts (1:18; 2:23; 5:16 [Eng. 17]; 7:3, 9). It has been translated as "anger" and that makes perfect sense here, although one should not think of a heated tirade. As the other instances suggest, something like "frustration," or better "agitation," is in view. Qohelet has often remarked that *kaʿas* is an emotion that may come and indeed seems to be unavoidable (2:23). But here he is telling the youth to do what he can to avoid such "irritation" from his heart.[10] So too, as we have seen throughout, *rāʿâ* is best not understood as "evil" in the moral sense of the word but here as "pain," especially since it refers to the body. Hence "unpleasantness" may be a more helpful translation.[11]

Finally, the reason Qohelet gives for the avoidance of these things is that youth and "vitality" are הֶבֶל/*hebel*. Two things are worth noting here. First, "vitality" is a translation of Hebrew שַׁחֲרוּת/*šaḥărût*, which occurs only here and whose meaning has been disputed in the history of interpretation. It is, however, most often understood as related to youthfulness in some sense, perhaps because the root שׁחר/*šḥr* means "black," as in the black hair of youth.

Second, here *hebel* may best be translated as "fleeting" or "transient" rather than "absurd."[12] After all, Qohelet is speaking of the fact that youth will give way to old age. Youth should not dwell on frustration or pain, since

---

9. In 8:5-6 מִשְׁפָּט/*mišpāṭ* is best translated "custom." See the discussion there.

10. So, Fox (*Time to Tear Down*, 316). Seow has "vexation" (*Ecclesiastes*, 346) and Longman "frustration" (*Ecclesiastes*, 261).

11. Fox, *Time to Tear Down*, 316; Seow, *Ecclesiastes*, 346. Longman has "pain," but by it he means essentially the same thing (*Ecclesiastes*, 261).

12. Miller understands *hebel* here in 11:10 as a metaphor for transience ("Qohelet's Symbolic Use of הבל," 448).

those glory days (such as they are) will come to an end. However, our base meaning of *hebel* (absurd) is still relevant in this context, since this very situation, that youth departs and old age comes home to roost, is the very kind of absurdity Qohelet has been discussing throughout the book.

Still, youth and vigor do hold out the possibility of finding something worthwhile about youth, that one should grab for the gusto while one can, because a time is coming when all such things come to an abrupt end. It is in this sense that 12:1-7 should be understood. As 12:1 indicates, Qohelet is still discussing youth. But the admonition to "remember your creator" is not meant to have a calming effect, or perhaps motivate one to faithful service to God while one is young. Rather, "to think on one's creator is to think of death, for the life-spirit returns to its giver (12:7)."[13] What follows is a litany of events that presumably occur after youth, and this subsection ends with an explicit reference to death (12:5b-7). It stands to reason that what occupies Qohelet's attention in vv. 2-5a is the intervening period between youth and death, that is, old age. Hence the heavenly referents in v. 2 are metaphorical of the ending of life. Yet the difficulty with pursuing this line of reasoning is the very content of vv. 3-5a, indeed, even v. 2. Rather than speaking simply of the ravages of old age, Qohelet's scope seems a bit broader. What we have in these verses is *cosmic* imagery that harks back to the very beginning of the book, where cosmic imagery was first used to indicate the absurdity of life (1:4-8). There is one important twist here, however, at the conclusion of Qohelet's monologue. In 1:4 the futility of life is expressed in that the world goes on and on (לְעוֹלָם/*lĕʿôlām*). Now what Qohelet envisions is a time when the world itself will come to an end: its heavenly lights, daily activities, the very daily rhythms of life.

More specifically, I take the cosmic imagery to describe death, though not simply in the sense of the individual, but of humanity in general. As Seow has persuasively argued,[14] this passage refers to the end of life in general as we know it, in its social and economic dimensions. The sun makes its final appearance here in Ecclesiastes and it is darkened: the sun's routine described in 1:5 comes to an end. Men of valor tremble with terror. "Grinders," likely referring to women working at the mills, become few (they die?), and so the daily and necessary work of bread production is affected. Women looking out the window "is a literary convention used to depict the dashed hopes of mothers,

---

13. Fox, *Time to Tear Down*, 322.

14. Seow, *Ecclesiastes*, 368-69, 372-82; idem, "Qohelet's Eschatological Poem." My comments here follow Seow's analysis. See also Fox's extended excursus on the subject (*Time to Tear Down*, 333-49).

wives, and lovers."[15] They grow "dim" because they have lost hope. The doors of the street (i.e., street bazaar) are closed, and so the center of social and economic activity shuts down. Related to this is that the sound of the mill lessens; again the daily production of bread becomes a whisper, and is a sign of death: "all economic and social activities are suspended (the doors of the marketplace are closed), and even life-sustaining activities are stopped (the sounds of the mills drop). Something disastrous is happening."[16] In place of the bustling noise of human activity, we hear the sound of birds swooping down, a picture of death and mourning.[17]

The imagery in v. 5b is difficult, but many commentators consider it symbolic of old age, since the description of the almond tree, locust, and caperberry are followed by a reference to humans going to their "eternal home."[18] The silver cord and the golden bowl both come to destruction. The latter probably refers to an oil lamp, which, when smashed, ceases giving light. The silver cord is either the cord that suspends the lamp,[19] the lampstand itself,[20] or simply a symbol of life being cut short. In any event, once again, the light goes out. There is nothing but darkness. Finally, pots are smashed, which represents the destruction of life.

We have, therefore, a series of comments that is nothing less than eschatological in scope, envisioning a time when all of life will stop dead in its tracks. How much more, therefore, should we consider our own mortality "in the days of our youth"? Thus Qohelet's monologue ends with both a symbolic/eschatological reference to the end and a clear reference to death, which should give us pause to consider how central a theme death is in the book as a whole. We return to dust. That is all. That is where we came from and that is where we are going. It should be clear by this point that, unlike the use of this verse in funerals, Qohelet is not submitting himself to the sovereign will of a good God who reminds us of our brief time on this earth. Rather, Qohelet remains here, as he has throughout the book, in a state of vexation and agita-

15. Seow, *Ecclesiastes*, 378.

16. Ibid.

17. Fox suggests that the birds and "daughters of song" in v. 4 are mourners who sing a dirge and who "bow low" (*Time to Tear Down*, 326).

18. The Hebrew is בֵּת עוֹלָם/*bēt ʿôlām*, but this should not be understood as heaven or the afterlife, which are wholly out of the question for Qohelet. It is, rather, a reference to the grave (Longman, *Ecclesiastes*, 266) or the dark underworld from which there is no return (Seow, *Ecclesiastes*, 381).

19. Fox, *Time to Tear Down*, 330.

20. Seow argues for this option, stating that as a lampstand, it would symbolize the tree of life, thus adding another dimension to the eschatological interpretation of this passage (*Ecclesiastes*, 381).

tion over what God has done. Breath returns to God who gave it in the first place. Qohelet's words begin and end with the futility, indeed, the absurdity, of the life God has given us.

12:8-14: Epilogue: Qohelet Is Wise, but There Is More

The role of the epilogue has already been treated at some length in the introduction, but now, at the end of the exegetical portion of the commentary, it is well worth another visit. The epilogue, which, along with the prologue (1:1-11), forms the frame of the book, holds the key to our understanding of the theological value of Qohelet's words. This is not to say that Qohelet's words should form a center point for an OT theology. It is simply to say that, for the frame narrator, Qohelet had something very much worthwhile to say, even if he encourages his son (12:12) to heed a warning. Indeed, it is fair to sum up the frame narrator's words in the epilogue as follows: "Qohelet is wise, my son. Listen carefully. But this is not all there is. Qohelet's words, as wise as they are, are not the final word on your existence as a follower of God."

The epilogue begins with a virtual repetition of 1:2. I take 12:8 as the first of the frame narrator's words rather than the closing remark of the previous passage.[1] We are reminded in no uncertain terms of the theme of Qohelet's words, especially following on the heels of his most relentless reminder of our fate in 12:1-7. A naïve reader of Ecclesiastes might think that the reminder of v. 8 will be followed by a censure of Qohelet, but that is not at all the case.[2]

Verse 9 has a couple of exegetical issues that we need to address before moving on. The verse begins "additionally," "furthermore," or "moreover."[3] Any of these English equivalents works, as they all mark off v. 9 as beginning a

---

1. See Fox, *Time to Tear Down*, 332; Seow, *Ecclesiastes*, 382.

2. Carasik points out that the recurrence of 1:2 in 12:8 "is not merely for stylistic reasons, but is intended to alert the reader, if only in subliminal fashion, to the repetitiveness and circularity which, in Qohelet's view, characterized the world" ("Qohelet's Twists and Turns," 195). Carasik's overall point is also worthy of consideration, that Qohelet's style throughout is marked by turning and returning, whereas "straightness" is the more valued theme in the Bible. "One must follow not the straight and narrow path suggested by the sages of Proverbs, but must turn and turn again, following the long and winding road mapped out by one's own imagination. If you seek true understanding, according to Qohelet, you cannot march. You must meander" (203).

3. The word is וְיֹתֵר/*wĕyōtēr* (see also 2:15; 6:8, 11; 7:11, 16; 12:12) followed by the relative particle שֶׁ/*še*. The point is that this marks off a new section, as can be further supported by the disjunctive accent *zaqeph gadol*.

new section. Having just recounted the words of Qohelet, the frame narrator now aims to give the reader some additional and valuable information. A second issue is the function of the relative particle שֶׁ/*še*, prefixed to the verb הי׳ה/ *hyh*, and the meaning of עוֹד/*'ôd* (whether it means "also" or "constantly"). Fox and Seow handle these issues similarly. Seow translates v. 9: "Additionally, because Qohelet was a sage, he constantly [*'ôd*] taught the people knowledge."[4] Fox's literal rendering is: "and something remaining is (the fact) that Qohelet was a sage." Fox points out that *'ôd* can mean "constantly," "additionally," or "also"; here he interprets it to mean that Qohelet's wisdom was "extensive" and his sayings "went beyond those quoted in this book."[5] It does not seem to mean that (1) Qohelet was wise, and (2) in addition (*'ôd*) he taught the people knowledge.[6] Qohelet's teaching is a function of his sagely role, and Seow's translation above brings this out most clearly.

More specifically, Qohelet's sagely role is outlined at the end of v. 9. He is said to have "listened" (אִזֵּן/*'izzēn*),[7] "searched/investigated" (חִקֵּר/*ḥiqqēr*), and "put in order/edited/composed" (תִּקֵּן/*tiqqēn*) many proverbs. These verbs are important for getting the force of the frame narrator's meaning throughout the epilogue. First, I do not think that listening and searching are ironic, that is, that these are things Qohelet tried to do, albeit unsuccessfully (hence justifying a subtle critique of Qohelet's words).[8] Rather, as Seow puts it, Qohelet "listened and deliberated," and having done that, "edited many proverbs."[9] There is little question in my mind that this editorial work in-

---

4. Seow, *Ecclesiastes*, 382. He understands שֶׁ/*še* causally, hence "because Qohelet was a sage . . ." (383).

5. Fox, *Time to Tear Down*, 350-51.

6. For the opposite point of view, see Longman, *Ecclesiastes*, 275.

7. Longman observes that this root occurs in the Piel only here, likely for aural reasons, i.e., all three verbs in this sequence are Piel (*Ecclesiastes*, 275). See also Seow, *Ecclesiastes*, 384.

8. Bartholomew takes a different angle on this issue. For him, Ecclesiastes is a wisdom teacher's ironical exposure of "an empiricist epistemology which seeks wisdom through personal experience and analysis without the 'glasses' of the fear of God" (*Reading Ecclesiastes*, 263). In his assessment of *Reading Ecclesiastes*, Fox summarizes Bartholomew's position: "the author uses the fictional Qohelet to demonstrate the failure of empiricism to make sense of life" ("Review," 196). For another presentation of ironic qualities in Ecclesiastes, see Sharp, "Ironic Representation." She argues that Ecclesiastes is not a skeptical book given its stamp of approval by a pious editor, "but is instead a brilliantly unified, thoroughly ironic discourse that represents its anti-hero as a sinful Adam [i.e., Genesis 2–3] who strove from knowledge apart from obedience to God" (62). Although my own view certainly departs from Sharp's, her discussion is both subtle and stimulating. Similarly, Spangenberg argues that Qohelet "takes an ironic look at the claims and hopes of the [traditional] wisdom teachers ("Irony," 58, 60). He cites 4:13-16; 7:1-4; and 9:1-10 as examples.

9. *Ecclesiastes*, 384-85.

cludes but also goes beyond what we read in Ecclesiastes. The frame narrator is establishing Qohelet's sagely credentials.

This continues in v. 10. By saying that Qohelet "sought to find pleasing words," we should freely presume that the referent is the words of Qohelet from 1:12 through 12:7. Moreover, as the context of this entire epilogue makes clear, we should not think of this "search" as a failed one. It is certainly true that elsewhere in the book we see Qohelet searching and not finding (7:28; 8:17), but that has no bearing on v. 10. "Seeking" here simply means that Qohelet was deliberate in communicating his words in a manner that was "pleasing," not in the sense of "feeling good" but that which is both effective as well as "timely" (taking our cue from 3:1). To put it more simply, Qohelet was very deliberate and intentional about what he said (v. 9), and he did a good job pulling it off (v. 10): "he wrote words of truth rightly."

The problem with v. 10 is the verb כָּתוּב/*kātûb*. As it stands, it is a passive participle. Many ancient translations have the perfect, כָּתַב/*kātab*, "he wrote," perhaps in an effort to address the difficulty. Contemporary scholars have tended to understand it as an infinitive absolute, כָּתוֹב/*kātôb*, which requires only a slight vocalic change. What is important to remember, however, is that the general sense of this verse is not affected either way. Allowing the passive participle to remain would yield a translation (albeit a bit awkward): "what is written [is] upright, words of truth." If the infinitive absolute is preferred, more options are open to us, since the infinitive absolute can perform a variety of functions. A good translation would be: "he wrote words of truth rightly."[10] Either way, the point is still that the written words of Qohelet are "words of truth" and have an "upright" quality to them. And when we remember how important the roots אמת/*'mt* and ישׁר/*yšr* are in Proverbs, we can conclude only that the frame narrator is making a very positive evaluation of Qohelet's wisdom.

It does not matter that these words are difficult to swallow. The "words of the wise are," after all, "like goads, like firmly embedded nails are the masters of [proverbial] collections"[11] (v. 11). This is shepherding language, and the image conveyed is that sometimes wisdom hurts. Wise sayings to those who hear them are likened to a shepherd[12] poking and jabbing at the sheep

10. See ibid., 385.

11. Hebrew בַּעֲלֵי אֲסֻפּוֹת/*ba'ălê 'ăsuppôt* regularly vexes commentators, but the phrase is certainly parallel to "words of the wise" and so refers here to "masters of collections," i.e., those who do the collecting of proverbial sayings. The point of both is the same: wise sayings hurt.

12. Some take מֵרֹעֶה אֶחָד/*mērō'eh 'eḥād* as a reference to God, i.e., "a certain shepherd." The reference to God, however, is out of place and the shepherding metaphor should be taken at face value. Fox argues that *'eḥād* functions simply as an indefinite article (*Time to Tear Down*, 355).

with a long stick with a nail embedded at the end. To put it another way, if Qohelet's words make you cringe a bit, that is precisely the effect they are supposed to have, being wise sayings. It is hard to escape the positive evaluation that Qohelet is given here by the frame narrator.

Having said that, however, is not to say that Qohelet's words do not deserve some sort of qualification, and this is where vv. 12-14 come into play. "Beyond these,[13] my son, be warned,"[14] begins v. 12. Beyond what? Presumably the words that Qohelet has just been uttering for eleven chapters.[15] "There is no end to the making of many writings," the narrator continues, meaning that one could go beyond Qohelet's words ad infinitum; one could go on speculating and arguing without stop. But "much study wearies the body" just as many words are wearisome in 1:8 (יגה/*ygh*). One should not, in other words, go on as Qohelet has done, making observations on the absurdity of life. One must, at some point, bring such things to an end. It is worth emphasizing that nowhere does the frame narrator in any way condemn Qohelet or his words. What he warns his son about is continuing on in the same vein.

To put it another way, Qohelet the sage has journeyed to the very edges of despair and found only absurdity and death, with a small "portion" thrown in along the way. The son is not warned *about* Qohelet, but warned about going *beyond* Qohelet. Thus the frame narrator puts an abrupt halt to any thoughts the son might have in doing Qohelet one better. The son is in no position to outdo "the king" Qohelet, who was not only wise but had at his disposal the royal means by which to carry through his quest. "Learn from him,"

---

13. As distinct from 12:9, the idiom וְיֹתֵר/*wĕyōtēr* is followed by the preposition מָן/*min* (מֵהֵמָּה/*mēhēmmâ*). This is a well-attested postbiblical idiom and means simply "beyond these," meaning the words of the wise (Seow, *Ecclesiastes*, 388).

14. Although in terms of the message of the epilogue as a whole the point is not of great consequence, Shields makes a strong case for tying "be warned" (הִזָּהֵר/*hizzāhēr*) to the subsequent clauses, hence "In addition to these things, my son, beware of excessively making books . . . and of excessive study" ("Re-examining the Warning"). Shields's reading is supported by the Targum of Qohelet (125).

15. Shields argues that the reference to the wise in v. 11 includes the words of Qohelet but moves beyond a focus on him, as we see in v. 9, and now begins a severe critique of the wisdom genre as a whole (*End of Wisdom*, 70-71). I agree that v. 11 expands the reference to the class of sages in general, but it is important not to drive a wedge between the focus in v. 9 on Qohelet as sage and the focus on the class of sage of which Qohelet is a member. Distinguishing the two as Shields does allows him to further his thesis that the epilogue is a call to reject conventional wisdom teaching and fear God and keep his commands instead. Shields summarizes this point at various junctures, but see esp. 108-9. As I argue throughout this commentary, I do not think the epilogue is critical of wisdom, but rather acknowledges this very wisdom as that which engages the difficult questions of life.

the son is told (12:9-11), but do not follow in his footsteps. Indeed, Qohelet has trodden that path for us. The sage has adequately given his instructions.

Hence, as the narrator continues rather abruptly in v. 13, "end of [the] matter; everything has been heard." And now the narrator tells the son the proper response to all of this. It is not to discredit Qohelet as some jumbled and heterodox thinker; neither is it to idolize him and follow in his footsteps. It is, rather, "fear God and keep his commandments." As I laid out in more detail in the introduction, rather than suggest a new approach to handle the difficulties Qohelet enumerates, the son is told to do something that would seem perfectly normal to any Israelite, yet seems somewhat anticlimactic in view of the book as a whole. What the son has before him, in view of the absurdity of life, is nothing less (and nothing more) than the tried and true traditional formula of fear and obedience. The son is told, in other words, to be an Israelite — no matter what is happening, no matter what he is thinking, no matter where his observations lead him in his mental exercise. He is not told to fear and obey *because* it makes sense, but whether or not it does. This is the beauty of the epilogue: Qohelet is both affirmed and relativized; he is praised as sage, yet the son is told that the answer is beyond what the sage has written.

The term "commandments" (מִצְוֹת/*miṣwōt*) is found only here in Ecclesiastes, but the linking of wisdom and torah is known to us through Second Temple sources (e.g., Sir 1:26-30; see also Ezra 7:25).[16] For the frame narrator, to be a faithful Israelite likewise links fear of God (wisdom) and keeping of the law (torah). This brief phrase in v. 13, therefore, is not a throwaway line, but strikes at the heart of Israel's developing notions of what it means to be faithful to Yahweh. And the narrator could not put the matter more strongly than he does at the end of v. 13, "indeed, *this* is 'all the man'" (כִּי-זֶה כָּל-הָאָדָם/ *kî-zeh kol-hā'ādām*).[17] Despite whatever troubles and struggles his readers might have, even to the point where they, like Qohelet, point their fingers at God and blame him for the whole mess, their chief "duty" (as the NIV puts

16. Dell puts the point succinctly: "the epilogue to Ecclesiastes functions to make a link between wisdom and torah and reflects an interpretation of Ecclesiastes as wisdom in a new sense that characterized the period of redaction" ("Ecclesiastes as Wisdom," 313). She connects Ecclesiastes to Ben Sira, as other scholars regularly do, but adds: "the emerging authority of wisdom is in connection with torah," and that it is that factor "that made it [Ecclesiastes] authoritative when it came to canonization" (311-12).

17. The other three uses of כָּל-הָאָדָם/*kol-hā'ādām* in Ecclesiastes are in 3:13 and 5:18, where they pertain to our portion in life, the pleasure experience, and in 7:2 with respect to death. See the introduction and the commentary at these passages for a fuller discussion of the interplay between the uses of this term.

it), what sums up their existence as Israelites, is now as it always has been, fear and obey.

This brings us to the final verse of the book, which provides the reason why fear and obedience are to be front and center: "for God will bring every activity into judgment." This does not necessarily imply an eschatological judgment, although the possibility should be left open. To be sure, Qohelet leaves little room, if any, for such a thing, but that does not necessarily hold for the frame narrator. He may have the long view in mind. But, at the end of the day, it is much more likely that the frame narrator is remarking on how God, despite appearances, will not allow any deed, even those hidden,[18] whether בֹוט/ṭôb or רָע/rāʿ, to evade his scrutiny. God's view, in other words, is comprehensive, including deeds as well as those things hidden, that which is ṭôb and that which is rāʿ. It is entirely proper to say that the thoughts expressed here are at odds with Qohelet's own thinking. For Qohelet, God is the problem, and ṭôb and rāʿ lack their moral focus as compared with much of the rest of the OT. For the frame narrator, however, God will put all things right, and ṭôb and rāʿ most certainly retain their moral focus. Qohelet pronounces ṭôb and rāʿ, understood as "enjoyment of good things" and "bad things that happen," as those things in life over which people have no control. The frame narrator, without discounting Qohelet's observations, turns the focus, as he has since v. 12, on the individual Israelite's responsibility amid this state of affairs. To put it another way, even though, to be sure, ṭôb and rāʿ happen (as Qohelet has been saying), it is still true that the morality of people's actions, even hidden ones (cf. Deut 29:29), will be judged by God as ṭôb and rāʿ.

At the end of the book, therefore, we find not a reversal of Qohelet's theology but an affirmation while going one better.[19] The frame narrator allows Qohelet to paint a very dark picture indeed, one that people of faith can attest to and analogues of which are found in the lament psalms and in Job.[20]

---

18. The phrase is עַל כָּל-נֶעְלָם/ʿal kol-neʿlām, and the preposition ʿal "indicates the basis of divine judgment" (Seow, *Ecclesiastes*, 391). See also Longman, *Ecclesiastes*, 281; Fox, *Time to Tear Down*, 363. See also Eccl 11:9.

19. See Enns, "כל-האדם."

20. In this respect, and as stated throughout the commentary, my view of Qohelet's perspective on God differs from those such as de Jong ("God in the Book of Qohelet"). De Jong suggests Qohelet does not "intend to offer a complete doctrine of God, but only show those aspects which Qohelet considered useful for elaboration of the central theme of his work [which is, limitation of man in comparison to God's greatness]" (167). I would simply replace "Qohelet" in this quote with "frame narrator." It is certainly the case that neither Qohelet nor the frame narrator intends to offer a complete doctrine of God, but Qohelet's observations cannot be described as a controlled description of God to suit his purpose. Qohelet is a crushed man, undone by what he sees under the sun.

But, having reached the precipice, he calls his reader back, not despite the pain but through it. To summarize, Qohelet says, "Life happens. You live and you die — at an old age, if you're lucky. What is God doing?!" The frame narrator answers, "Yes, your wisdom is evident, but go no further. Fear and follow God anyway." There is no weapon that can stand up against such a view of life.

This tension between affirming Qohelet's harsh criticisms of God while affirming traditional Israelite theology lies at the heart of the interpretive difficulties with Ecclesiastes throughout Jewish and Christian history. Yet it is this very tension that stokes the fires of theological and practical reflection, to which we now turn.

Theological Horizons of Ecclesiastes

It is heuristic but also artificial to "do exegesis" apart from an implicit or, better, explicit engagement of a book's theological themes. One does not exegete and then say, "Okay, let's do some theology now." As discussed briefly in the introduction, how one understands the theology of Ecclesiastes and how one handles the matter of exegesis are interdependent. Throughout the exegetical section I have mentioned pervasive theological themes as an attempt to make sure a particular exegetical suggestion is given adequate support. Such interdependence between exegesis and theology is unavoidable, I feel, and holds true for any serious engagement of any biblical book. It is all the more relevant, however, for a book such as Ecclesiastes, with its exegetical conundrums and meandering theological themes.

All this is to say that, in laying out the theological themes of Ecclesiastes below, we will be revisiting some concepts that should already be familiar from the previous section of the commentary. There will be no surprises here, although I do hope to achieve succinctness and clarity. My focus will also be on Qohelet's theological themes more so than those of the frame narrator (although here too complete separation is artificial). The frame narrator's role in 1:1-11 is to support and crystallize Qohelet's words. In the epilogue (12:8-14) he helps readers understand the rightful impact Qohelet should have on readers. This has already been discussed at length in the introduction, but it has important implications for how the theology of Ecclesiastes can be accessed today. Hence the epilogue will be brought to bear more directly in the final section below, on contemporary praxis.

How Does One Know? Life "under the Sun"

The first theme I would like to address is foundational to many of the themes we see in Ecclesiastes. It is the issue of Qohelet's epistemology. In a word, Qohelet is a no-nonsense, "I call it like I see it," evidentialist. I do not mean "evidentialist" in the popular sense of the word, that one can only prove or disprove things by looking at neutral evidence. The term simply means that Qohelet's conclusions about God and the world are drawn not on the basis of revelation but on his own vast ("under the sun") experience.[1] These experiences are not necessarily limited to actual events he himself has lived, but extrapolating from those experiences to make universal pronouncements on the nature of reality. For example, the declaration in 1:10, that there is *nothing* new despite appearances to the contrary, does not mean that Qohelet claims to have experienced all things. Rather, in his mind's eye, he can see how things will play out. Perhaps one can say that there are no new "event categories," that is, even though this event may have never happened before in exactly the same way, the category has. No two trees ever fell in the forest in exactly the same way. No two trees are exactly alike. But the various instances of "tree" and "falling" hardly constitute anything new, especially in the sense that no new event can come along and undo Qohelet's ultimate declaration that all is absurd. No number of trees falling can change that.

Michael Fox puts it well when he says that Qohelet's personal experience differs from that of Israel's sages in that his experiences are a "source of knowledge"[2] rather than confirming or supporting a body of wisdom-knowledge that is accepted as authoritative and exists independently of the observer, such as we find in Proverbs. For Qohelet, what is knowable is that which can be observed, either in time and space or in the mind's eye. He has little patience for considering that, perhaps, there is more to reality than meets the eye. What is beyond our ability to experience is unknowable, plain and simple (e.g., what happens after death, 3:18-22).

His scope, as we have seen, is limited to what happens "under the sun." As we discussed in the exegetical section, this is not an expression that imputes a faulty epistemology to Qohelet (see 1:3). The book does not imply that, if only Qohelet had stopped navel gazing, he would not find himself in such a bind. Rather, Qohelet's gaze is, in his own estimation, *exhaustive* in that he has looked everywhere under the sun. This notion implies not only the here and now, but, as Qohelet remarks (3:11), knowledge of the expanse of

---

1. Crenshaw speaks of Qohelet's "denial of revelation" (*Whirlpool of Torment*, 79-80).
2. Fox, *Time to Tear Down*, 80.

time stretched incalculably backward and forward (i.e., עוֹלָם/'ôlām). Qohelet has "seen" it all, not literally, but in his mind's eye. He has left no stone unturned, and he will now offer his wisdom to any willing to hear. Alternate epistemologies are a priori out of bounds. He bids his readers to take a seat and listen, and the frame narrator concurs.

What is so intriguing about Qohelet's theology is that he undermines his own epistemology in the sense that, at the end of the day, there is very little we can know with certainty, and what one does know collapses into absurdity. The only certain knowledge Qohelet seems to give us is that everything is absurd, not just the things we cannot know, but the very things we *can* know. After his expansive gaze through time and space, Qohelet comes to the harsh conclusion that there is precious little knowledge out there. He is, in a word, a skeptic (hence the theory of some that Qohelet's unique view of the world, biblically speaking, is influenced by developments in Greek philosophy).[3] He is skeptical of everything, not the least of wisdom and God himself, the next two themes we will consider.

Qohelet and Wisdom: Friend or Foe?

One of the more difficult conceptual theological matters to iron out in Ecclesiastes is how Qohelet understands wisdom: what is wisdom for Qohelet? Does he see wisdom as an ally or an enemy? These are important questions for understanding the theology of the book as a whole, for how we handle these questions is invariably bound up with the evaluation of the frame narrator in 12:8-14.

Unfortunately, as we have seen, this question of Qohelet's understanding of and relationship to wisdom is an ambiguous matter. Still, there seem to be a couple of anchors that can hold the ship in place somewhat. First, in Qohelet's self-description in 1:12–2:26, although not without its own frustrating interpretive challenges, we see someone presented to us as a seeker of wisdom and who seeks by wisdom. This wisdom-laden quest is partly demonstrated by Qohelet's kingly accomplishments in 2:4-8. His observations are guided by wisdom, as he understands it, and his resulting conclusions are wise.

What is theologically crucial is to decide whether Qohelet's claims to wisdom are to be understood at face value or whether the very means by which he engages his wisdom quest is an indication of his lack of wisdom.

---

3. For a recent articulation of the Hellenistic influence on Ecclesiastes, see Perdue, *Sword and Stylus,* 198-255 (ch. 5, "Wisdom during the Ptolemaic Empire: The Book of Qoheleth").

This is a very legitimate issue and deserves due attention. There is no question that Qohelet's wholly experiential epistemology, as discussed above, is out of accord with what Israel's sages express in Proverbs. On the surface, this would seem to lend some credence to the second option, that Qohelet actually lacks wisdom despite his claims. But here is where the frame narrator's evaluation comes into play: how one understands 12:8-12 is crucial for how one understands the theology of Ecclesiastes. It is in this epilogue that the frame narrator praises Qohelet for his wisdom, although not without some qualification, as we have seen. Still, the sagely character of Qohelet in the epilogue is clear enough, and I am of the mind that the frame narrator's evaluation serves as a surer point of departure for assessing Qohelet's relationship to wisdom than appealing to an alleged standard notion of wisdom, such as might be gained from Proverbs, and then judging Qohelet's words on that basis.

In order to maintain the view that Qohelet was indeed not wise, the frame narrator's evaluation would have to be understood as a subtle but searching condemnation of Qohelet: "Sure, he is 'wise' (but we know better)."[4] The trouble with this evaluation, as I see it, is that the behaviors of Qohelet that the frame narrator describes are indeed sagely activities (12:9-11). Also, the qualification he adds in 12:13 only has its force if the positive evaluation beginning in v. 9 is taken at face value. And, perhaps most importantly, if Qohelet is not truly wise, and if the epilogue is simply a sweeping condemnation of Qohelet, then one wonders why eleven plus chapters are spent rehearsing Qohelet's observations and struggles.

What we have here, then, is a choice between two interpretive models. In one model, the frame narrator's evaluation is taken at face value and then used as the foundation for theological interaction with Qohelet's words. In the other, the interpreter comes to Ecclesiastes with a base definition of wisdom, assesses Qohelet on that basis, and therefore concludes that the frame narrator's evaluation has more to it than meets the eye. There really is no objective way of adjudicating between these two options. I have adopted the former model for the reasons cited above. But which model will ultimately prove more persuasive will only be judged by how well the model can achieve the more pleasing accounting of Ecclesiastes as a whole, that is, which does a better job of explaining why Ecclesiastes looks the way it does and why Qohelet says what he says. Stripped of all its flourish, this commentary, along with any other, is simply one concerted attempt to seek coherence by one of these models.

4. For example, Bartholomew argues that the epilogue exposes the ironic use of "wisdom" in Qohelet's speeches (*Reading Ecclesiastes*, 236).

Hence, rather than concluding that Qohelet was not wise because of the tensions we see between his thoughts and those expressed in Proverbs (not to mention Deuteronomy, with its seemingly unquestioned acceptance of the deed-consequence connection),[5] I think it is more reasonable to understand Qohelet's words as sagely observations that expand our notion of biblical wisdom. This is not too hard to accept when we add Job to the mix. The three biblical wisdom books have certain similarities, but they have differences that should encourage us to hold to a more diverse notion of wisdom, rather than allowing one of those books (Proverbs) to set an absolute standard. I will expand on this notion in the next chapter.

Moreover, it is worth remembering that the wisdom expressed in Proverbs is hardly simple or monolithic. To be sure, it holds out the expectation that certain behaviors, whether wise or foolish, will tend to yield corresponding consequences. But, as most scholars acknowledge, Proverbs falls short of guaranteeing such results. Rather, what Proverbs shows is a pattern of living that wise people should invest themselves in, to gain more and more wisdom, and so to bring themselves into alignment with God's pattern of behavior. It is not a rulebook or owner's manual for Christians, as is sometimes assumed in popular Christian circles. Rather, as Prov 1:1-6 make clear, it takes effort and discipline to become wise.

That Proverbs presents a real-world rather than simplistic view of wisdom is seen in the very content of the book. (The ideas expressed here are expanded in the next chapter.) Well known are the injunctions of Prov 26:4-5, where the reader is told, in two successive verses, to answer a fool and then not to answer a fool. Both proverbs are wise and true. Both are meant to be applied. The question is, however, *when* and *how*. It takes wisdom to know the *situation* and so to know *which* proverb to apply in the here and now. This situational dimension of Proverbs is often lost on readers, who see it as more of a "rules to live by" book. In a sense the proverbs are, but these rules are to be "lived by" wisely, which means the reader gains more and more wisdom by living life and seeking out more and more how his/her actions and speech can conform to the divine pattern. This type of situational diversity is seen throughout Proverbs. Another example concerns wealth. Wealth can be a source of pride (18:11) or security (10:15). Its worth can be wholly determined by the character of the person (10:16; 11:4). Wealth seems to guarantee friendships (19:4), but trusting in riches results in failure (11:28).

My purpose for talking about Proverbs is that, although to be sure Prov-

---

5. The influence of wisdom on Deuteronomy is well documented. See Weinfeld, *Deuteronomy and the Deuteronomic School*.

erbs is a different type of book than Job or Ecclesiastes, its character is by no means so different that one can draw a thick line between them. There is an elusive dimension to Proverbs, so much so that readers are admonished to *seek* wisdom (e.g., Prov 8:17), though it cost them all they have (4:7). Hence, when we turn our gaze to Ecclesiastes, it will not do to set up a stark contrast between them, as if Proverbs presents a simple "A will lead to B" world and Qohelet is rejecting that teaching. There is little doubt in my mind that Qohelet is indeed frustrated with how the world, under God's direction, works. He may even be highly skeptical of and even frustrated with some of the wisdom expressed in Proverbs specifically. But I feel that Qohelet's problem goes beyond Proverbs and touches on a more sensitive nerve: the trustworthiness, even goodness, of God. We will look at this more below, but here I just want to remark that Qohelet's jibes cannot be said to be directed simply toward the "conventional" or "traditional" wisdom that Proverbs supposedly represents. Qohelet's anger and disappointment have a broader target.

Rather than contradicting and canceling out the concept of wisdom, one purpose of the book seems to be to challenge readers to broaden their notion of wisdom. In this sense the author has much in common with Job and lament psalms, which we will look at below. Qohelet's quest is one that he and the frame narrator consider wise, even if it challenges certain dominant strands of Israelite wisdom. The reason for such a challenge is not that a grumpy old man woke up one morning and decided he had had enough. Rather, a certain social/cultural location would breed such a tone. That location, as is widely recognized, is one that began with Israel's sages trying to make their way against the backdrop of Israel's rejection by God in the exile, and this spiritual/intellectual journey continued to Israel's return to its homeland and the subsequent challenges that surfaced in the centuries that followed (Persian influence, Hellenism). Qohelet, in other words, represents not simply a diverse opinion about wisdom, but a *development in the nature of wisdom itself.* Such developments in the concept of wisdom are documented later in the Second Temple period, articulated famously by Ben Sirach and the author of the Wisdom of Solomon. For the former, wisdom and torah are virtually equated. Also, as we see in Sirach 44–50, the role of the sage is to explain Israel's past for the benefit of a contemporary audience, just as we see in Wisdom 10–19 and Pseudo-Solomon's rehearsal of Israel's experiences in Egypt, the exodus, and wilderness.[6] In other words, the sage's task is expanded to include the engagement of Israel's tradition, namely its written tradition, Scripture.

6. See Phua, "Wise Kings of Judah"; Enns, *Exodus Retold.*

Qohelet's connection to Israelite wisdom is not easy to define, but it is certainly best to avoid a stark, either/or contrast between Qohelet's role as sage and what we see in Proverbs. Israel's wisdom tradition is complex and hardly static. To put it simply, Qohelet's claim to following wisdom coupled with the frame narrator's strong support of Qohelet's sagely activity should lead us to *include* Qohelet in forming our definition of Israelite wisdom rather than contrasting it with a supposed core or norm. Qohelet's theology of wisdom, therefore, contributes to a broader theological discussion of (1) what wisdom is and (2) how wisdom relates to biblical theology, both of which will be addressed later.

God, the Problem: Injustice and Unpredictability

Another very important aspect of Qohelet's theology is his view of God, especially what he perceives to be God's unpredictable and unjust behavior. I do not think this dimension of Qohelet's theology receives as much attention as it should. Reasons for this neglect likely include the epilogue's positive evaluation of Qohelet, which would seem to make criticism of God out of place, and the sometimes subtle, or even equivocal, manner in which Qohelet expresses himself.[7]

Still, Qohelet's overall frustration and even anger toward God are announced quite plainly already in 1:13, the second verse attributed to Qohelet's own mouth: "It is a grievous task God has given to humanity to occupy him." This task refers to the previous sentence, Qohelet's wisdom investigation of all that is done "under the sun." He announces himself in v. 12, and in v. 13 he explains his task and gives the evaluation, all in summary fashion. Not only is his task grievous, but it is one that *God* has given to humanity. One might say that for Qohelet, God poses a theological problem. He does not seem to be so much concerned *whether* God is just, can be trusted, and so on. Nor does he seem eager to defend God's justice, as one might in a theodicy. He seems already to have made up his mind.

As we have seen in the above commentary, this view of God is maintained throughout the book. It is not that Qohelet never has anything positive to say. But his reflections and observations lead him to the theological con-

---

7. Of Qohelet, Ehrman comments, "God is not responsible for his pain as he is in Job" (*God's Problem*, 195). I understand the point with respect to God's overt role in Job, but technically it is the accuser who is responsible for Job's pain; God allows it. For Qohelet, more so than Job, God is to blame. Ehrman's picture of Qohelet's God is too generous.

clusion that God is not a source of comfort but the one ultimately responsible for his distress. This conclusion must be connected with his epistemology (discussed above). What Qohelet values is what is known by observing and reflecting on what he sees. Again, it might be easy to dismiss Qohelet's epistemology as being too narrow (i.e., if only he would look beyond himself), but such a dismissal is difficult to square with the evaluation of Qohelet in the epilogue. Rather than judge Qohelet's observations as inadequate, the book as a whole suggests another conclusion: "My, that Qohelet has certainly done his homework. His research is very thorough."

In view of Qohelet's overt and more subtle criticisms of God combined with the epilogue's acknowledgment of Qohelet's status as sage, we are faced with a theological dilemma: how can a sage talk like this? We should not presume, however, that such a dilemma is a failure on our part to read carefully or faithfully — as if we are missing some key that will allow all of this tension to go away. Rather, the tension is part of the fabric of the book itself, and ancient readers were no less struck by it than we are — indeed, perhaps more so. To miss this theological tension is to miss the plain meaning of the words in front of us. The tensions are not there for clever persons to come around and assuage what the author has put there. The book seems designed to throw ancient and contemporary theological categories for a loop.

This is not to say, by any means, that Qohelet represents the dominant biblical voice about God. But his is a legitimate, canonical voice. In the same way that Ecclesiastes drives us to expand our understanding of wisdom, it also helps us to see part of the theological diversity by which ancient Israelites expressed their relationship with God. Qohelet's words are not distant observations on "the nature of God." He is no philosopher or even theologian in the contemporary sense of the word. He is, rather, a man with both feet firmly planted on the ground who calls it the way he sees it. His gaze is vast, but not comprehensive, to be sure. Still, it is legitimate and valued enough to find its way into Israel's self-defining writings, the Hebrew Bible.

What allows us to take Qohelet's words with the utmost seriousness while also achieving a greater degree of coherence with the OT as a whole is to draw an analogy between Qohelet and both Job and the lament psalms. I will leave further discussion of this point for the next chapter. I only wish to point out here that in various portions of the OT Israel's struggles with their God come front and center. Job, lament psalms, and Ecclesiastes are not equal to one another, but they do form a similar collection of texts, which Walter Brueggemann refers to as Israel's "countertestimony."[8] Israel's daily experi-

8. Brueggemann, *Theology of the Old Testament*, esp. 317-403.

ence finds itself in tension with what we see in Israel's "core testimony" (to use another of Brueggemann's terms).

In other words, the God of Israel is not the God of philosophers or systematic theologians. He is a God who is in relationship with his people, and, as in any relationship, there are peaks and valleys. The predominant biblical notion to describe this relationship is summed up in the word "covenant." The OT describes this relationship both in terms of its divine initiation and God's responsibility to his people. It also speaks often of the people's failure to maintain its responsibility due to rebellion. With Ecclesiastes, however (as with Job and the lament psalms, I would argue), what we have is an honest expression of human finitude. We should note that in all three texts, there is an "answer" to the frustration. Lament psalms end in every case but one (Psalm 88) with some sort of statement of renewed faith. Job gets a different answer, but encounters God all the same, and there is movement toward resolution. The epilogist of Ecclesiastes brings Qohelet's observations into the larger context of traditional fear and obedience, although without suggesting that this will alleviate one's internal struggles. The point we are considering here, however, is not the ultimate solution to the struggle, but the fact that Scripture spends so much space entertaining the struggle to begin with. In a sense, it may not be too far off the mark to say that Israel's suffering is a vital portion of its self-identity, perhaps even that Israel's calling is to suffer in some sense. This identification is not seamless, since Israel's sufferings are often brought on itself by disobedience. In Ecclesiastes, Job, and lament psalms, Israel's suffering seems to be out of Israel's control, and Israel's Scripture is not timid about addressing this too. We will explore this in detail in the next chapter.

So, for Qohelet, God poses a very practical problem. Life, Qohelet says, is absurd. His observations lead him to question — even accuse — God of setting up a no-win situation. You cannot count on wisdom to come through from day to day, and death assures that any moment of success is seen for the fleeting folly that it is. These thoughts, however distressing they may be, are familiar to all who have ever tried to understand their suffering in the context of their faith in a wise and just God. Rather than shaming such sufferers for their lack of faith, the Bible itself, in such places as Ecclesiastes, lets us know that the struggle is an old one. We are not alone.

Everything Is Absurd, a Chasing of the Wind

As is well known, הֶבֶל/*hebel* is one of the dominant themes in Ecclesiastes. It appears with great emphasis at the beginning of the frame narrative, occurs throughout the book in numerous climactic statements, and comes to us one final time in the first line of the epilogue, thus framing Qohelet's words. Qohelet is all about *hebel.* He is determined to demonstrate it.

As discussed in the introduction, I have chosen to translate *hebel* consistently as "absurd" for reasons indicated there. I would like to flesh out the meaning and use of *hebel* by Qohelet a bit more here, and I begin by offering Seow's definition as a way of rounding things out a bit. When Qohelet says that everything is *hebel,* he is saying "everything is beyond human apprehension and comprehension."[9] There is nothing about which one can say "I have it" or "I understand it." All is outside our control, our mastery. Seow's definition expands our scope, for thus far I have been focusing on the psychological/emotional dimension of Qohelet's struggle. What Seow's definition does is help us see what drives Qohelet to such a psychological disposition that can be called "absurdity."

What further fleshes out the notion of *hebel* is the companion phrase, "chasing of the wind" (in its various forms).[10] I certainly understand this phrase as adding further definition to *hebel.* That which is *hebel* (which is everything) is a complete and utter waste of time. It gets us nowhere and leads to no demonstrable, efficacious result. We end up where we begin, with nothing to show for our frenzied activity — and we need only visualize someone actually chasing the wind around to grasp the ridiculousness of Qohelet's imagery. In this respect, we can see how intertwined are the notions of "absurd" and "no profit." Everything is absurd because, at the end of the day, we cannot grasp life, as we cannot grasp the wind. There is, therefore, no profit in any of our activities, regardless of whatever temporary results we might see. For Qohelet, any profit we experience is real but temporary, and hence no profit at all. What seals the argument, as a stone seals a tomb, is the inevitability of death.

What is relevant for our discussion of the meaning of *hebel* is its distribution throughout Ecclesiastes. The term appears thirty-eight times in thirty verses. Not all uses are equal, however. Some have a decided climactic force — they bring to a conclusion a point on which Qohelet has been laboring. Other uses of *hebel* have less of a climactic force and seem to summarize more a point that is about to come. All occurrences of *hebel* are as follows: 1:2, 14; 2:1, 11, 15, 17, 19, 21, 23, 26; 3:19; 4:4, 7, 8, 16; 5:7, 10 (MT 6, 9); 6:2, 4, 9, 11, 12; 7:6, 15; 8:10, 14 (bis); 9:9 (bis); 11:8, 10; 12:8. We can play with these numbers a bit. Let us first eliminate both 1:2 and 12:8, which are the frame narrator's evaluation.

---

9. Seow, *Ecclesiastes,* 59.
10. The phrase is first used in 1:14. See the comments at 1:14 and 2:11 above.

They most certainly have a climactic/summarizing force, but they are not the words of Qohelet, which is the focus here. Of the remaining instances, in my estimation several do not have the climactic force of the others: they do not summarize as absurd an extended portion of Qohelet's observations, but rather appear within the flow of Qohelet's monologues. So from this list I would bracket: 4:7; 5:7 (MT 6); 6:4; 7:15; 9:9; 11:8, 10. What remains is the following: 2:1, 11, 15, 17, 19, 21, 23, 26; 3:19; 4:4, 8, 16; 5:10 (MT 9); 6:2, 9, 11, 12; 7:6; 8:10, 14 (bis).

So, assuming the validity of bracketing some of the uses of *hebel* (and I will grant the matter is debatable), we can begin to see an interesting pattern. There are twenty verses that contain a climactic use of *hebel*.[11] Nine of those appear in 1:14–2:26. To put this is statistical terms, 1:14–2:26 (thirty-one verses) is 14 percent of the 222 verses in Qohelet's words, yet nine of the twenty climactic verses appear in these verses. In other words, nearly half (45 percent) of the climactic uses of *hebel* appear in the first 14 percent of Qohelet's words. The conclusion I draw from this is that the opening of Qohelet's own words — where he gives his own introduction (1:12-15), reviews his kingly pursuits and accomplishments (1:16–2:11), and alerts his readers that there is no profit to wisdom, folly, or labor (2:12-26) — is vital for understanding Qohelet's theology. Qohelet seems to have a point he wants to hammer home, in rapid succession, at the outset. Note especially 2:11-26, where *hebel* appears seven times in sixteen verses. I find this to be of some importance, and suggest, based on the uses of *hebel* in the opening section of Qohelet's words, that 1:12–2:26 are vital for understanding the claim made by the frame narrator in 1:2, that everything is absurd. Note too that the exact phrasing of 1:2 is found elsewhere only in 2:11. Given the central importance of *hebel* for understanding Qohelet, it seems that chapters 1–2 set the tone in ways that should be kept in mind, if not even control our thinking, as we engage the remainder of the book.[12]

Perhaps the point can be sharpened a bit by taking note of two other issues. First, 1:12–2:26 ends with the first carpe diem passage in Ecclesiastes. In this section, where *hebel* is found in such a concentrated fashion, Qohelet concludes in a manner that will become familiar throughout the book: *hebel* is the case, and the best humanity can do — what we have to settle for — is to

---

11. One might also take note of 1:17, which I see as another climactic statement, though without the use of *hebel*. There the phrase is, "This too is a chasing of the wind." In my view this is no less climactic than the uses of *hebel* discussed here, although I will leave it aside for statistical purposes.

12. I would add that of the twenty climactic verses, all but three (2:11, 17; 3:19) employ the demonstrative זה/*zh,* thus further demonstrating their climactic function.

enjoy one's work and accept this as coming from God's hand. Second, the opening chapters of Ecclesiastes introduce readers to the ambiguous nature of wisdom for Qohelet. In 1:16 and 2:9 wisdom is descriptive of kingly attributes, but in 1:18 it brings pain. In 1:17 and 2:12 it is the object of Qohelet's search, and it is then contrasted to folly (2:13-14a), but in 2:14b-16, 19, and 21 it is neutralized by death. Wisdom is both a trusted ally and an undependable business partner, as much a victim of death as anything or anyone else.

A close look at the uses of *hebel* throughout Ecclesiastes, not only in isolation but in conjunction with other important concepts, shows the pivotal role that chapters 1–2 play in setting the trajectory for the remainder of Qohelet's words, and by implication, helps us to see more clearly the stunning declaration of the frame narrator concerning Qohelet's sagely character. As unsettling as his words may be, as difficult as they may be to coerce into an overall view of the "proper" nature of "biblical teaching," Ecclesiastes 1–2 are quite clear as to the intention of Qohelet's words and the frame narrator's comprehension of that intention: our labors are ultimately in vain, there is no payoff for anything we do, we all die, wisdom is only a temporary help at best, and this is God's doing. Hence everything is *hebel*.

Work, Labor, Deeds: That Which Passes the Time

Human existence is filled with all sorts of activity. Qohelet refers to these activities in various ways, and the key terms are עשׂה/*'śh* and עמל/*'ml*. The former occurs in various forms sixty-four times, and thus makes it one of the most common lexemes in Ecclesiastes.[13] I do not think that the two roots are synonymous, but they clearly have significant semantic overlap for Qohelet. The former denotes more or less anything we do in this life, whereas the latter seems more focused on activities that require the expenditure of some effort ("toil"), perhaps more akin to how we might use the word "work," although any notion of a contemporary "work day" seems out of place.

Almost universally, these roots are used in Qohelet to indicate what such efforts *cannot* bring, namely something of lasting value. They may be of temporary benefit (e.g., 2:21, 24; 5:18), but the ultimate inefficacy of such activity is immutably pronounced already, and most emphatically, in 1:3. In-

---

13. In addition to the ubiquitous ו/*w* and definite article, the most common lexemes are the prepositions ל/*l* (230 times) and ב/*b* (159 times). Rounding out the most common lexemes are: כָל/*kol* (91 times), אֲשֶׁר/*'šr* (89 times), כִּי/*kî* (87 times), מָן/*min* (75 times), אֶת/*'ēt* (74 times), שֶׁ/*šĕ* (66 times), and לֹא/*lō'* (65 times). The importance of the notion for work, activity, etc., is clear for Qohelet: עמל/*'ml* occurs 35 times.

deed, the only benefit such activities have is temporary, and that only if we turn a blind eye to the reality of death. The perceptive observer, the one who is wise and takes the time to investigate all that is under the sun, sees that the inherent fruitlessness of one's activities and labor is a daily, pervasive reminder of the absurdity of our existence. That is why, as Qohelet announces in the so-called carpe diem passages, the *best* one can do is to enjoy what one has here and now. This is what we have. Giving a thought to where all this is eventually and inexorably headed will only result in grief and anger (1:18).

In addition to the act of laboring, the nominal form of the root '*ml* also represents that which is earned. The product of his earnings is what gives Qohelet pleasure, at least temporarily. What is stressful for him is the *exertion* needed to procure what he earns. This underscores an important point we have seen with respect to *hebel*. Qohelet's issue is not so much that gaining material things is of no value (that they are fleeting, or some similar notion), and certainly not that it is somehow beneath him or even wrong. What is *hebel* is what needs to be *done* in order to get his material reward. It is the effort exerted that is *hebel*, because the material things do not last, hence the effort is for naught. They are either lost at death, or, as Qohelet laments elsewhere, are given over to one who himself has not exerted the effort. If, in other words, Qohelet were to win the lottery, or be handed a treasure chest out of the blue, without any toiling on his part, he would not see his ultimate separation from these things as *hebel*. His problem is not that these material things waste away, are ephemeral, but that his efforts ultimately produce no lasting results. This is what he laments. There is nothing unfair about losing something you did not earn. There *is* something dreadfully unfair if what you earn slips *inevitably* away (because of death).

I think we would be going down the wrong path if we condemned Qohelet here as a crass materialist. Understood in a more generous way, he seems to expect nothing other than just compensation for his efforts, proper consequences for his deeds, as one can deduce from Proverbs or Deuteronomy. What Qohelet is questioning, however, is that this compensation has no ultimate benefit as he sees things, since death will ultimately separate him from what is rightfully his. And the patriarchal blessing of living through your offspring is of absolutely no use to Qohelet. If Qohelet is radical here, and he is, it is not in his expectation of just consequences for effort exerted. It is that all the benefit of his compensation comes to an end at death. Unlike Abraham, Qohelet takes no comfort in leaving all of this to his own offspring. In some respects, therefore, the climactic passage in the first two chapters (as discussed above), 2:18-26, is among the more radical in the entire book. He turns what was a sign of blessing for his ancestors on its head and declares it absurd. One is left wondering whether this royal author (albeit a persona) has had any misgivings about how he himself has benefited from the labor of his own father, but that is a matter that must be left to speculation.

All Our Deeds Are Leveled by Death

We have visited this theme in the introduction, throughout the exegetical section, and at several points above, but it bears repeating here. If one could summarize Qohelet's problem, including the problems he has with God, it would be that people die. Death is what inevitably takes away anything you have to show for your labor. You spin your wheels for whatever *hebel* days you are given (by God) on this earth, and then you die and are forgotten — quickly.

With Qohelet, we have the only OT author who openly questions death, at least with this sustained degree of intentionality. Of course, other biblical authors speak of death quite freely, whether it is the glorious passing of an ancient figure such as Abraham or Moses, or the lament of a psalmist, asking God to preserve him in the face of his enemies. Job is in such pain, emotional and physical, that he even wishes for his own death. But Qohelet is not like any of these. *Death is for him a fact of life that makes all human activities absurd.* It brings to naught anything that looks, to the unwise eye, as if it might bring some sense to it all. Death is not a solemn affair where words of wisdom (and possessions) are passed down to one's offspring. Nor does the temporary preservation from death at the hands of one's enemies bring praise to his lips. For Qohelet the problem is not that death comes too quickly or not quickly enough; it is not that it may come at the hands of an enemy; it is that death comes — period. And when he does wish for death, unlike Job, it is not to be rid of his inexplicable torment. Rather, to be dead — better, never to have been born (4:2-3) — means that you are not in a position to be able to ruminate over the divine injustice of it all. Since all die, you are better off nonexisting and not having to try to think about it. It is in this context that the opening summation of the frame narrator finds its full force: "'Utterly absurd,' says Qohelet, 'Utterly absurd. *Everything* is absurd'" (1:2).

Unlike *hebel*, which appears most frequently in the opening chapters of the book, it is the concept of death that permeates the whole. We see it first on the part of the frame narrator, where he declares that there is no memory of those who have died, as there will be no memory of those who will die by those who come after them (1:11). Indeed, the whole notion of death is already captured in 1:5-7, where we read of the profitless cycles of nature. In 2:16-26, what I am calling the climactic passage of the *hebel* section (chs. 1–2), it is precisely death that figures into the equation quite prominently. We have seen how the cycles of nature in 1:5-7 are paralleled in the cycle of humanity in 3:1-9, a list of activities over which humans have no control, and which is headed by the declaration "a time to be born, a time to die" (3:2). Justice is not a certainty among the living, and thereafter humans and animals both die alike (3:18-21). Oppression is a fact of life, and oppression makes one yearn for nonexistence (4:2-3). A stillborn is better off than someone who, even having a hundred children, does not derive satisfaction from his life experiences — and does not get a decent burial to boot (6:3). Even living a lengthy life (1,000 years twice over) means nothing if one does not experience enjoyment (6:6). It is better to go to the house of mourning than feasting, for after death no more "spoilage" (as with fine oil) can happen to you (7:1-2). Being excessively bad or foolish yields premature death (7:17). "The woman" of 7:26 is more bitter even than death (which is quite a statement for Qohelet). No one is master over the days of one's death (8:7-8). Everyone suffers the same fate, regardless of their deeds or status, and the dead will never again have a portion with those under the sun (9:2-6). In Sheol there is no activity or calculation or knowledge or wisdom (9:10). A poor but wise man rescues a city, but he is not remembered (9:15). The eschatological poem of chapter 12, which itself speaks of the end of all life, culminates in a final, painful swipe at our ultimate destiny (12:5-7).

There are precious few places to hide from the specter of death in Qohelet's words. Even where some respite may be found (all of ch. 5, for example), you need only keep reading a little further before Qohelet slams your face against the mortuary's front window.

Then What Does Life Have to Offer Us? Our Portion

Since all of our activities are rendered ultimately nonprofitable because of the finality of death, Qohelet laments the absurdity of life. Still, whereas ultimate meaning is wholly allusive, what we do have is temporary (provisional) meaning. The key word here is חֵלֶק/*ḥēleq*, "portion." This is what Qohelet declares as good, or at least, "there is nothing better than."

What is clear in Qohelet's uses of *ḥēleq*, especially in the carpe diem passages, is that he does not allow us the option of resting in this provisional meaning as if it were some respite from an otherwise threatening reality. Quite the opposite. That which is our *ḥēleq* is the best we can settle for in the face of absurdity and death. If there is any escape Qohelet offers, it is in not being too wise, since wisdom counts you among those who ponder such things to the point of grief (1:18), although even here he counsels his readers that being wise is still better than not being wise (2:13-14; 7:16-17).

This is particularly pertinent with respect to the carpe diem passages (3:22; 5:18-19), which are sometimes adduced as examples of a more positive message of Qohelet that balances out his pessimism. But here, too, the opposite is the case. Qohelet's affirmations about eating, drinking, and enjoying the good are not a cause for celebration, but an act of resignation. It is the best we have before us. It is God's "gift" to humanity. The same God has given us the "grievous task" of taking a good hard look at the absurdity of it all; the same God has given us the consciousness of the grand expanse of time, forward and backward, so that our terrible plight is made more plain to us. The carpe diem passages are, in other words, not a respite from absurdity but further confirmation of it.

Our *ḥēleq* is what we can glean in the here and now. The term occurs eight times in Ecclesiastes. In addition to 3:22 and 5:18-19 (MT 17-18), with its note of resignation, its other uses will help us round out the theological scope of this word. In 2:10 one's *ḥēleq* is to find joy in one's labor (עמל/*'ml*). Similarly, in 2:21 *ḥēleq* refers to the produce of the one who labors wisely which he winds up giving to one who has not worked for it. This relinquishing of one's *ḥēleq* is *hebel*. In 9:6 Qohelet declares that the dead have no portion, which is here a reason to lament death (even though elsewhere Qohelet greets death as the more favorable state). In 9:9 Qohelet stresses that one's days are essentially *hebel* and so enjoins his reader to take pleasure in the woman he loves as his portion, what God has given him in his labors. In 11:2 Qohelet advises to give one's *ḥēleq* liberally, for one does not know what disaster might befall.

All of these uses of *ḥēleq* hold in common that this is all one has in the face of an existence that will come to an absurd end in death. One's portion is not the generous provision of a gracious God. It is humanity's only recourse in carving out an island of provisional "meaning" in the face of an ocean storm of divine injustice.

The Role of the King

The royal persona of Qohelet plays a central role in Ecclesiastes, particularly in the first several chapters, where the identification is explicit. It is also true with respect to the book as a whole, even though the royal persona is dropped well before we arrive at the end of the book.

Qohelet's Davidic lineage is announced by the frame narrator in the very first verse of the book: "The words of Qohelet, son of David, king in Jerusalem." The identification of Qohelet with an actual Israelite king is not the purpose of this announcement, as discussed at some length in the introduction. Rather, what is being established is a royal persona for bringing greater force to the author's theological argument. Qohelet himself echoes the frame narrator's announcement in his own opening statement (1:12). By mimicking the ancient Near Eastern genre of "royal testament" ("I am Qohelet. I have been king over Israel in Jerusalem"), Qohelet begins to outline his deeds of self-glorification.[14]

This royal testament continues explicitly through 2:11, and indeed throughout "the king's" first person monologue to 2:26. As we have seen above, the opening two chapters of Ecclesiastes are important for establishing the more important theological themes of the book. In the same way that הֶבֶל/*hebel* makes a disproportionate appearance in these chapters, the royal persona is found in concentrated fashion here as well. Ironically, however, and as we have seen already, by the time we reach 4:1-3, not only does the royal persona recede to obscurity, but the connection between Qohelet and the king seems to be somewhat strained. In 5:8-9 Qohelet warns his readers not to be surprised at corruption in the land, and the king's role in benefiting from it. Then in 10:20 the reader is warned not to speak ill of the king, lest a "winged creature" report it to him.

It is unreasonable — or at least very unlikely — to consider that Solomon or any king would write such a self-evaluation. The purpose of the royal persona is not to identify Qohelet with any particular king. Rather, as I argue in the introduction, the writer is signaling to his audience, "think of wise Solomon when you read all this." A Solomonic/royal persona is adopted by the writer, without deceptive intention, to drive home the utter futility of the quest for meaning. The king is more suited than anyone to make the claims Qohelet makes. At his disposal are supreme wisdom, a supply of resources, and the luxury of time. No one else is so equipped to carry out so thorough and searching a critique of the human predicament.

Even though the royal persona becomes self-critical and then collapses altogether, it comes to bear on the epilogue, particularly 12:12, where the reader is warned not to add to Qohelet's words. There is no end to the making of books, and there is no need to, seeing that one such as this Solomonic figure has done the work for you. He is a sagely king, you are not. There is nothing you can add to his insights, which have been gleaned from a thorough

---

14. See Seow, *Ecclesiastes*, 119; Fox, *Time to Tear Down*, 170-71; Longman, *Ecclesiastes*, 76.

grasp of all that happens "under the sun." In other words, what the frame narrator is telling his son (12:12) is to take Qohelet's word for it rather than duplicate his quest. It has all been done already. There is, as we see as early as 1:9-10, nothing new under the sun, nothing about which one can say, "Look at this. It is new."

Hence the purpose of the kingly persona is to lend authority and finality to the musings outlined in Qohelet's words. The reader is warned to accept their wisdom but not to continue in the same vein. To me, Qohelet's observations are *more* extreme and striking than anything a "lesser" Israelite could concoct. There truly is nothing more that can be said (12:13a), for Qohelet has said it all. He has taken his reader not only to familiar places of emotional struggle, but also much further than readers (ancient and modern!) wish to go. And dismissing Qohelet's words is not an option left open for us. We are forced into his world of despair, and then we emerge, hearing:

> You have gone to the edge, much further than you have ever gone, and peered over. It does not get any worse. But even here, especially here, you are to continue as generations before you have done: fear God and keep his commandments.

Our Lives Simply Mirror the Larger Picture

The final theological trajectory in Qohelet to be discussed here is, like the previous one, a theme that unites beginning and end. As noted in the exegetical section, Qohelet's "eschatological poem" in 12:1-8 seems to provide a frame of its own with the references to nature and humanity in 1:3-8. The latter passage is an extended illustration from nature of the absurdity of life: if you want proof that there is no profit and that everything is absurd, just open your eyes, go outside, and take a walk. Nature itself depicts the futility of humanity.

With the former passage, Qohelet himself returns to this theme and brings it to a conclusion, which is a fitting end to the despair of the book as a whole. As we have seen, Qohelet here is depicting the end of life as we know it, the end of humanity and the world around us, in its social and economic dimensions. To remember one's creator in the days of one's youth (12:1) is not a call to vigorous service of Yahweh when young, but a reminder that youth will not last. Death comes to all. Hope will be lost. Have, therefore, a sober existence, one that is tempered by the knowledge that death awaits everyone and everything.

It is this final stamp on Qohelet's words that should also influence our understanding of the carpe diem passages as providing no more than temporary meaning. The best we have is our day-to-day "pleasure," which can be experienced only by either a mighty effort on the part of the wise to bracket their understanding of the absurdity of it all, or by being only wise enough to be better off in the here and now than a fool but with no real comprehension of ultimate absurdity. By ending his observations as he does, Qohelet, who we may have thought could not plummet any further, reaches a state of awareness that moves beyond any previous assertions about the absurdity of our individual lives. Here his view is broad and deep, all-encompassing and relentless. It is like a teacher at the beginning of a school year outlining in painstaking detail an overload of course requirements, only to punctuate his words with a wholly unreasonable assignment that has the class abandoning all hope. The older, graying teacher leans over the desk, brings his reading glasses to rest at the end of his nose, and asks in purely rhetorical fashion: "Have I made myself clear? Are there any questions?" It is clear to everyone that the teacher's goal of bringing some discomfort to the room has been realized, and people walk out stunned.

Indeed, Qohelet has made himself clear, and it is only by allowing Qohelet to have his way, here and throughout, that we can participate in the depth of his struggle. And it is only by participating in his struggle that we can feel how liberating — and even commonsensical — the frame narrator's admonition in 12:13-14 is. Ecclesiastes is a brutally honest book, and we will not profit from it if we tame it according to another standard, be it one gleaned from elsewhere in Scripture or of our own devising.

The Contribution of Ecclesiastes to Biblical Theology (and the Contribution of Biblical Theology to Ecclesiastes)

Toward an Understanding of Biblical Theology

Since the latter half of the twentieth century, the subject of biblical theology has been variously defined and has seen various articulations. As I engage the topic of Ecclesiastes and biblical theology, I should express at the outset my understanding of what biblical theology entails.

First, we have already been engaging in the biblical-theological task. Central to this task is an understanding of a given text in the context of (1) its historical setting and (2) the book as a whole. Of course, very often we know very little of the original setting of a passage or book. Moreover, a distinction often needs to be made between the context of the instigating event/utterance and the context of the final form of the larger corpus of which that text is a part. This is notably the case with the formation of the Pentateuch, but also affects every other segment of the OT (Former and Latter Prophets, Psalms, Wisdom Literature). At any rate, in exegeting particular passages we are already engaged in doing biblical theology. Exegesis is not a preliminary, neutral step. Rather, the very questions we bring to any text are already informed by a variety of implicit factors that reflect the limited nature of all human knowing (e.g., cultural setting, theological categories). Put simply, exegesis has a circular dimension, although the exegetical exercise also helps us be more critical of some of our commitments (or prejudices). The image then, as others have said, is more of a hermeneutical spiral than a circle.

The task of biblical theology is to put the exegetical pieces of the whole together. This is a synthetic task and it begins with biblical theology on the book level, which is how the term "biblical theology" has often been understood. It is assumed, and rightly so, that any book has a theological integrity of its own (regardless of its oral or literary prehistory), and the task of exegesis is to try to bring that theology to the surface. In that sense it is "biblical" rather than applying dogmatic or other types of categories onto the ancient text (although realizing, again, the complex issue of how our own context informs us in our exegetical task). With Ecclesiastes, the relationship between the parts and the theology of the book as a whole is a bit more complex than we might find in other books, due to its tensions and ambiguities, and what role we assign to the frame narrator in summarizing Qohelet's thought. Hence it is necessary for interpreters to be much more intentional in moving back and forth between the trees of exegesis and the forest of biblical theology.

With an understanding of the theology of the book of Ecclesiastes — which we have seen is both complex internally and in some tension with other books of the OT — we can consider the task of biblical theology on the broader canonical level. Such a move assumes that the books of Scripture can and should be in conversation with one another. This is my assumption as well, although I would quickly add that this canonical conversation can just as easily be filled with tension as harmony. Indeed, this is to be expected, since a canonical *conversation* does not aim to obliterate the distinctives of any particular book — even one as difficult to pin down as Ecclesiastes. I do not assume, therefore, that harmony is preferable to tension, especially when dealing with Ecclesiastes, although I have no predilection to exaggerating diversity. The reason I have come to embrace the tensions between Ecclesiastes and other portions of Scripture is that the integrity of those other books demands it. If we impose a unity (which is not to say that all unity is imposed), we will find ourselves in the unfortunate position of deflating other books of their life, while also needing to defend forced readings of those texts that militate against unity. Rather, I would prefer — as best as I can — to allow the parts of Scripture to play off of one another. Such a conversation allows the various biblical voices to speak from the context of their own historical particularities. A biblical theology in the broader sense of the word is an attempt to capture the nature of this biblical conversation. And since it is a theological conversation, it is also understood that any biblical-theological construction we may offer must remain open to further clarification: biblical theology is a journey as much as it is a destination — perhaps more so.

Even though we all approach Scripture with preconceptions, we must at the very least be hermeneutically self-conscious enough to know how those preconceptions affect our understanding of Scripture. This is very different from saying that our preconceptions *should not* affect us. They always do. But by being aware of the hermeneutical process we will hopefully be more open to allowing that process to be critiqued and corrected if need be. So, for example, as we have seen, we may all have a notion of what wisdom is, and then judge Ecclesiastes on the basis of that notion. That is fine as an entryway to the hermeneutical spiral, but there must also come a point where a reading of Ecclesiastes should affect one's preconceived notions of wisdom, especially since it is *biblical* (i.e., all the canonical books) wisdom that is being discussed. With Ecclesiastes, the overarching theological issue that comes into play is one's theology of God and whether he would inspire texts that say some of the things Qohelet says, that offer such a different perspective from other OT books. The problem, however, is that even our doctrine of God — especially our doctrine of God — should be driven by the witness of Scripture as a whole rather than by our own theological preferences and the inevitable privileging of certain texts that follows.

The voice of Scripture can easily be muted when a confession or tradition determines Scripture's proper interpretation rather than being in conversation with Scripture, that is, when an external authority becomes the truth rather than being subject to the Scripture, the alleged subject of study. In such cases biblical theology, and with that a proper understanding of Scripture, is cut off at the knees. Misplaced notions of what God does or does not do or allow can adversely affect our ability to hear the very tensions that the author of Ecclesiastes seems intent to lay before us. A rigid and constricting view of what is appropriate for God to do can, ironically, distort the message of the book that is claimed to be inspired by God. All of this reflects my conviction that we must be ever diligent to allow Scripture to take us where it will, to be willing to explore new avenues and to take theological risks, if that seems warranted by the text. Thus a biblical theology that involves Ecclesiastes will not see its task as alleviating tension in favor of a theological unity that, supposedly, is more consistent with God's character. Rather, it will explore the unique contribution of a book like Ecclesiastes to our understanding of what the Bible *as a whole* is saying about God and humanity.

In the broadest sense of the words, I understand biblical theology to come to its final statement in the person and work of Christ and in the life of the body of Christ, the church. Christians confess Jesus as God's final declaration of who he is by which all previous declarations (the OT) receive their ultimate context of interpretation. This is the pinnacle of theological interpretation. This is not to say that we now can dismiss Qohelet's struggles in light of the gospel, as some Christian interpreters, contemporary and otherwise, have implied. Indeed, the exact opposite is the case. We now bring the voice of Ecclesiastes into conversation with the gospel, realizing in somewhat paradoxical fashion that in Christ we see the climactic (and therefore final) revelation of God, while also realizing that the God presented in Ecclesiastes may help us understand better what that final revelation means.

I develop this in a bit more detail in the introduction ("Reading Ecclesiastes Christianly"), so this point will not be repeated here in full. Perhaps, though, it is worth highlighting my understanding of what a Christotelic understanding of Ecclesiastes entails. It is not an exercise in "seeing Jesus" in every verse of Ecclesiastes. Nor is it an exercise in comparing and contrasting Ecclesiastes and the gospel to see where the former falls short. Rather, it is allowing the gospel to orient us to the types of questions we bring to Ecclesiastes, as well as seeing how the theological contours of Ecclesiastes contribute to our understanding of OT theology as a whole and what the God presented in Ecclesiastes later did in Christ. That Ecclesiastes is at best alluded to perhaps only once in the NT presents us, however, with the possibility that Ecclesiastes did not work itself into the first Christians' theological reflections.[1] Genesis, Psalms, Deuteronomy, and Isaiah were very popular texts for drawing out the significance of Jesus the Messiah vis-à-vis the OT story, but Ecclesiastes is at best an echo. Still, the absence of Ecclesiastes from the NT is by no means a deterrent for its implicit value for the biblical-theological task. It is, rather, an invitation. It is the church's obligation, in view of the biblical-theological trajectories already set by the NT writers, to bring all of the OT into this larger theological conversation.

The Christian canon consists of "two parts," the OT and NT, but the biblical-theological task is brought into sharper relief if we articulate the relationship between the Testaments somewhat differently. The NT can be understood as a *commentary* on the OT in light of the person and work of Christ. In other words, the NT explains Christ in light of Israel's Scripture while at the same time modeling how Israel's Scripture is now to be understood in light of that reality. The reality of the coming of Christ puts all of Scripture (the OT) in a fresh light by placing it in the broadest redemptive-historical context. The event complex that towers over and gives final definition to all others is the death-resurrection-ascension of the Son of God, which resulted in the creation of a new people of God, made up of Jew and Gentile together, who are now not divided by law but united by the grace of Yahweh through faith in his Messiah.

To illustrate the point, it may help to think of the NT as analogous to developments in Judaism. For Jews the reality of the exile, followed by subjugation to foreign rule in their own homeland, then the destruction of the

---

1. Romans 3:12 may echo Eccl 7:20. The "frustration" of creation in Rom 8:20 may echo Qohelet's "absurd" (ματαιότης/*mataiotēs* of Rom 8:20 is the word used in the LXX of Ecclesiastes for הֶבֶל/*hebel*). See also Jas 4:14, "What is your life? You are a mist that appears for a little while and then vanishes."

temple in A.D. 70, were all events that needed to be understood in light of Israel's Scripture. These events were then brought to bear on their reinterpretation of Scripture. The resulting theological efforts for classical Judaism were eventually the Talmud and other important Jewish works such as the midrashim. (I am leaving out of the picture here other, earlier developments in Judaism such as those of the Qumran community and other early Second Temple literature.)

Judaism is a response of a people to its own Scripture in light of changing circumstances. The NT is, in this sense, a Christian Talmud. I am not saying that the Talmud and NT are interchangeable, and we can all walk hand in hand into an ecumenical sunset. To be sure, classical Judaism still found its ultimate purpose in Torah whereas the first Christians understood God's purposes now to be summed up in the Messiah. I am suggesting, however, that both share a similar hermeneutical posture, that of rethinking Scripture in light of paradigm-shifting events. Both faiths answer a similar question of self-definition at the intersection of ancient Scripture and contemporary events that recast Scripture. For Christians, however, that contemporary event is not exile but the death and resurrection of the Son of God: "Now that Jesus has come, how do we understand what it means to be the people of God?" That question necessarily and invariably becomes a deeply hermeneutical one, as God's antecedent revelation must be drawn into the answer. To be "God's people," after all, implies an understanding of the inviolable relationship between Jesus and his fulfillment of Israel's Scripture. This is why the OT is cited well over three hundred times, and is alluded to at least a thousand times, in the NT.[2]

To put it yet another way, both postbiblical Jewish and Christian literature are exercises in biblical theology, of bringing the past to bear on the present and vice versa and presenting a coherent picture of the whole. For Christians this task is one where all of Scripture is brought under the authority of the risen Christ and where the work of Christ is understood more deeply on the basis of Israel's Scripture. Moreover, that the NT, especially those books that deal explicitly with the post-Easter church (i.e., everything but the Gospels), is so focused on the belief and praxis of the church indicates that the biblical-theological task is not complete until one has understood its implications for the reconstituted people of God. In other words, bringing Scripture to bear, in Christ, on the life of the church is the final dimension of biblical theology. It addresses the question, "How are we *today* the people of God?" This is precisely the same question asked in Scripture at various junctures, for

---

2. My source for these statistics is Aland, *Greek New Testament*, 887-901.

example, by the Chronicler living in the postexilic period and by Paul living at the outset of the post-resurrection period. It is the very practical question of "Who are we?" that gives Scripture itself its developmental, progressive trajectories. The climax of those trajectories is seen not only in how Christ brings them to their final expression, but in how those trajectories are realized in the body of Christ, the church. The application of God's antecedent revelation in an "in Christ" way is an extension of the biblical-theological work evinced in Scripture itself. This is what the Christians today have in common with the NT writers. Both are living in the post-Easter universe; they participate in the same eschatological moment. The church, therefore, puts itself under apostolic authority by following the lead of the NT writers in continuing the biblical-theological project they began under the Spirit's guidance.

My comments thus far are not a digression from the task at hand. Such an approach to a biblical theology of Ecclesiastes will help us see how the various hermeneutical horizons interplay while also giving necessary supremacy to God's final statement in Christ. I wish to avoid, though, a facile notion of supersessionism, which could imply that the OT is of no theological value. It certainly is of indisputable value, as the NT itself shows again and again. However, if we learn anything from the NT's commentary on the OT, it is that the OT does not ultimately stand on its own. In view of the resurrection, it *must* now be seen in light of the gospel, that which the OT authors strained to see but could not (1 Pet 1:10-12; Heb 1:1-3). This is what it means to understand Ecclesiastes or any other OT book Christianly. To be sure, there are those who might consider any Christian reading supersessionistic in that it subsumes Israel's story under the authority of the risen Son of God, but to lose the climactic nature of the gospel for reading Israel's story is to lose the very message of the gospel — it is a sub-Christian reading.

In what follows, we will explore the intersection between Ecclesiastes and biblical theology, first by seeing Ecclesiastes in the context of biblical wisdom, and second by looking at the contribution Ecclesiastes makes to the broader redemptive-historical impulse of the OT. Then we will expand the biblical-theological task by exploring how Ecclesiastes can be in conversation with Christ and the church as described in the NT.

Ecclesiastes and Wisdom

First, let us flesh out a bit more what we glimpsed earlier of the biblical-theological conversation between Ecclesiastes and Israel's wisdom traditions. Here we will focus, rightly so, on the canonical material, but with a brief comment on developments in Second Temple Jewish wisdom. Biblical wisdom is a diverse path. It is important to allow that diversity to stand, especially since such diversity reflects inner-biblical historical developments in the nature and task of wisdom for ancient Israelites.

Ecclesiastes, Proverbs, and Job

As mentioned earlier, comparing and contrasting Ecclesiastes to Proverbs and Job results in broadening our definition of biblical wisdom rather than privileging one expression as standing guard over another. To put it another way, we must allow the descriptive task to inform our prescriptive conclusions. This is the legacy of any theological task that attempts to be faithful to Scripture.

How, then, can Ecclesiastes contribute to our notion of wisdom? This can first be seen in observing the inner-biblical conversation among the three biblical wisdom books. The difficulty is that these three books are quite different from one another. On one level it may be legitimate to ask whether the term "wisdom" can do justice to these three books. But as I see it, we should neither allow the diversity of these books to cast doubt on their belonging together, nor should the common label "wisdom" justify seeking an artificial unity. I would prefer to maintain the conventional designation and then ask what it is about these books that permits the common designation. Can we offer a definition of "wisdom" that is both sufficiently broad yet meaningful enough to hold the biblical wisdom books together? The following definition of wisdom can provide one entryway to that discussion: *Wisdom is concerned with mastery of life.*

How one masters life, amid all the ups and downs, when things go well and not so well, is a question that captures the essence of wisdom literature.[3] Each of the biblical wisdom books contributes to the discussion in its own way. We bear in mind, however, that these books do not function as "how-to" books or Christian owner's manuals. It is common to think of Proverbs, for example, as the book we run to that "tells me what to do." This is not how wisdom literature works. A "how-to" approach can be particularly problematic in reading Ecclesiastes, for it encourages readers to go to the supposedly

---

3. For a similar view, although approached from a different angle, see Packer, "Theology and Wisdom." Packer's point is that all of theology should rightly be focused on right living, and so he proposes the term "sophiology" to describe the centrality of wisdom for any theological endeavor.

"less skeptical" passages, such as the carpe diem passages, to find some safe guidance, and to jettison the less favorable passages (which is most of the book). But as we have seen, this does not capture the force of these carpe diem passages. They are not Qohelet's more sober moments that are worthy of emulation but notes of resignation.

Following the path of wisdom is more than citing a few passages. The nature of wisdom, God's wisdom, is deeper and subtler than this. We have already seen this with Proverbs. On the surface, Proverbs seems to be a book of "wise sayings to live by," a tendency seen, for example, in publications of the NT that include Proverbs and Psalms. But a close reading of Proverbs shows that the issue is much more complex. Again, Prov 26:4-5 (NIV) illustrates the point succinctly.

> 26:4 Do not answer a fool according to his folly, or you will be like him yourself.

> 26:5 Answer a fool according to his folly, or he will be wise in his own eyes.

Already here we get a hint of the complexities involved in handling wisdom literature. Proverbs is not a rulebook that simply tells you what to do. These are *both* wise sayings, to be sure, even though they give contrary advice. It is because they are both wise sayings that it takes *wisdom* to know how — indeed, when or even if — to apply them. It takes wisdom to discern what situation calls for which proverb. Wisdom requires that we read not just the proverb but the situation.[4]

Such situational elements are not hidden in a few corners of Proverbs. Earlier I pointed out briefly the diversity of what Proverbs says about riches. Simply scanning the passages below (all NIV) illustrates the point.

> 10:15 The wealth of the rich is their fortified city, but poverty is the ruin of the poor.

> 18:11 The wealth of the rich is their fortified city; they imagine it an unscalable wall.

---

4. Waltke has argued that Prov 26:4 and 5 do not reflect differing life situations but both must be understood as "absolutes and applicable at the same time" (*Proverbs*, 2:349). Longman's view is much more convincing and represents the mainstream of scholarly opinion: "This proverbs pair is prime evidence leading toward the proper understanding of the proverbs genre. Proverbs are universally true laws but circumstantially relevant principles" (*Proverbs*, 464). See too Van Leeuwen's treatment of Prov 26:4-5 in *Context and Meaning*, 102-6.

The first half of each proverb is the same, but the second half of each tells a very different story. For some, wealth as a fortified city is a security against poverty, for others, a source of arrogance. The applicability of the proverbs depends on context.

Consider also the following pair:

10:16 The wages of the righteous bring them life, but the income of the wicked brings them punishment.

11:4 Wealth is worthless in the day of wrath, but righteousness delivers from death.

In 10:16 we see that wealth is more or less neutral and that its benefit depends on the quality of the person possessing it, whether righteous or wicked. In 11:4 any benefits of wealth are neutralized "in the day of wrath." Only righteousness can deliver from death.

11:28 Whoever trusts in his riches will fall, but the righteous will thrive like a green leaf.

Here we see that one's downfall is in trusting riches. The righteous, however, will survive, although there is no mention whether the righteous have wealth. As in 10:16, wealth seems to be neutral, and what counts is one's character. But then in 19:4 we see an endorsement of wealth regardless of other factors.

19:4 Wealth brings many friends, but a poor man's friend deserts him.

What Proverbs has to say about wealth is diverse and demands a mature understanding of the circumstances of the individual. You cannot isolate one of these statements and make it absolutely valid, applicable to each and every situation. Nor can these statements be harmonized to say the same thing. Wealth can be a sign of blessing or it can be abused to the individual's peril. Which proverb applies right now? *It depends.* And it is these two little words that help us get to the heart of the situational dimension of Proverbs.

This raises the issue of biblical authority, which is not only relevant for Proverbs and Wisdom Literature, but other portions of the OT such as the Psalms. In what sense is Proverbs authoritative? The issue as I see it is more the nature of that authority. We should observe that Proverbs has a largely descriptive quality rather than being overt commands. To be sure, this is wisdom, hence it is not merely observations but it has an implicit prescriptive function — still, the mode of presentation is significant. Both their descriptive form and diverse content suggest that "authority" for the book of Proverbs must mean more than just "Do what it says," "Obey this verse because it is in the Bible." Proverbs is one book of the OT that seems to invite proof-texting, but it is precisely Proverbs that, when properly understood, seems to be designed to resist proof-texting. Individual proverbs are not meant merely to be "cited" or "read" to get the information content: they are meant to be pondered, lived with, meditated on, and acted upon. It is necessary to do so in order to understand them. Their meanings are not obvious, nor is their relevance. They can be general, vague, obscure, and so it takes effort to know how to use them. Proverbs, in other words, is not just a book of wise sayings to make the simple wise (Prov 1:4). It is also a book for wise people (1:5) who are on a life-long journey to gain more and more wisdom in order to attain a more godlike life, or, as I suggested above, to master life.

It may help to come at this by using creation as a metaphor. To master life means to live according to the *order* in the universe that God has laid down, the order that reflects his nature, his wisdom. Wisdom is order, just like creation.[5] Genesis 1 speaks of God ordering the chaos. Wisdom, likewise, is God's order, not on the cosmic level but on the level of everyday life. This is one way to understand such passages as Prov 3:18-20 and 8:22-31, where creation and wisdom are closely connected concepts. The purpose of wisdom literature is to pull back the curtain to let us catch a glimpse of the pattern, the order that God has laid down for life, even if our perception and understanding of that order are incomplete. The wisdom quest, according to Proverbs, is to seek diligently this order that God has established and to conform our lives to it. In doing so, one is living in such a way that mastery of life is being realized more and more.

How, then, does Job fit into this definition of "mastery of life"? Job is one who *struggles to discern this order.* Unlike Proverbs, the book of Job does not focus on explicating this order more clearly through wise observations. Rather (and this is true of Ecclesiastes as well), Job focuses on the intersection of divine order and human experience and the tensions between the two.

Job is a complex literary and theological work. For the purpose of fleshing out the relationship between Ecclesiastes and Proverbs and Job, however, I will restrict my focus to the theological tension represented by the speeches of

---

5. The intersection of Wisdom and order, including the created order, is a common observation. See Murphy, *Tree of Life,* 115-21. Important studies of this theme include Zimmerli, "Concerning the Structure"; Hermisson, "Observations on Creation Theology"; Perdue, *Wisdom and Creation.*

Job's four friends. In brief, Job's friends say what one would expect an orthodox Israelite to say. Anyone grounded in the teaching of Proverbs or Deuteronomy would immediately recognize the validity of their words. Take the following four representative examples (all NIV).

> 5:17-18 (Eliphaz): Blessed is the man whom God corrects; so do not de-
> spise the discipline of the Almighty. For he wounds, but he also binds up;
> he injures, but his hands also heal.

> 8:20-22 (Bildad): Surely God does not reject a blameless man or
> strengthen the hands of evildoers. He will yet fill your mouth with laugh-
> ter and your lips with shouts of joy. Your enemies will be clothed in
> shame, and the tents of the wicked will be no more.

> 11:13-20 (Zophar): Yet if you devote your heart to him and stretch out
> your hands to him, if you put away the sin that is in your hand and allow
> no evil to dwell in your tent, then you will lift up your face without
> shame; you will stand firm and without fear. You will surely forget your
> trouble, recalling it only as waters gone by. Life will be brighter than
> noonday, and darkness will become like morning. You will be secure, be-
> cause there is hope; you will look about you and take your rest in safety.
> You will lie down, with no one to make you afraid, and many will court
> your favor. But the eyes of the wicked will fail, and escape will elude them;
> their hope will become a dying gasp.

> 36:5-7 (Elihu): God is mighty, but does not despise men; he is mighty, and
> firm in his purpose. He does not keep the wicked alive but gives the af-
> flicted their rights. He does not take his eyes off the righteous; he en-
> thrones them with kings and exalts them forever.

Much of what undergirds the comments of Job's friends is the belief that the
universe is ordered. It is God's universe and things happen for reasons; actions have consequences. Is this not what we read all through Proverbs and
the Law? Job's circumstances, which we see, are actually *consequences*. They
have causes, even if we do not see them.

For some, the observations of Job's friends are neutralized because they
reason from consequence to cause rather than from cause to consequence. Because they *infer* due cause, whereas Proverbs and Deuteronomy move from
cause to consequence, one might be tempted to render invalid the observations of Job's friends. But this strikes me as a superficial objection. Job's friends
are perfectly within their "biblical right" to say what they do. Since God is just,

Job's friends reason that, if certain behaviors lead to certain consequences, the presence of those consequences must be a result of certain behavior — lest the justice of God and the truth of Scripture be called into question.[6]

Job's friends are not absolutely wrong in making this reverse connection from consequence to deed. But they lack wisdom in that they merely proof-text, that is, they make a superficial appeal to a theology of retribution such as we find in Proverbs or Deuteronomy (note that the appeal is superficial, not the theology of retribution). It is not wrong to appeal to traditional categories (the frame narrator of Ecclesiastes does this very thing in 12:13-14). But one has to appeal to them wisely, keeping in mind the "it depends" factor. Job's friends needed to exercise wisdom to know how — indeed, if — these categories applied to Job *in this instance*.[7] There are circumstances concerning Job that they are not aware of, circumstances that are outlined in chapters 1–2. Readers know why Job is suffering: "the accuser" (Heb. הַשָּׂטָן/*haśśāṭān*) challenges God to test whether Job is a worshiper of God or a fair-weather believer. We know this, but Job and his friends never do. Instead, the book goes into great detail describing how Job and four of his friends struggle to interpret Job's suffering. Job's friends understand the traditional categories of wisdom, but they fail in applying them rigidly to Job (in a "how-to," owner's-manual way). For Job, confidence in the functionality of the traditional categories is precisely what is now in question. He does not doubt that bad actions lead to bad consequences. The problem for Job is that he is experiencing the latter, but has not engaged in the former. He is having a theological/faith crisis.

So how is Job a wisdom book? It too concerns mastery of life — how to live well. The specific problem being addressed is the all too common experience of the biblical portrait and the everyday world failing to align. The divine pattern of conduct is not reflected in one's experience. Although they are very different kinds of books, Proverbs and Job share at least one important aspect, that the wise God has ordered the world not only physically but so-

---

6. We might recall here John 9:2. Before Jesus heals the man born blind, he is asked, "Rabbi, who sinned, this man or his parents?" Jesus puts such thinking to rest, but it is worth noting that the question was raised somewhat naturally. The notion that some negative circumstance (such as suffering) is a result of sin is perfectly reasonable. Jesus' response should be seen not as correcting the errant theology of his readers vis-à-vis biblical teaching, but as realigning an OT expectation.

7. On this see Albertz, "Sage and Pious Wisdom." Albertz describes the theology of wisdom embodied by Job's friends as "a conscious synthesis of the sapiential mastering of life and piety, or as reason's permeation of personal piety, fashioned by the perspective of the upper class" (260). It is flawed in that it "seeks to penetrate and explain the living relationship of God and humanity in a rational manner" (261).

cially/behaviorally. Proverbs helps us see this order, if only in glimpses. Job is wrestling with the common human experience of the divine order not being reflected in the human drama. It is worth repeating that nowhere does Job reject the pattern on the basis of his experience. Rather his agony reflects his commitment to assuming the validity of the pattern. This disconnect is what fuels Job's distress.

With Job in mind, we can now return to Ecclesiastes. How does Ecclesiastes address the issue of wisdom and the mastery of life? Like Job, the issue in Ecclesiastes is the disconnect between the divine pattern and human experience. Our author, however, is relentless in not letting God off the hook. Job's sufferings, both physical and emotional, are deep, but he is silenced in the end by God's voice. Qohelet's God is distant and hardly worth the effort to bring into the conversation, and so Qohelet does not bother; he simply accuses. It is not until we get to the frame narrator's conclusion that we see the solution offered to Qohelet and those who might participate in his despair. There is no answer given to Qohelet as we see given to Job, from God's mouth, stunning the complainer to silence. Rather the complaints are *affirmed as wise,* but the reader is challenged to move *beyond* this state, even against all reason, to one of fear of God and obedience to his commands — to continue being a faithful Israelite regardless of the absurdity. Rather than "How dare you question me" as we see in Job, here we read, "Yes, it *is* tough, but follow God anyway."

Despite the differences between Job and Ecclesiastes, they are united in one overarching notion: in the end it is all about who God is and what is required of his people. But whereas the book of Job offers a defense of God's character, no such thing is found in Ecclesiastes. No attempt is made to dull the scalpel of Qohelet's incisive observations. The reader is simply told to keep going, not by ignoring the pain but by looking right at it. As Winston Churchill reportedly said, "If you are going through hell, keep going." Job's complaints receive their answer from God out of the whirlwind, although, in a way, it was no answer — at least not the one readers might expect ("Well, you see Job, let me explain. An accusing member of the divine council came up to me and challenged me, and I just could not let it rest.") Still, at least Job got an answer. The readers of Ecclesiastes, however, are left to ponder how "fear and obedience" can actually bring meaning to life in the face of Qohelet's relentless skepticism concerning the very system that he spends roughly twelve chapters undermining. To that question they get no answer. They are only told to fear and obey, and to know that God will set all things right.

One should sense at this point how inadequate the frame narrator's answer would be for Qohelet himself! Throughout his monologue he has been pecking away at the very notion that the frame narrator here declares with confidence. Qohelet has been saying, "Life is unjust, and therefore God is unjust. So why bother?" The frame narrator responds by acknowledging Qohelet's observations as nothing less than wise, but then says in effect, "Bother anyway. God is just. Obey him." On one level this borders on the nonsensical, but this is precisely where the strength and wisdom of Ecclesiastes can be seen, not despite the despair but through it. In Proverbs and Job there is still the expectation that all things find their final answer in the wise God. Qohelet offers no such resolution, but readers are told to fear and obey anyway, not because they have seen the just God, but as a precondition to seeing the just God.

This is the unique contribution of Ecclesiastes to the wisdom conversation of Proverbs and Job. For Proverbs, things are not necessarily crystal clear, but the wise God is seen in the pattern of conduct laid out for humanity. Job's struggles are a function of his ultimate trust in the pattern; his despair comes as a result of his inability to see how his sufferings follow from any unrighteous behavior. *Qohelet has given up on the viability of the pattern altogether,* and so shows no hesitation in giving God an earful. And the frame narrator's evaluation is, "Good point, Qohelet. Fear and obey anyway." Against such a posture of faith in the face of the utter impossibility of faith there is no defense. The frame narrator's final two verses are a cold slap in the face — they are against not childish cynicism but a true, legitimate, "wise" despair that comes from peering into the darkest well of absurdity of the human drama. Qohelet has given it his best shot, but the answer remains the same.

To master life is not a program of several steps, where each success leads to others. Life is hard. All three wisdom books make this point in their own way, and Ecclesiastes takes it as far as it will go. One hears, perhaps, a distant echo of the famous saying, attributed (falsely?) to Tertullian, "I believe because it is absurd," or countless others who have obeyed even when it truly renders asunder every shred of common sense they have. To live wisely, to master life, is to expect to be redressed by the most challenging of circumstances imaginable — and to emerge steady and sure. In this sense Ecclesiastes is indeed wisdom literature. Even in the face of undeniable evidence to the contrary, where every shred of evidence says that God is either absent or unjust, wisdom reigns.

Ecclesiastes as Second Temple Wisdom

As discussed in the introduction, Ecclesiastes is nearly universally accepted as a text of Second Temple provenance, and linguistic factors are one important reason why. Qohelet's skepticism toward God and criticism of kingship also seem to support this conclusion. The notion of wisdom in general also underwent a transformation of sorts during this period, and these developments can be summed up by observing the growing importance of the role of the sage.[8]

There is little question that Israel's wisdom tradition was quite old, famously associated with Solomon and no doubt influenced by ancient and ubiquitous sapiential traditions of the ancient Near East, particularly Egypt. The ultimate rise of Israel's sages to a role of greater prominence, however, is a result of its exile. With the exile, Israel's central institutions of kingship and cult were, for all intents and purposes, neutralized. On foreign soil there is no enthroned king, nor is there the Jerusalem temple, the only place prescribed by Deuteronomic law where Israel's rituals could take place. In the absence of such time-honored means whereby Israel could connect with Yahweh, Israel's devotion to God shifted to another means: study Scripture.

This is no small development. The extent to which preexilic Israel had an explicit canonical consciousness is debated, but in the postexilic period such a consciousness can be documented. It is axiomatic in contemporary biblical scholarship that the exilic and postexilic periods are responsible for developments that eventually gave us the Hebrew Scriptures, and the role of Israel's sages was central to these developments. Briefly stated, whereas the institutions of the past were neutralized, Israel's rich literary heritage (which would include oral tradition) was as alive as ever, and indeed came to prominence. Whereas the voices of the king, priest, and prophets had either ceased or receded, what remained was their voice that echoed in Israel's written and oral memory. That memory became codified eventually in the Hebrew Bible, and so became the means by which present-day Israelites could identify with their preexilic heritage, and so with God himself. As a result, the role of the sage shifted somewhat from that of purveyor of wisdom in general — recording observations on the nature of life and reality — to that of accessing divine wisdom through Scripture. Sages, in other words, became very interested in Scripture and its interpretation as a means to becoming wise. To put it with only slight exaggeration, the exegete was born, and exegesis became a sagely occupation.

This development in wisdom is seen very clearly in two extracanonical Jewish works, Ben Sirach (Ecclesiasticus) and Wisdom of Solomon. As distinct from Israel's canonical wisdom literature, in which Israel's past is hardly in view, these two books actively engage Israel's history and the significance

8. For a summary of this development with reference to other secondary literature, see Enns, *Exodus Retold*, 144-54.

that that history has for their time. Ben Sirach, for example, is explicit in identifying wisdom with law (Sirach 24, especially v. 23), thus placing wisdom at the very heart of Israel's self-understanding.[9] He also rehearses the flow of Israel's history in his famous paean to "famous men" in chapters 44–50, which begins with Enoch and ends with "Simon the high priest, son of Onias" (50:1), thereby connecting wisdom with Israel's grand narrative.

Likewise, roughly half of Wisdom of Solomon's nineteen chapters are devoted to rehearsing Israel's history, focusing mainly on Israel's exodus and wilderness experience.[10] In 10:1-14 the author reviews wisdom's role in the lives of prominent figures in Israel's history: Adam, Cain, Noah, Abraham, Lot, Jacob, and Joseph.[11] The general point being made is that wisdom was with these figures (curiously, including Cain), guiding and/or protecting them. In 10:15 and going to the end of the book, the author's attention is on the exodus and wilderness wanderings. Here too the author's point is that wisdom was with the Israelites in the most challenging and central of Israel's historical moments. In addition to fusing Israel's history with the role of wisdom, the author's focus on the exodus also seems to be an exercise in biblical theology. Wisdom's protection of the exodus community is seen as a paradigm for wisdom's protection of the author's contemporaries, who are facing persecution and an "exodus" of another sort — the passage from death to life (see the author's use of ἔξοδος/*exodos* as "death" in Wis 3:2 and 7:6). The author reminds his readers that, just as wisdom was with the prototypical exodus community, so is she with his readers now in their moment of their enslavement and eventual release in death, their exodus.

In both Ben Sirach and Wisdom of Solomon, wisdom is given a role that is at best only hinted at in the OT — a partner in Israel's legal and narrative traditions. For these authors, handling Scripture and bringing the lessons of Scripture to bear on God's people was a sagely activity, for it takes a wise man to discern the lessons of the past.

Ecclesiastes, although sharing a Second Temple historical context, has little in common with Ben Sirach or Wisdom of Solomon. Not only is there no clear reference to Israel's history in Ecclesiastes, but also Qohelet's despair and pessimism concerning God's justice and wisdom's benefits are a far cry from what undergirds Ben Sirach and Wisdom of Solomon. The latter books praise wisdom and place wisdom at the very heart of Israel's story, a tone that is only suggested in the OT (e.g., Prov 8:22-31). Whereas much of earlier-

---

9. On this see Sheppard, *Wisdom as a Hermeneutical Construct*, 19-71.
10. Enns, *Exodus Retold*, 43-134.
11. Ibid., 17-41.

twentieth-century OT theology was notorious for not knowing what to do with wisdom, these ancient authors knew exactly what to do: she guided Israel along its long and arduous journey. By contrast, Qohelet's words call into question all that these other authors hold dear. Indeed, it seems that Wis 1:16– 2:11, with its full confidence in the reality of the afterlife as the locus of God's judgment (and therefore his ultimate justice), may have been fashioned by the author as a countervoice to Qohelet's complete skepticism (Eccl 3:18-22).[12]

Having said this, however, there is one element of Ecclesiastes that, although briefly stated, is nevertheless a point of contact with Ben Sirach and Wisdom of Solomon: the epilogue, Eccl 12:13-14. As we have seen, the frame narrator reflects on Qohelet's words and concludes for his son that (1) Qohelet is wise, (2) do not add to his words, (3) fear God, keep the commandments, and trust that God will, despite appearances, bring all things to judgment. Qohelet's words may be sui generis in the OT and among other Second Temple developments in wisdom, but Ecclesiastes taken as a whole is not entirely unique.

Fearing God and keeping the commandments represent two central Israelite theological themes: wisdom and law. And the call to trust God's ultimate justice in the affairs of humanity is a reiteration of these two themes. Ben Sirach and Wisdom of Solomon bring wisdom to bear on contemporary issues by forging the connection between wisdom and Israel's redemptive history, whether Torah as in Ben Sirach or the great figures of the past, as in both Ben Sirach and Wisdom of Solomon. The frame narrator does not go in quite this same direction, but he does give similar sage advice: the final response to Qohelet's despair over God's covenant faithfulness and justice is, simply put, to reiterate those very same things. What Wisdom of Solomon says to its readers is that wisdom is now poised to come through for you just as she did throughout Israel's history. Ben Sirach puts it a bit differently, that wisdom pays off as can be seen in the list of those from Israel's past who have been righteous and just. For both, the ultimate message is that wisdom works. It is in the face of Qohelet's despair that the frame narrator calls on his readers to embrace the same attitude.[13] For all three, the final affirmation of Israel's tra-

---

12. Enns, "Wisdom of Solomon," 213-14.

13. Sheppard remarks, "Qoheleth has been thematized by the epilogue [12:13-14] in order to include it fully within a canon conscious definition of sacred wisdom, one that is remarkably close to Sirach and Baruch. . . . Therefore, the epilogue provides a rare glimpse into a comprehensive, canon conscious formulation concerning the theological function of biblical wisdom. When the assumed ideological coherency of the wisdom books is clarified in such a manner, the complementarity between the canonical function of the biblical wisdom books and the func-

dition is clear. They differ in the situation to which they apply that affirmation. Even though Ecclesiastes lacks the deliberate and extended engagement of Israel's traditions that we find in Ben Sirach and Wisdom of Solomon, all three see that tradition as being of irreducible value for addressing matters of importance for their Second Temple audience.

Ecclesiastes and Israel's Story

Ecclesiastes as Counterpoint

Ecclesiastes is one of several strands of Scripture that serve as a counterpoint to Israel's dominant picture of God. Throughout Israel's narrative and prophetic traditions, although there is certainly diversity of focus and content, we are presented with a God who fits numerous well-known descriptions: he is creator, redeemer, king, just, holy, warrior, father, righteous, judge, shepherd, and so on. These images are so dominant in Israel's literature that, when confronted with alternate descriptions (e.g., when God is grieved), one is hard-pressed to see how the various images can be held together. This is the case regardless of the fact (or at least, of my opinion) that the more common depictions of God as creator, redeemer, and so on are indeed dominant, or what Brueggemann helpfully calls "Israel's Core Testimony."[14] These form the complex of images that define the heart of Israel's conception of God.

But the dominance of Israel's core testimony does not neutralize Israel's likewise documented testimony of taking that core testimony to task.[15] Brueggemann refers to this as "Israel's countertestimony" in which Israel's core testimony is "cross-examined." Brueggemann's *Theology of the Old Testament* takes as its organizing principle the metaphor of the courtroom, where testimony is answered by countertestimony ("dispute").[16] This countertestimony is

---

tion of certain other inner-biblical sapientializing redactions becomes all the more obvious and compelling" (*Wisdom as a Hermeneutical Construct,* 127, 128-29). Sheppard demonstrates the last point by looking at Hos 14:9 (MT 10), Psalms 1 and 2, and 2 Sam 23:1-7 (129-58).

14. Brueggemann, *Theology of the Old Testament,* 115-313.

15. Ibid., 315-403.

16. Brueggemann's appeal to the court metaphor of testimony, dispute, advocacy (i.e., core testimony, countertestimony, unsolicited/embodied testimony) owes much to the notion of the dialectical and dialogical nature of the theological articulations of the OT (a characteristic of Jewish theology) rather than the transcendentalist (a characteristic of Christian theology) (ibid., 83). Brueggemann finds here a fresh and imaginative way of doing OT theology today in the wake of the collapse of historical criticism, a journey he lays out from the Reformation to the contemporary situation on pp. 1-114.

an interrogation of the core testimony, and Brueggemann treats under this rubric the hiddenness, ambiguity, and negativity of God as seen in lament psalms, Lamentations, Job, and of course Ecclesiastes, among other portions of Scripture. Ecclesiastes in particular he refers to as "The Far Edge of Negativity." Far more so than even Job, "At the very edge of the Old Testament, culturally and epistemologically, the Book of Ecclesiastes gives us the residue and outcome of that shrill and incessant voicing of negativity. . . . [It is] a hostile witness, going through the paces but not really caring if anyone is persuaded by this utterance of guarded negativity."[17] I am not particularly persuaded that Qohelet's negative witness is all that "guarded," but the overall courtroom imagery is certainly a helpful way to access the theology of Ecclesiastes and its place in OT theology and biblical theology. Qohelet is a relentless prosecuting attorney cross-examining the dominant portrayals of God in the OT.

We have already glimpsed the relationship between Ecclesiastes and Job, a book that offers its own countertestimony. Moving outside the wisdom corpus, a group of texts that demands our attention is the lament psalms. These psalms are so called because they, on some level, utter some degree of questioning, of pain, of disappointment, and even despair. As is well known, Psalms 1 and 2 are a gateway to the Psalter. Psalm 1 orients the reader to expect a very clear, seemingly unalterable, relationship between deed and consequence. You are blessed if your life conforms to Torah. If it does not, you are like an uprooted plant. There is an orderly pattern to the world, a rhythm by which to gauge one's life. Psalm 2 continues this articulation of God's pattern by announcing that the king, the Messiah, God's son (by which David seems to be meant), is on the throne. All is as it should be.

What follows, however, is a collection of poems and songs that at best intermittently support the vision just articulated. Rather than the idyllic, black-and-white order of Psalm 1, things in many of the remaining psalms are regularly not as they should be, and the psalmist finds himself in the position of having to plead with Yahweh to make good on his own promises. And having Yahweh's anointed on the throne (Psalm 2) is, apparently, no guarantee, since it is the king himself who pleads with God to protect him, to deliver him from his enemies, and so on. Moreover, the king himself fails to uphold the standard, and so finds himself pleading with God for his mercy (e.g., Psalm 51). Psalms 1 and 2 seem to present the ideal, whereas many other psalms provide a counterpoint. This counterpoint is not an occasional blip on the screen, but a pervasive element in the Psalter — one that reflects Israel's own experiences and is richly documented in Israel's own Scripture. This counterpoint, which

17. Ibid., 393. The entire section on Ecclesiastes is found on 393-98.

bears testimony to the disjunction between ideal and real, would seem to be of significant value in any biblical-theological task that includes Ecclesiastes.

Psalm 73, for example, is a strong echo of the theology of Ecclesiastes.[18] Here the writer affirms the fundamental correctness of the "order" of the world (v. 1).

> Surely God is good to Israel, to those who are pure in heart.

The difficulty he addresses, however, is that his experience does not support how things should be (vv. 2-5).

> But as for me, my feet had almost slipped; I had nearly lost my foothold. For I envied the arrogant when I saw the prosperity of the wicked. They have no struggles; their bodies are healthy and strong. They are free from the burdens common to man; they are not plagued by human ills.

The psalmist continues in this vein for several more verses and then gets to the heart of the struggle (vv. 12-14).

> This is what the wicked are like — always carefree, they increase in wealth. Surely in vain have I kept my heart pure; in vain have I washed my hands in innocence. All day long I have been plagued; I have been punished every morning.

The pivotal point in the psalm follows (vv. 15-17 NIV).

> If I had said, "I will speak thus," I would have betrayed your children. When I tried to understand all this, it was oppressive to me till I entered the sanctuary of God; then I understood their final destiny.

The psalmist's internal struggles are beginning to surface more clearly. The psalmist's observations are, in his estimation, too troublesome to communicate to others, lest he "betray your children," injure their faith. Likewise he says, "When I tried to understand all this, it was oppressive to me." What is unsettling here is not simply that the unjust prosper. His deeper struggle is that *God lets it happen.* How can it be, he asks, that God allows all this? It is too much to take in. Is God truly just? Is the world truly as it should be? The similarities between this psalmist and Qohelet are suggestive. Although Qohelet's "lament" goes on much longer than that of the psalmist, and al-

---

18. For an exposition of Psalm 73 that likewise focuses on the clash of religious belief and reality, see Crenshaw, *Whirlwind of Torment*, 93-109.

though Qohelet articulates his distress with greater determination, both share the same basic view that life is not as it should be, and that God's reputation is at stake (for the psalmist) or that God's reputation has already been lost (Qohelet).

We can also juxtapose the solutions each offers. For the psalmist, all of what he saw was oppressive to him until he "entered the sanctuary of God" and so understood the final destiny of the unjust. Qohelet does not offer anything resembling such a solution, but the frame narrator most certainly does, albeit using different imagery. For the psalmist, resolution emerges in worship. It is in submission to Yahweh that he begins to see that patience is required of him, that God will right all wrongs. His present observations are not discounted. They are quite perceptive, but they do not determine ultimate reality. The frame narrator of Ecclesiastes paints a similar picture, although it is somewhat more disarming, given the previous eleven chapters of Qohelet's relentless, unbending despair. The difference between the two, however, is that the psalmist gets his answer in the here and now. The frame narrator likewise affirms that God will bring every deed to judgment (which, as we discussed, is not an allusion to eschatological judgment). But it seems that Qohelet's readers are primed for a much longer period of unsettlement. There is no actual resolution, only the continued promise that such a resolution is forthcoming. In the meantime, they are to act in accordance with that future resolution: fear God, obey his commands.

Although each lament psalm has its own characteristics, they tend to end with a similar note of resolution (except Psalm 88, which ends on a strong note of despair). Praise is given to God, and his ultimate goodness and faithfulness are proclaimed. With respect to Ecclesiastes, however, that no such resolution is given should not obscure the point that similar moments of struggle are well documented in Israel's self-definition, beyond Ecclesiastes and Job. It is worth stressing again, therefore, how Israel's own understanding of what it means to be a follower of Yahweh carries with it such a clear element of struggle and lament. Most often, Israel's experience of struggle is not anything brought upon them by their actions, but is a function of their observations of the way of the world. And it is certainly central to this discussion that — even with Ecclesiastes — Israel's very real reflections on the nature of reality are claimed to find their ultimate resolution, either now or later, in God himself. The overall message is not that God's people should not experience such struggle if they are on good terms with God, but that even people who are on good terms experience the darker side of being in covenant with God. Again, let us be clear that this dark side is not to be understood as the simple observation that things do not work out as one might expect. Rather it is the unsettling notion that God allows such an unjust state of affairs to exist. If we forget this, we forget the anguish of this biblical countertestimony.

One might ask what the difference is between Ecclesiastes or a lament psalm and the complaints of the exodus generation (e.g., Exod 15:22–17:7; Num 11:1–14:45). There is a world of difference between the grumbling or murmuring tradition of disgruntled Israelites, who had just been delivered from slavery and Israelites who observe the disjunction between God's alleged unalterable justice and righteousness, and the fact that wrong often seems to come out on top. The former is truly rebellion in the sense that the murmurers had just seen God's faithfulness firsthand and in dramatically concrete fashion. They are not observing digressions from God's pattern and crying out to God for justice. They are living in the moment of resolution the psalmists cry for — God breaks through and is present with his people — and still they complain. Any similarities between murmur and lament are superficial. The spiritual orientations are completely different.

One reason why this distinction is important to highlight will be addressed in more detail in the final chapter of this commentary, but is worthy of mention here. What the struggle/lament tradition, the counterpoint of Israel's Scripture, shows us is how acceptable, even expected, it is to give honest articulation to those struggles. It is not the case that those who truly believe are never to question God. The murmurers question God because they do not trust him. The psalmists, however, complain because on some level they do or at least want to trust him. Too often I run across well-meaning people who insist that a truly mature follower of God will not allow doubt to enter his/her mind. Scripture, however, embodies a very different perspective, one that anyone who has ever suffered will quickly recognize. The entire struggle can be summarized in the psalmist's utterance, "How long, O LORD?" In this phrase is captured both the acceptability of the lament and the trust — however fractured — in God's faithfulness that the psalmist yearns for. The same posture is seen in the frame narrator's call to fear God, obey his commandments, and trust his justice despite the circumstances observed by Qohelet. What raises interesting theological possibilities for Ecclesiastes is when this dialogue is transferred to the national level, to which we now turn.

Ecclesiastes and Israel's National Lament

Israel's tradition of struggle and lament seems to exist quite comfortably on the level of the individual Israelite. After all, most of the psalms, including the lament psalms, speak of the sufferer in the first person singular. Likewise, Job and Qohelet are individuals. But already here, the psalms open a window to seeing the whole matter from a different angle. Ever since the pioneering work of Hermann Gunkel, we have understood that the "I" of the Psalter is not meant to focus on a single individual but reflect the cultic life of the Israelite community — not unlike how "I" hymns function in churches today.[19] To be clear, the "I" psalms have a long tradition of being appropriated by individual worshipers, which hardly seems remarkable. However, the presence of this collection of psalms in Israel's national defining document suggests that there is more at work here than merely a collection of poems that recount individual experiences. The Psalter speaks to Israel's corporate, national solidarity. My contention is that what holds for the lament psalms holds for Job and Ecclesiastes, too. Although both books have been read with great profit as expressions of individual suffering, they too speak to Israel's corporate, national life.

One way of drawing out the national, corporate dimension of both Job and Ecclesiastes is to broaden our discussion to that section of the Hebrew canon in which we find those books: the Writings. To be sure, the Hebrew Bible as a whole is a grand historical narrative that recounts Israel's journey from creation to exile and beyond. This narrative focus is seen throughout the Torah and Former Prophets (i.e., historical books). The prophetic corpus (Latter Prophets) either carries forward this narrative or at least reflects the prophetic voice from various points in time within this redemptive-historical framework. The Writings, however, particularly Israel's poetic and wisdom traditions, do not seem to fit easily into redemptive history, but I suggest that this is only on the surface.

We should remark first off that, quite obviously, a number of books in the Writings do indeed contribute to Israel's redemptive-historical narrative. First and Second Chronicles retell Israel's preexilic history from a postexilic point of view. Ezra, Nehemiah, and Esther overtly extend the redemptive-historical drama to the postexilic period. Ruth is a preface to the story of David, as can be seen in the genealogy in Ruth 4:18-22.[20] Lamentations reflects

---

19. Gunkel classified the Psalter into several genre categories that reflected Israel's cultic life (*Psalms*). These categories have not remained static in subsequent years, nor has Gunkel's student, S. Mowinckel, convinced all by his attempt to locate many psalms in specific cultic settings, e.g., New Year's festival (*Psalms in Israel's Worship*). Nevertheless, the function of the Psalter as a communal, cultic text rather than mere recollections of individual piety is certain.

20. I do not mean to suggest that this is the sole function of Ruth. For example, Ruth is called a "virtuous woman" (חַיִל-אֵשֶׁת/'ēšet-ḥayil) in Ruth 3:11, as is the woman of Prov 31:10. Ruth's placement immediately after Proverbs in the Hebrew Bible canon suggests that Ruth is to

on the fall of Jerusalem. Daniel, although apocalyptic, is nevertheless a continuation of redemptive history as it proclaims the role of God in national and world events.

The redemptive-historical connections with these books are obvious, but the remaining books of the Writings — Psalms, Proverbs, Ecclesiastes, Song of Songs, and Job — seem less willing to be brought under the redemptive-historical umbrella. Some connection to Israel's story is often made, somewhat uneasily, on the mere basis of authorial ascriptions, namely David (Psalms), Solomon (Proverbs, Ecclesiastes, Song of Songs). But this hardly constitutes an integration into redemptive history. One is left wondering what it is about these books that rendered them worthy of being included in *Israel's* sacred story.

Let me suggest that these five books, like the other Writings, afford a deeper redemptive-historical connection than is sometimes appreciated. For example, rather than seeing the Psalter simply as a collection of Israel's communal worship songs, think of it as a commentary on the collective sufferings and triumphs of the nation. In Psalms 1 and 2 put the entire Psalter in the context of redemptive history, not simply by loosely connecting the Psalter to David, but by encouraging readers to approach the Psalter with redemptive-historical categories in mind.[21] Psalm 1 is not an abstract description of individual piety, but a declaration of what it means to be an Israelite (or perhaps, too, what an ideal Israelite king looks like). By meditating on the law day and night, one will find oneself planted firmly by streams of water — a double entendre of Israel's possession of the land in view of Torah obedience. Psalm 2 is a declaration of the status of Yahweh's king, the favor bestowed on the son, his status vis-à-vis the nations. Law and king begin the Psalter, and it is Israel's failings with regard to these interconnected themes that will prove to pose such difficulties for the nation. Psalms 1 and 2 portray what Israel *should* look like.

The interpretation of the Song of Songs has been a puzzle throughout much of the modern period, and I do not want to give the impression of providing the last word here. Still, throughout the history of interpretation for both Jews and Christians, the Song has been connected directly to redemptive history allegorically. That allegory sees the lover and beloved as representing Yahweh and Israel, or Christ and the church. I will not digress here to discuss

---

be understood as a woman who exemplifies the idea of Prov 31:10-31. Interestingly, such an identification not only makes Ruth an example of a virtuous woman, but also provides a link between redemptive history and wisdom.

21. For fuller treatments of the redemptive-historical and eschatological arrangement of the Psalter, see Vos, "Eschatology of the Psalter"; and Mitchell, *Message of the Psalter.*

how compelling such an allegory is from a modern vantage point, only to say that it is not as superficial as many in the more modern history of interpretation have argued. Allegorical interpretation is not an embarrassed effort to neutralize the sexual language and imagery of the book. Rather, allegorical interpretation, ironically, has a deep redemptive-historical impulse. The allegorical interpretation is consistent not only with the redemptive-historical framework of the OT, but with the apparent characteristic of the Writings to comment or otherwise be connected to redemptive history. The redemptive-historical connection can also be seen by viewing the Song in light of the garden of Eden: healthy sexuality is a return to the "pre-fall" state. This connection further draws into the discussion Israel's understanding of the temple, particularly the Holy of Holies, as somehow representative of or reflecting sexual union.[22] Both allegory and the "return to Eden" motif connect the Song with redemptive history on a deep level.

Proverbs, being essentially a collection of sayings, is not as amenable to a redemptive-historical reading, but here too we should not rush to judgment. An important theological element introduced in Proverbs and developed further in Israel's noncanonical wisdom tradition is, as mentioned above, the intimate connection between wisdom and creation. To speak of wisdom as a "tree of life" (Prov 3:18; 11:30) clearly evokes images of the very beginning of Israel's redemptive-history journey, the Garden of Eden. Attaining wisdom is to attain the very life forfeited by Adam and Eve. The more explicit creation connection is developed in 8:22-31, certainly one of the focal moments in chapters 1–9. Having just extolled wisdom as the source of power and wise rule (8:14-17) and wealth (vv. 18-21), the writer presents his final case for why wisdom is to be followed at all cost: she is from of old, the firstborn of Yahweh, with him before any created thing existed. This connection between wisdom and creation provides the motivation for the son in Proverbs 1–9 to listen to wisdom, hence the concluding call for the son to listen to wise instruction and by doing so to find life rather than to love death (vv. 32-36). Proverbs, in other words, is far more than a collection of "wise sayings to live by." The one who is wise is intimate with all of creation (recall Solomon's activities in 1 Kgs 4:29-34) and the Creator himself. This, I would argue, is an articulate redemptive-historical statement. The one who is wise is, like Wisdom herself, intimate with the Creator-God. The moral maxims that fill the remainder of the book are to be understood in terms of this foundational, generative, redemptive-historical act. To be wise is not to be "good" or "moral" but to participate in the Creator-God's pattern of social order. The end goal of Israel's redemptive-historical journey

22. Davidson, "Theology of Sexuality"; idem, *Flame of Yahweh*, 545-605.

is to reflect the presence of God, to embody moral and social order, in every corner of reality. The book of Proverbs gives glimpses of what this fully formed, redemptive-historical, in-tune Israelite looks like.

We now move to Job, which is most like Ecclesiastes. Both have as their literary focus an individual, and that individual is the vehicle by which the author makes his theological point. As much as Job is presented as a story of an individual sufferer,[23] the story also contains some redemptive-historical impulses. I do not mean to argue that one reading must necessarily dominate the other. I do, however, wish to draw out legitimate redemptive-historical impulses of the book that others have already commented on, but that do not always enter into the discussion. In brief, Job, read on a nationalistic level, is a "return-from-exile" story. Many of these redemptive-historical connections are observed by juxtaposing Job and Isaiah.

For instance, consider that in 42:7-17 Job receives back literally double for his sufferings, whether sheep, camels, oxen, donkeys, and his seven sons and three daughters are replaced. Many have noted how unsatisfying this would be on an individual level to receive "replacement children" for those lost. But perhaps the individual level is not primary here.[24] Note that according to Isa 40:2 Israel, in returning from exile, has received double for all their sins, meaning the redemptive situation is twice as good as the preexilic situation. Further, Job 42:10 provides an inviting redemptive-historical connection. This verse is translated in the NIV: "After Job had prayed for his friends, *the* LORD *made him prosperous again* and gave him twice as much as he had before." The italicized portion is translated in other English Bibles: "The LORD restored Job's fortunes" (NASB, RSV, NRSV). The Hebrew phrase, however, suggests a different translation.

וַיהוה שָׁב אֶת-שְׁבִית [Qere שְׁבוּת] אִיּוֹב/wayhwh šāb ʾet-šĕbût ʾîyôb

A more literal translation would yield something like: "Yahweh turned the captivity of Job," which is in some sense reflected in the translations above. What is of interest, however, is the use of שָׁב אֶת-שְׁבִית/שְׁבוּת/šāb ʾet-šĕbît/ šĕbût elsewhere in the OT to refer to Israel's restoration from exile. For example, in Deut 30:1-3 we read that if Israel "turns" (שׁוּב/šûb) to God (repents), then God will "turn with respect to your captivity" (וְשָׁב . . . אֶת-שְׁבוּתְךָ/

---

23. Well known, for example, are the "Babylonian Job" (*Ludlul bēl nēmeqi*) and the "Babylonian Theodicy" (Lambert, *Babylonian Wisdom Literature*, 21-62, 63-91, respectively).

24. Note, however, Balentine's comment that "Job's possessions are a tangible confirmation of his unparalleled piety" and that reward "eventually comes to those who remain faithful to God" (*Job*, 715).

wĕšāb . . . *'et-šĕbûtĕkā*), that is, he will have "compassion" and "gather" the people he scattered. This language is picked up by the prophets, namely Jeremiah and Ezekiel, and used to describe the reversal of the conditions of exile in general,[25] and especially the reversal of Israel's "Babylonian captivity."[26]

Where does this leave us? We should be careful not to overread these data, as if they demonstrate a nationalistic reading of Job.[27] We should remember that Job is a non-Israelite, a man from Uz, and so one might well question whether Job is capable of bearing a redemptive-historical interpretation. On the other hand, just as quickly as Job is introduced as Gentile, he is brought into an Israelite sphere, being the topic of conversation in Yahweh's council. Moreover, he is also presented as a worshiper of Yahweh. Recall, too, that Job is referred to by Yahweh as "my servant Job" in 1:8 and 2:3, and then again in 42:7 and 8. A number of individuals are referred to this way,[28] but given the nationalistic tone struck thus far, this evokes images of the Suffering Servant of Isaiah. J. C. Bastiaens observes that "Job's speeches in chapters 16, 17 and 19 contain lexical units and syntagmatical patterns that are reminiscent of the texts about the Suffering Servant" of Isaiah.[29] The fact that Job and the Suffering Servant share the "language of suffering"[30] suggests that Job's status as suffering servant also reflects nationalistic concerns. This reading was adopted by Rabbi Eliezer b. Elijah Ashkenazi (1513-1586), who identified Job with Israel:

---

25. Jer 48:47 (Moab); 49:6 (Ammon), 39 (Elam); Ezek 29:14 (Egypt).

26. Jer 29:14; 30:3, 18; 31:23 (Qal); 32:44; 33:7 (bis), 11, 26 (Hiphil); Ezek 16:53 (3 times, Qal); 39:25; Hos 6:11; Amos 9:14; Zeph 2:7; 3:20 (Qal); Joel 3:1 (MT 4:1) (Hiphil).

27. This very matter has not received its due attention, in part because this precise Hebrew phrasing noted in the previous paragraph is nowhere else used with an individual as its subject (Hartley, *Job*, 540).

28. For example, Abraham (Gen 26:24), Moses (Num 12:7), Caleb (Num 14:24), and David (2 Sam 3:18). Nebuchadnezzar, another non-Israelite, is called "my servant" in Jer 25:9; 27:6; 43:10.

29. Bastiaens, "Language of Suffering," 421.

30. Ibid., 432. Working from a wider range of connections, Hartley comes to a similar conclusion: "The interplay between Isaiah and Job leads to the hypothesis that one of these two authors was well acquainted with the other's work. . . . It seems most likely that the author wrote before Isaiah, for he only alludes to the vicarious merit of innocent suffering; Isaiah develops this theme fully. If this position is correct, the message of the book of Job prepared the people to receive and understand Isaiah's bold new message that God was going to redeem his people and the world through the innocent suffering of his obedient Servant" (*Job*, 15). Hartley's point is well taken, although I am not as confident in positing Isaiah's dependence on Job. If anything, Job's suffering servant makes more sense as a brief allusion to a well-established motif, rather than the impetus for such a developed tradition as one sees in Isaiah.

Now you will also find that the rabbis said that Job was only created as a symbolic figure. In other words, he was a symbol for Israel as a consolation for them, in that first he prospered in every respect, then he was more abased than anyone who had gone before him, and finally he was raised up with his prosperity redoubled. So too the Israelite nation was once decidedly prosperous, then humiliated in this miserable exile. In the messianic age, their prosperity will be redoubled.[31]

More specifically Ashkenazi makes the connection with Isaiah's Suffering Servant: "Look, and you will discover that all of Isaiah's words in this passage [Isaiah 53] can be found precisely among the words of Job." He adduces no less that eighteen verbal correspondences between Job and Isaiah 53.[32]

The issue is whether these signals warrant reading Job nationalistically (without excluding the traditional individualistic dimension). In my view a nationalistic reading is signaled strongly enough in Job to yield such a conclusion. Still, not everyone will be convinced by such signals, gleaned as they are by broader and subjective canonical observations. I respect this criticism; indeed, I have little quibble with it. Biblical theology is not restricted to the theological limits of the text in its precanonical state. The biblical-theological task opens up responsible, possible readings of *canonical* (OT and NT) Scripture.

---

31. See Cooper, "Suffering Servant and Job."

32. Ibid. (1) "Behold, *my servant* will prosper" (Isa 52:13) // "*my servant* Job" (Job 1:8; 2:3; 42:7, 8); (2) "Many were *appalled* at you (Isa 52:14)" // "Look at me and be *appalled*" (Job 21:5); (3) "His appearance was marred, unhuman" (Isa 52:14) // "When they saw him from a distance, they could not recognize him" (Job 2:12); (4) "They shall *look upon* what they have not heard" (Isa 52:15) // "I wait, but you do not *look upon* me" (Job 30:20); (5) "Upon whom has the arm of the Lord been revealed?" (Isa 53:1) // "God revealed himself to Job and told him of all His mighty acts"; (6) "He was *despised,* shunned by men" (Isa 53:3) // "The *contempt* of families shatters me" (Job 31:34); (7) "A man of *suffering*" (Isa 53:3) // "His *suffering* was very great" (Job 2:13); (8) "The Lord has *afflicted* him" (Isa 53:6) // "Why make me the object of your *affliction?*" (Job 7:20); (9) "*Crushed* by our iniquities" (Isa 53:5) // "If only God wanted to *crush* me" (Job 6:9); (10) "He had no beauty, that we should *look upon* him" (Isa 53:2) // "The eye that *looks upon* me will not see me" (Job 7:8); (11) "As one who *hid* his face" (Isa 53:3) // "To the man whose way is *hidden*" (Job 3:23); (12) "His *grave* was set among the wicked" (Isa 53:9) // "My days have run out; the *grave* awaits me" (Job 17:1); (13) "Though he had done *no injustice*" (Isa 53:9) // "For *no injustice* on my part" (Job 16:17); (14) "And had spoken no *falsehood*" (Isa 53:9) // "My tongue will utter no *falsehood*" (Job 27:4); (15) "Out of the *anguish* of his soul" (Isa 53:11) // "Nights of *anguish* are allotted to me" (Job 7:3); (16) "He exposed himself to *death*" (Isa 53:12) // "I prefer strangulation, *death*" (Job 7:15); (17) "He was numbered among *sinners*" (Isa 53:12) // "My *sins* are wrapped in a bundle" (Job 14:17); and (18) "He shall see offspring and have long life" (Isa 53:10) // "[Job] also had seven sons and three daughters. . . . Afterward, Job lived one hundred and forty years" (Job 42:13, 16).

Even for those who do not share that same hermeneutical conviction, the less ambitious point I wish to make is that each of the Writings evinces some redemptive-historical quality, even if that quality rests beneath a surface reading of the text. As I see it, Job is more than a book of private significance — or of the "problem of suffering" in general. It is, rather, a book that seems to lend itself to be read on one level as a parable of the struggles of the Suffering Servant in exile.

With this digression into Job, we are prepared to take a look at Ecclesiastes and its contribution to this aspect of biblical theology. Since Ecclesiastes was written sometime in the postexilic period, we must consider this period to understand the theology of the book. Although a postexilic date for Ecclesiastes is about as firm a conclusion as one can achieve in biblical scholarship, the specific era during that period remains debated. Following Seow, I accept the basic position of a date in the Persian period, as outlined in the introduction. Others prefer a Hellenistic date, a position that has been ably defended in the history of modern scholarship, most recently in a monograph by Leo G. Perdue, in which he attempts to place Ecclesiastes and all of Israel's wisdom traditions in their historical contexts.[33] Without wanting to minimize these scholarly differences, I do not think it is absolutely vital to the biblical-theological task to settle on either option. True, greater clarity in terms of historical setting would yield greater theological clarity, but a firm date cannot be fully determined.

What is known, however, is the postexilic dating of Ecclesiastes. The central theological issue raised for Israel during this period is its national and religious self-definition amid the utter cataclysm of their exile from no less than the promised land and subjection to Gentile rule. It is a truism to say that the significance of the events preceding and following the exile to Babylon cannot be overstated for our understanding of Israel's struggles to understand how, if at all, they are still the people of God, still God's chosen vessel to bring blessing to the nations, that the God of Abraham, Moses, and David remains their God.

Unlike the other Writings, the contribution of Ecclesiastes to biblical theology is in its relentless probing of the justice and even goodness of God. We will look more below at the personal/spiritual implications of such a theological posture, but here I want to focus on what this says about a nation in crisis. Israel's exile ended in 539 B.C. only in terms of its location. Functionally the exile continued as long as the land was not under Israelite rule.[34]

33. Perdue, *Sword and Stylus*, esp. 219-55.
34. The claim that Israel's exile did not functionally end with the return from Babylon is

They may have occupied the land. They may have rebuilt the temple, a shell of its former self. But as long as the king is not seated on the throne in Jerusalem ruling God's chosen people as his earthly representative, then "Israel" in the biblical sense does not truly exist. And the longer this state of affairs continues, the longer they remain alienated from their divine purpose.

Moreover, the more comfortable the people feel in their new circumstances, the greater the disconnect is with their past. The temptation to assimilate to Gentile ways was indeed ever-present for Israel. The story is told in Daniel and is recounted in other stories throughout the Second Temple period. What was at stake was not simply having Gentiles rule over Jews and Jews adopting Gentile ways, thus becoming less distinguishable. What was at stake was that this process of assimilation threatened Israel's role among the nations as expressed to Abraham in Gen 12:1-3. Israel was neither to assimilate with the nations nor was it merely to be separate among the nations. The children of Abraham were to have been a holy (separate) nation that would embody Yahweh's pattern of conduct and in doing so would be blessed by God and be a blessing to the nations (Gen 12:1-3). Israel's role was to be a missionary one simply by being a holy people of the true God. Or, to put it in the words of Exod 19:6, Israel was delivered from Egypt in order to be a "kingdom of priests and a holy nation." As a holy nation of priests, Israel's mediatory role vis-à-vis the nations is stressed. Israel was never meant to be like the nations, and certainly not ruled by them. They were the children of Abraham, the redeemed of Egypt, who were to be the light on the hill for the nations to see and stream toward them.

This redemptive-historical context is one in which we can consider the theology of Ecclesiastes, particularly Qohelet's complaints. Our author finds himself in a postexilic setting, which, as mentioned above, is still an "exile" of sorts. But rather than asking "how long?" or repenting and renewing his commitment to Torah obedience, he is pondering a much darker scenario: What if God is the problem? What if he is not just? What if everything we have heard about Yahweh, his goodness, is all a sham? What if we are born, live lives of toil and stress, and then die, like animals? What if God is responsible

---

debated. The position is argued quite energetically by Wright (*New Testament and the People of God*, 280-338). The debate is well summarized by Fuller, who interacts with Wright and focuses on the theme of regathering in early Jewish literature (*Restoration of Israel*). Although only a small percentage of Jews may have been affected by the exile, it was "remembered as *the collective experience of all Jews*" (1-2). Continued domination by Greeks and Romans led Jews to reevaluate the restoration of Ezra-Nehemiah in the sixth century and push back "Israel's definitive return" to the "eschatological future" (22-23). See too Evans, "Jesus and Continuing Exile." The debate is summarized in more detail in Newman, ed., *Jesus and Restoration*.

for all of this? The cauldron of suffering can cook a mean brew, one that a landed people, comfortable in their daily existence, may never taste. This book expresses, through the voice of the king, the despair of a *people,* far removed from the relative serenity of the monarchic period, who have had enough. It is only with the frame narrator that the readers are told to move toward Torah obedience rather than remaining in such a state.

The writer of Ecclesiastes speaks to Israel through the Solomonic/royal persona, which permeates the book despite the tone of criticism toward kingship that Qohelet takes after the opening chapters.[35] The king speaks and the implied audience is the people. Perdue puts it well when he describes the writer as portraying himself "as Solomon who speaks from the grave."[36] Solomon is back, addressing a people who had gone through much in the intervening centuries. Or perhaps better put, the exasperation of a people is put on the lips of the great and wise king from days of old. This royal dimension already goes a long way to putting the book as a whole in conversation with redemptive history. Ecclesiastes is a book for the people, to speak to Israel's self-definition in some way. It is not a book that simply describes the inner psychology or spiritual despair of a single Solomonic figure or of individuals who suffer similarly. Rather, the inner psychology and despair of King Qohelet are used to speak of Israel's plight.

What Ecclesiastes says on a nationalistic level is that, despite the ravages of the exile and the subsequent generations, Israel is still connected to God, even though every impulse is to the contrary. To be sure, the only place where that constructive connection to Elohim is made is in 12:13-14 — when the frame narrator admonishes Israel to continue fearing God and keeping his commandments — but that is enough. The book's relentless focus is on the deeply felt sense of disconnect between Israel and its covenant God. Qohelet gives voice to the people's anger at being abandoned by God. This abandonment is not simply a matter of being captive in a foreign land or being subject to Gentiles. It is a much deeper sense of resignation that flows from these things. We can only imagine the emotional toll of the paradigm shift that occurred in the Israelite psyche in the generations following the departure from the promised land. Who are we? Where do we belong? Where is God when you need him? What happened to all the promises? The words of Qohelet are

35. I suspect that one of the reasons for the "misplaced" third person reference in 7:27 is to remind readers that King Qohelet is still speaking, despite the critical turn he has already begun to take.

36. Perdue, *Sword and Stylus,* 249. Incidentally, such an understanding of the royal persona would suggest that 1:12 be translated, "I, Qohelet, *was* (הָיִיתִי/*hāyîtî*) king over Israel in Jerusalem," rather than "am" (as I argue) or "have been."

a vehicle through which the captives lash out at God, questioning such previously unquestionable things as God's ultimate goodness and justice, the benefits of wisdom, the meaningfulness of life vis-à-vis death, the benefit of wealth and hard work, the enjoyment of simple pleasures. Qohelet takes no prisoners. The relentless complaint of Qohelet is a high-speed, supercharged version of any lament found in Scripture, going as far as one can conceivably go — declaring that God himself is the problem. Qohelet's lament gives voice to the lament of the people.

To read Ecclesiastes is not simply an exercise in glimpsing someone's internal spiritual struggles. It explicates, from one vantage point, a moment in redemptive history. Ecclesiastes participates in the overall drama of the people of God. It presents a tone of utter despair prompted by Israel's reflection of its own place in God's economy in light of disorientation — and reorientation — of the exile and its aftermath. None of this is to suggest that Ecclesiastes can and should be read only on this nationalistic level. Ecclesiastes certainly has significant value as a theological statement on the individual level, as we will explore later. Nevertheless, as Scripture, we must presume that Ecclesiastes is not dissociated from Israel's redemptive-historical metanarrative. Like other books among the Writings, Ecclesiastes can and should be read as contributing to our understanding of Israel's journey as the people of God. A redemptive-historical reading is a dimension of the theology of Ecclesiastes that should not be neglected if one is aiming at recovering the theology of the OT for the church.

Moving Forward

Thus far we have looked at the contribution of Ecclesiastes and the other Writings to the biblical-theological scope of the OT. There is always much more that can be said, but I have restricted myself thus far to two important biblical-theological issues concerning Ecclesiastes: (1) Ecclesiastes and wisdom, and (2) Ecclesiastes and Israel's story (Ecclesiastes as a commentary on Israel's national lament). On the second point, I have offered some reflections on how a redemptive-historical understanding of the OT affects our reading of Ecclesiastes, and consequently how Ecclesiastes contributes to our understanding of redemptive history.

As we continue our theological reflections, it is important to remember that Israel's Scripture was an expression of self-definition, that is, what it meant to be the people of God, particularly when God and Israel seemed so distant from each other. As with any religious expression, modern or ancient, such separation is felt on a deeply personal level. But again, Israel's Scripture was not focused on telling individual stories for individual benefit, but on telling the story of Israel as the people of God. As far as the church is concerned, Israel's story does not end with Israel but continues in the crucified and risen Christ and how he successfully embodies Israel's mission, and how his newly constituted people of God participates in that mission. By saying that Israel's story, including Ecclesiastes, reaches its climax in the death and resurrection of Christ, I am not arguing that one should read Ecclesiastes to point out superficial Christological connections or to "see" Christ in Ecclesiastes. Rather, I am advocating a process of understanding anew the various chapters of Israel's story in the light of how Christians confess that God himself chose to end that story, and of allowing the earlier chapters of that story to deepen our understanding of the meaning and significance of that climactic episode. Such a "Christotelic" exercise (see the introduction, "Reading Ecclesiastes Christianly") is not mechanical, nor are its results exhaustive or final. Rather, entering through the hermeneutical door that the NT authors themselves have opened for us, we seek to be ever more faithful in understanding Christ according to the Scriptures, and the Scriptures according to Christ. This is how, hermeneutically speaking, we bear witness to the centrality of the death and resurrection of Christ for all of life, including, most certainly, how we engage Scripture.

Ecclesiastes and the Son of God

Having just briefly explored the theology of Ecclesiastes vis-à-vis the other wisdom books, the lament psalms, and the exile, we will now expand our scope to the NT. In this section we will look at how several theological themes in Ecclesiastes can be brought to bear on our understanding of Christ's climactic role of embodying Israel's mission. In the next section we will explore how some of these theological themes can bring greater clarity to our understanding of what it means to be the body of Christ.

Jesus, the Suffering King

As we move to a consideration of the biblical-theological connections between Ecclesiastes and the NT, it is understandable that we will reflect on what the NT has to say on the life of the NT *believer*, highlighting perhaps issues of suffering and doubt that are part of the Christian life. Before we explore that avenue, however, there is another biblical-theological possibility before us, one that may not come immediately to mind. Rather than thinking first of the connections between Qohelet's and the Christian's despair and doubt, could we find any value in exploring how Jesus embodies the role of Qohelet? On one level this may strike us as utter nonsense, as it is hard to imagine nearly any of Qohelet's words ever falling on Jesus' lips. There is, however, at least one aspect of Ecclesiastes that lends itself to some Christological connections, and that will also bring into sharper relief the more overt theological connections between Ecclesiastes and the church.

This connection is seen in Qohelet's kingly identity and how that king has explored suffering and despair on a far deeper level than any of his subjects could hope to. This is the theological force behind the royal identification of Qohelet. As the king, he has at his disposal the needed resources to explore everything under the sun. Not only would these be natural resources, but also the requisite wisdom (e.g., 1:12-18). This is why the son is warned not to add to Qohelet's words, and, although Qohelet is deemed wise by the frame narrator, he also shuts off further discussion (12:12-13). Qohelet has already explored the depths, peered over the edge, gone as far as one can go in despair. The son is told, "observe well, but you cannot go where the king has gone." Qohelet's royal persona is not simply a rhetorical device. He is the wise Solomonic king entering into a state of alienation from God that is unique in Israel's Scripture. His suffering is in no way vicarious, but it is *representative*, as any king of Israel was representative of his people.

We have in Qohelet a wise king who at every turn, like his subjects, feels the abandonment of God. Do we hear any echoes between the wise king, with his sense of gaping distance between himself and his God, and Jesus, likewise a son of David, a wise king, and his sense of God's abandonment? Even though Qohelet is not a "type" of Christ to the same degree as one might want to argue for many other OT figures, I see considerable value in posing Qohelet's "dark night of the soul" with that of Jesus.

I am suggesting that inasmuch as we can see the suffering of the Davidic king in Psalm 22 (for example) as adumbrating in some sense Christ's sense of abandonment on the cross, so too can we read the words of Qohelet. I am not equating, say, "My God, my God, why have you forsaken me?" (Ps 22:1), with "it is a grievous burden God has laid on man" (Eccl 1:13). I am not suggesting that the words of Qohelet would be found on Jesus' lips, nor does drawing out this theological connection require it. I am suggesting, however, that the sense of utter despair that Qohelet experiences — which makes readers today wish to turn the page to get to the resolution more quickly — can help readers gain perhaps a sense of Jesus' experience of abandonment. For both, the experience was real. In neither case does a narrator interject that the fact of the matter is really different than the king's experiences. God did indeed abandon Christ. His reference to Ps 22:1 was not a flourish but a statement of fact (with atoning, vicarious results). It is most curious, as we have had occasion to remark at various junctures, that the frame narrator likewise does not neuter Qohelet's experience by casting doubt on his wisdom, blaming *him* for his experiences or denying his reality. Rather, the frame narrator says, "What Qohelet has written is upright and true. Now move on, my son, and remember your calling as an Israelite to fear and obey."

We may go so far as to suggest that Qohelet is *vindicated* in the epilogue. One might conclude with Qohelet's words in 12:7 and remark that such language is unbecoming of any follower of Yahweh, let alone a king, and so some criticism is in order. But none is found. Frankly, I find 12:9-10 to be wholly unexpected and among the more jarring words we find in all of the OT. After all that Qohelet has said, eventually attacking God and his ways, we read, "not only was Qohelet wise . . . he imparted knowledge . . . what he wrote was upright and true." The reader is left with little choice but to accept Qohelet's observations. I do not think, however, that Qohelet's vindication is simply a "historical" observation on the frame narrator's part concerning a Solomonic king. The entire point of Ecclesiastes — the reason, I would venture to say, it was included among Israel's self-defining documents — is what the *reader* is to do with the words of such a man who has been so vindicated. Qohelet's words were not recorded to give psychological insight into one man's struggles. Rather, they are meant to be understood as reflecting the thoughts of any Israelite anywhere when he/she walks down that lonesome road where God is nowhere to be seen (which includes the nationalistic level, as discussed above). Qohelet's experience is already a democratized experience, like that of the Psalms, when the focal point is not that of a biblical character but the Bible reader. This is why Eccl 12:13-14 is no mere pious addendum to keep Qohelet's words safe for consumption. They are the point for why Qohelet's words have been kept in Israel's embrace. The words of Qohelet are for "everyman," and when Qohelet's words find a home in one's life experiences, when the reader participates in the suffering of Qohelet, so to speak, that reader is reminded (1) that the experience is very real indeed and not to be neutered by pious nonsense, and (2) that the reader is to continue *through* the suffering in a continued posture of fear and obedience — keeping on being an Israelite, no matter what.

This is why Qohelet's experiences are catalogued for us in such relentless passion and detail. He truly has gone everywhere, and he everywhere comes to the same conclusion, at least eventually: God is not here. Jesus' alienation from God is not catalogued in similar detail, but the passion narrative is given paramount place in the four Gospels. The reason for this prominence is not simply to recount Jesus' suffering, but to remind the early church of the central importance of the community meal wherein the passion is not only recounted but actualized by the Christian community. According to Bo Reicke, it is this life setting of the early church that accounts for the coherence of the four passion narratives.[37] He attributes the absence of the Eucharist institution in John to the fact that his Gospel is directed to "outsiders and catechumens"; he cites John 20:31 in support.[38] To be sure, none of this in any way suggests that Jesus' suffering has merely exemplary force. Rather, the atoning and "wholly other" sense of Jesus' suffering is not merely an external act. The whole point of the Eucharist is how the church now participates in the suffering of Christ (regardless of how various church traditions have articulated the nature of this participation). In other words, in the Eucharist the church is answering the question, "What does the suffering of Christ have to do with us here?"

Both Ecclesiastes and the Gospels, therefore, are concerned to address not the experience merely of one, but of the many, in that the experience of the one is exemplary. Again, Jesus' suffering is not merely exemplary, but it is a model for the church, nonetheless — even to the point where the believers' suffering is participatory (Phil 3:10-11; Col 1:24). The question is not whether the believer will suffer, but when. And when that happens the believer understands something of what Christ himself endured, although not to its full extent. The full sense in which Christ was abandoned by God is inaccessible to any follower of Christ, but here again is the value of Qohelet's words — they model something of the depth of despair that comes from abandonment by God. They give believers a glimpse — only a glimpse — of the hopelessness and despair of Christ's passion. Even though readers of Qohelet's words may accuse him of being a bit over the top or even outright faithless (despite the frame narrator's evaluation), in a biblical-theological sense Qohelet does not go nearly far enough. He cannot. But he goes as far as one can go in painting a fierce, relentless picture of what such a state of alienation looks like. Readers then and now are told not to shy away from it, but to embrace it as their own — and to move on.

For Qohelet's Israelite audience, "moving on" means to continue down the path of faithful Israelite behavior. For the church, it means following the suffering King Jesus no matter what. Qohelet was "vindicated" by the frame

---

37. Reicke, *Roots of Synoptic Gospels,* 139-49, esp. 145.
38. Ibid., 149.

narrator in 12:9-12, and the way forward is recorded in 12:13-14. Jesus' vindication is of a very different sort but with similar implications. The true purpose of Jesus' passion is shown in his resurrection, and it is in the event complex of Jesus' passion *and* resurrection that his people are shown the way forward. Like Qohelet's readers, the church's dark night of the soul participates in that of the king, and in doing so is shown the pattern by which the lives of believers are to be governed. And as Qohelet's readers are told to fear God and keep his commands — that is, to continue being Israelites — those in Christ are told that they are united to the resurrected Christ and, even in despair, to follow him anyway — to continue being disciples — knowing that in doing so they will be more like him. For both the readers of Ecclesiastes and the church, the present and very real circumstances do not define ultimate reality. But the message of Ecclesiastes can hit home only if one accepts the suffering of Qohelet and passes through his despair with him. So too with Christ one will grasp the depth of the gospel message when one perceives more clearly the suffering of the king, how his suffering is truly "the end of the matter," and so see one's present suffering in the light of his greater suffering.

Jesus as Sage

The relationship between Jesus and Israel's wisdom tradition has received its fair share of attention.[39] In biblical-theological studies, however, the connections between Jesus and such OT offices as prophet, priest, and king have been more dominant. One reason for this, I suspect, reflects a larger problem of the absence of wisdom literature in the biblical-theological discussions earlier in the twentieth century, a problem that stems from the dominance of a strictly defined redemptive-historical paradigm in biblical theology.[40] I affirm that the role redemptive history plays is central to the structure of the OT, but I am also convinced that the Writings, including the wisdom literature, are not as out of alignment with redemptive history as some have assumed. Hence I would like to offer some suggestions concerning the general

---

39. For a valuable overview of wisdom's influences on Jesus and how Jesus influenced the wisdom tradition, see Witherington, *Jesus the Sage.*

40. For example, in von Rad's classic *Old Testament Theology* (approximately 900 pages), he devotes a scant forty pages to the topic (1:418-59). Of course, no one can accuse von Rad of neglecting the notion of wisdom altogether (see his *Wisdom in Israel*), but its relative absence from his *Old Testament Theology* is telling in its own right. Likewise, Eichrodt's equally influential and lengthy *Theology of the Old Testament* (over a thousand pages) devoted just over ten pages to the topic (2:80-92).

theme of Jesus as sage as a means of addressing the theological intersection between the sagely roles of Qohelet and Jesus.

First, as is well known, wisdom pervades the OT, and is not restricted to the so-called wisdom books. Significant scholarly work has been done in demonstrating the role wisdom plays in various sections and genres of the Hebrew canon: creation, the Joseph narrative, law, Deuteronomy, the Deuteronomistic History, the Chronicler's History, Psalms, prophets, apocalyptic, and others.[41] Wisdom continues to be a key theme in the NT.

One need only look at Jesus' early years, how in his youth he was "filled with wisdom" (Luke 2:40) and "grew in wisdom" (Luke 2:52). Wisdom marked his progression from boy to Messiah. One might say that becoming wise was part of his messianic calling — that Israel's sagely tradition informs Jesus of his messianic role. Wisdom also reflects on his kingly role (more typically connected with the notion of "messiah"), since kings were to be marked by wisdom. Think also of Jesus' parables. They show his understanding of the created order (birds, lilies, mustard seed, etc.), and how that order reflects on his hearers' sense of "moral order." And by speaking in parables Jesus spoke in such a way that people would *not* understand (e.g., Matt 13:13 and its use of Isa 6:9-10).[42] As announced in Prov 1:1-7, the words of the wise are for simple and wise alike, and involve the disciplined discernment of proverbs, parables, sayings, and riddles. It takes effort to understand wise words, and wise words are given in forms that reflect the profundity of the message. Parables are not "sermon illustrations" but part of Jesus' sagely repertoire.

Jesus' miracles can also be seen from the point of view of wisdom. Specifically, as Wisdom was with Yahweh from of old, from before any created thing (Prov 8:22-31), Jesus' ability to manipulate nature speaks to his intimacy with creation. The connection between miracles and wisdom is explicitly confirmed in Mark 6:2 (NIV), "What's this *wisdom* that has been given to

---

41. For creation see Alonso Schöckel, "Sapiential and Covenant Themes"; Perdue, "Cosmology and Social Order." For the Joseph narrative see von Rad, "Joseph Narrative and Ancient Wisdom." For law see Blenkinsopp, *Wisdom and Law.* For Deuteronomy see Weinfeld, *Deuteronomy and the Deuteronomic School.* For the Deuteronomistic History see McCarter, "Sage in Deuteronomistic History." For the Chronicler's History see Blenkinsopp, "Sage, Scribe." For the Psalms see Mowinckel, "Psalms and Wisdom." For the prophets see Lindblom, "Wisdom in Old Testament Prophets." For apocalyptic see Collins, "Wisdom, Apocalyptic, and Generic Compatibility."

42. Witherington refers to Jesus' sayings in ch. 13 as a "collection of narrative *meshalim,* further evidence that Jesus is Wisdom speaking and speaking in Wisdom form" (*Jesus the Sage,* 362). Further, this mode of "not understanding," according to Witherington, is descriptive of the "need for both revelation with further explication" in the development of mature disciples of Christ (363).

him, that he even does *miracles!*" (see also Matt 13:54). Miracles are a sagely activity.

Likewise we see Jesus' ability to confound the teaching of the Pharisees with little effort. Jesus was able to outwit them; despite their profound learning, they lacked wisdom. We see this presaged in his youth, where he amazed the teachers of Israel with his "understanding and answers" (Luke 2:47). It is typical to understand this aspect of Jesus' ministry as a dimension of his prophetic role: Jesus speaks authoritatively to rebellious leaders. There is certainly something to be said for this, particularly in view of the fact that prophetic and sagely roles are not mutually exclusive. Still, it adds a dimension of depth to see Jesus' effortless and attractive ability to confound the Pharisees as an aspect of his sagely role.

Likewise, Jesus roaming the countryside and calling people to repentance reflects Proverbs 1–9, where Lady Wisdom calls in the streets for the simple to heed her message. She is in competition with Lady Folly, who is also on the lookout to convince the simple to follow her. Jesus may be thought of as an itinerant "preacher" (a possible meaning of the name Qohelet), but again, focusing on the theme of prophetic proclamation can obscure the biblical-theological richness of Jesus' activity. Wisdom stood in the public squares and noisy streets, calling in a loud voice for any who would heed her call (Prov. 1:20-21; 8:1-11). Jesus too went where the people are, to show them the benefits of following him. His public proclamations were the final concretization of personified Wisdom's call in Proverbs 1–9.

The Synoptic traditions demonstrate the sagely dimension of Jesus' preaching. In Matt 7:24-29 (par.),[43] Jesus compares those who hear and do what he says to *wise* men who build their house on the rock. *Foolish* men build on the sand. This is a classic wisdom theme: putting into practice what is wise. And Jesus' words, unlike those of the teachers of the law, had authority because they reflect his wisdom. The teachers knew the law, but they lacked wisdom, as seen in their hypocrisy, their failure to put into practice what they say they believe and they themselves teach. Likewise, in Matt 24:45 (par.), Jesus praises the "faithful and *wise* servant" for *doing* what the master commanded. Again, this focus on right actions, that is, righteousness, is a ubiquitous wisdom theme from the OT, which Jesus simply seems to be carrying through in his own ministry. The parable of the ten virgins (Matt 25:1-13) likewise begins by describing five as foolish and five as wise. The wise virgins were those who remained alert and vigilant in bringing with them the necessary oil. The foolish ones did not

---

43. For a helpful book-length treatment of Matthew's portrayal of Jesus as personified Wisdom, see Deutsch, *Lady Wisdom*.

think to plan ahead. In Matt 11:19 (par.) Jesus is accused of being very unwise — a glutton and drunkard (e.g., Prov 23:20) — but Jesus responds, "wisdom is proved right by her actions" (NIV; Luke 7:35 has "all her children"). This indicates further the inextricable connection between true wisdom and behavior — wisdom will, eventually, be made plain, despite the unjust accusations and clever argumentation of a ruling party.

In one example, Jesus' self-attestation to his wisdom is particularly clear. In Matt 12:39 (par.) Jesus chides his hearers who ask for a miraculous sign. In response, Jesus appeals to the Queen of Sheba as an illustration (1 Kgs 10:1-13). She came from "the ends of the earth" (i.e., southwest Arabia) to pay homage to Solomon for his wisdom. Yet someone greater than Solomon was before them, and they were asking for a sign. A mark of his messianic identity was wisdom, a mark that was hidden from the foolish.

Highlighting the intersection between the OT wisdom tradition and Jesus not only adds biblical-theological depth to the person and work of Christ, but also offers insights into the canonical-theological contribution of Ecclesiastes. Qohelet is presented to his readers at the outset as a king and at the end as a sage. To be sure, Qohelet's wisdom, as we have seen the frame narrator declare, is not meant to be duplicated. This is an important and obvious difference between the wisdom of Qohelet's observations and Jesus' teachings and declarations. But Qohelet's wisdom is not called into question. This raises the issue that, in a way, encapsulates the entire debate over the meaning and interpretation of Ecclesiastes: In what sense is Qohelet wise, as the frame narrator claims? This question is particularly challenging when Qohelet and Jesus are juxtaposed. To be clear, the point of this comparison is not to make Qohelet into a Jesus-figure of some sort, least of all to redeem him somehow. The point is to see how true wisdom themes are evident in both of their activities, and so bring greater depth of theological understanding to both.

From several angles we can compare the sagely activity of Qohelet with that of Christ. For one thing, both make direct and unapologetic observations on the nature of life, based on "empirical" evidence, namely looking about and drawing conclusions from what they see. With Qohelet, this is adumbrated in the frame narrator's appeal to creation — sun, wind, and sea — to demonstrate the absurdity of life (1:5-7). Qohelet's appeal to nature echoes those of Jesus. "Consider the lilies, the bird, the mustard seed" is not that far removed from "consider the sun, wind, and sea." To be sure, they come to very different conclusions and they make their observations for very different reasons, but this does not mean that Qohelet is thereby unwise. The wisdom of these appeals to nature is in the nature of the appeals — lessons are drawn from the observable world. This is something the wise do.

Likewise, Qohelet's observations in 3:1-8 touch on the natural world ("a time to plant and a time to uproot," etc.). More often, however, they concern the realm of human activities. This is characteristic of Qohelet's speeches throughout: death, toil, kingly tasks, oppression, advancement, and so on. Much of what fuels Qohelet's speeches is his investigation of the daily activities of humanity, how all of them eventually come to naught. Jesus also finds the subject of his parables in the observation of human activity: debt, oil for lamps, sheep, coins, management of funds, widows, tax collectors, and so on. Drawing from common experience, Jesus uses those well-known features for the purpose of making a very profound, often counterintuitive, point about the kingdom of God. Qohelet's lessons are also counterintuitive for those versed in Israel's wisdom tradition, and more often than not move from the counterintuitive to the downright disturbing. Once again, the end effect of their speeches is different, but that does not mean that Qohelet is less a sage in the nature of his observations.

Another point of contact between Jesus and Qohelet is that both critique the power structures of their day. As we saw above, this is also a dimension of Jesus' prophetic role, since a central element of the prophetic voice is to call to account corrupt leadership (e.g., Hab 1:1-4; Malachi). I do not wish to minimize that aspect, but we have also seen how confrontation of corruption is a sagely activity as well. Proverbs has much for every reader, but a theme of Proverbs is whether those in some position of power are behaving righteously. This can concern topics like kingship, wealth, accurate scales, servants, justice, the poor, pride, and knowledge. Qohelet's criticisms of kingship in the latter portions of the book fall under this category (4:13-16; 8:1-17). Qohelet, the royal-sage figure, critiques kingship. So too Jesus, the Messiah (i.e., Davidic king), critiques the leaders of Israel for duplicity and hypocrisy.

Allowing the figures of Qohelet and Jesus to cast light on each other yields two theologically pertinent conclusions. First, it allows us to grasp more clearly the real sagely character of Qohelet. Again, this should not be misunderstood as a way of lessening the offense of Qohelet's words — which are themselves wisdom for the frame narrator. Quite the opposite: we are forced to comply with the frame narrator's intention for readers to pay attention to what this sage is saying. By seeing how Qohelet's words reflect genuine wisdom patterns, however, the frame narrator's evaluation of Qohelet may not seem quite as surprising — and may even seem self-evident, at least to a degree. Second, it puts certain aspects of Jesus' ministry in a slightly different light. By understanding his preaching as a Qohelet-like activity, we may be able to hear more clearly the offense of Jesus' words — their counterintuitive and countercultural character. This holds irrespective of the fact that Jesus does not come to the same conclusion as Qohelet, or, to put it more directly, Jesus does not share Qohelet's theology — but to connect Jesus to Qohelet does not require that we bridge this theological gap. This is typically carried out by dulling the offense and alleged heterodoxy of Qohelet's words, so as to bring him more in line with more dominant biblical expressions. Instead, the connection between Qohelet and Jesus is seen in the offensiveness and even heterodoxy of both *in their contexts*. Remember that Jesus' words were taken as blasphemy and otherwise counter to the Jewish tradition. Both are carrying out their sagely duties, albeit in very different ways. To mute that unique witness is itself unwise.

The End

The end plays a role for both Qohelet and Jesus, albeit once again in different ways. On one level, the end pertains to the death of the individual. As we have seen time and time again, death for Qohelet is the final and unavoidable stage of an absurd life — or better, the final stage that invariably renders all of life absurd. Qohelet is quite obsessed with death. Jesus is not, and where he does mention it, it does not hold the same note of despair as it does for Qohelet. Jesus sees death as the inevitable end, but, as distinct from Qohelet, he speaks of an afterlife and the reality of God's judgment there. As we have seen, Qohelet is adamant that such things are utterly unknowable, and therefore one would be foolish to look to such things to provide meaning. The only place where the two sages seem to intersect is that death is a sober reminder of what will be. For Qohelet, it is the end by which we gauge our daily affairs. Oddly enough, Jesus does something similar in the story of the rich man and Lazarus (Luke 16:19-31). There the reality of death and judgment is mentioned as a warning to live a life consistent with Moses and the Prophets. For Qohelet, death is what makes the pursuit of simple pleasures the best that life has to offer.

One of the places where Jesus parts company with Qohelet is in his unquestioned acceptance not only of an afterlife, but of the reality of judgment in the afterlife. The afterlife is not a central topic in OT theology at any rate, and certainly the matter of eschatological judgment for the individual is a sublimated theme at best (Dan 12:1-2 is the one lone example). Death is characterized as a state of "sleep" (Ps 13:3), a place where Yahweh is not praised (Pss 6:5; 30:9), as being "gathered" to one's people, meaning buried in one's homeland with great ceremony (Gen 49:29–50:14). It is not a place of final judgment. But, as we have seen in the introduction, death becomes a dominant concept in Qohelet's thinking, and he concludes that any attempt to paint a smiling face on all of this is utterly futile. So, although both Qohelet and Jesus use death as a teaching tool, so to speak, they employ it for very different purposes and for very different ends. The explanation for this difference seems to be twofold: (1) Qohelet's strictly empirical epistemology, where the afterlife is unobservable, and (2) developments in the Jewish notion of the afterlife during the Second Temple period, which formed the backdrop of Jesus' words.[44] If anything, this illustrates the critical importance of understanding the cultural setting of biblical writers in assessing their theological contributions. Reconciling Qohelet and Jesus on the issue of death is not where our theological energies should be focused, if our purpose to do so is to enforce superficial theological conformity between them. If, however, such an exercise is plainly called for what it is, a midrashic exercise in canonical theological creativity, then perhaps some theological value can result, not because a particular apologetic has been satisfied, but because the dialogue between portions of Scripture that evince such theological differences can encourage creative theological thinking.

This somewhat divergent point notwithstanding, the issue before us is that for Jesus the afterlife is a place of judgment. For Qohelet, since one cannot count on an afterlife, it is a useless theological category. Death is a central theological category because it is empirically verifiable; afterlife and judgment are not because they cannot be verified. The frame narrator does speak plainly of God's judgment in 12:14, but I understand this to reflect the common theology of, say, the Psalter, where God's judgment is expected eventually (here and now) to vindicate the righteous.

Where I see more direct overlap between sage Qohelet and sage Jesus is in their apocalyptic overtones, that is, "the end" on a grander scale. For both, the end of the age is an important concept, even though it does not form the dominant element in the thinking of either. For Qohelet, we have seen his "eschatological poem" in 12:1-7, which employs creation language to lay out the breakdown of social and economic realities, and culminates in a final reiteration of the central theme of death. Even though his immediate focus is on the death of all living beings, his final jab is to declare that all of reality as we know it will come to a "grinding" (12:3) halt. Death affects more than the in-

---

44. The resurrection scene in Dan 12:1-2 should not be assumed of Israelite faith throughout its history. Rather, it represents a development in later Judaism that is influenced by apocalyptic thought. Daniel, in other words, bears testimony to the development of notions of the afterlife in Judaism. It is not the canonical example that can be pressed into service to explain the "OT view" of death and the afterlife. Wright addresses expansively the issue of death and resurrection in the OT and Second Temple Judaism in *Resurrection of the Son*. See also idem, *Surprised by Hope*.

dividual. For Jesus, his eschatology can be glimpsed in the Olivet Discourse in Matt 24:1-51 (Mark 13:1-37; Luke 21:5-36), where he likewise expresses himself in apocalyptic language. Here we see that the temple will be taken down, one stone from upon another. This will happen in times of war, famine, and earthquakes, all of which signal the "beginning of birth pains" (Matt 24:8). The holy place will be desecrated by "the abomination that causes desolation" (v. 15), picking up on Daniel's language (Dan 9:27), and false prophets will be able to perform signs and wonders. Those days are described by Jesus in cosmic terms: the sun and moon will become dark, the stars and heavenly bodies will be shaken loose from the firmament (Matt 24:29). Indeed, of two women "grinding" with a hand mill, one will be taken (v. 41).

It should be clear that here too the imagery used by Qohelet and Jesus is similar. I am not suggesting, of course, that Jesus got his ideas from Qohelet. If anywhere, he got it from the prophets (Isa 13:10; 34:14; Joel 2:1-11) and common theological categories of his day, but explicit dependence is not the issue, here or elsewhere. The point is that both sages employ cosmic and cultural catastrophic images to make their points, and this seems to build a biblical-theological bridge between Qohelet and Jesus. For Jesus it is clear that actual future events are being discussed, as most will conclude, the events surrounding the destruction of the temple in A.D. 70. Qohelet's forward gaze is not as explicit, nor would we expect it to be, given his commitment to an empirical epistemology; how can he be expected to embrace a future event and not the afterlife, since both are outside our experience? I would say that in Eccl 12:1-7 Qohelet is simply drawing a general inference of where all this is headed from what he has seen in the here-and-now.

But again, despite these important differences, the end plays a role in how one perceives the present, for both Jesus and Qohelet. For Qohelet, the end (both on the personal and societal levels) demonstrates that the here and now is ultimately of no value. For Jesus, although the interest in the end is shared, the end is a motivation to examining one's life in the here and now. The theological differences between them are clear, but it is the task of biblical theology to see how the divergent theologies can speak to each other, revealing perhaps a stark contrast or in other cases a higher level of coherence. In this case, Qohelet's views in the end seem driven by cultural/contextual factors that make some of the sublimated promises of his Scripture ring hollow. In Second Temple Judaism, and with Jesus, death and the afterlife began to be a powerful theological entity worthy of attention. The differences between them, therefore, are historical/developmental ones, and this fact reminds us that a responsible biblical-theological approach must take into account historical setting.

Merging the teaching of Qohelet and Jesus together on this topic, on the assumption that, since both are Scripture, they cannot diverge in this stark manner, is to miss the riches, diversity, and contextuality that are reflected in all of Scripture. Neither finding a (superficial) unity between the two nor casting wise Qohelet aside in favor of Jesus does justice to the canonical witness. Instead, we will move in the right direction when we ask not how to "unify" these divergent theologies, nor how to pick one over the other, as if the two are static. Rather, we are best off if we ask how these theologies can cohere. Coherence is not a systematic theological category that seeks to align or prioritize the varied witnesses of Scripture. It is a term of biblical-theological value in that it allows the theologies of Scripture to be calibrated against their individual historical moments, and thus make broader theological statements that respect the diversity while also asking, What, now, does the whole say to us? Biblical theology does not seek the "unity" of the biblical witness, but its ultimate narratival coherence.

The theological issue is expressed well by Larry Helyer, who, following David Hubbard, observes that "the train of revelation, at the end of the Old Testament period, enters an intertestamental tunnel. Upon reemerging in the New Testament period, it obviously carries additional cargo."[45] Developments in NT theology are not meant to be taken as interacting with the OT *solely,* but interacting with an OT that itself had been interacted with for some time. The NT authors, to put it differently, had an "interpreted Bible" that formed the basis of their theological observations on Jesus and the church. This same movement is found on the lips of Jesus himself, and perhaps one of the more interesting examples is Jesus' understanding of realized eschatology, or as it is sometimes put, "the already/not yet," where the end is upon us but has not yet been fully realized. Geerhardus Vos, the Princeton biblical theologian of the first half of the twentieth century, investigates this issue against the backdrop of Second Temple Judaism. His focus is on Paul's articulation of this theme, and he concludes that Paul's eschatology is to a certain degree dependent on this earlier theological development — even though Paul certainly has distinctive marks.[46] Both Pauline and Second Temple Jewish eschatology have their basis in the OT, but this common basis

> can not wholly account for the agreement between it [Second Temple Judaism] and Paul as to data going beyond the O.T. There is no escape from

---

45. Helyer, "Necessity, Problems, and Promise," 597.

46. According to Vos, Paul's eschatology is distinct from Jewish eschatology in that the former is nonpolitical, more individualistic, and less elaborate/imaginative (*Pauline Eschatology,* 28 n. 36).

the conclusion that a piece of Jewish theology has been here by Revelation incorporated into the Apostle's teaching. Paul had none less than Jesus Himself as a predecessor in this. The main structure of the Jewish Apocalyptic is embodied in our Lord's teaching as well as in Paul's.[47]

Vos states that, although there is an ultimate OT root for both Jewish and Pauline eschatology, they share elements that are not OT concepts. Since the Jewish eschatology preceded Paul, Vos observes that Paul incorporated the Jewish eschatology into his teaching, albeit by revelation. Moreover, what Paul did, Vos argues, Jesus already did with respect to his own apocalyptic thought. Now, what is very important for Vos is that this *incorporation* of a Second Temple theological development is in no way hostile to *revelation*. For Vos, revelation and historical development are not mutually exclusive concepts. Biblical theology does not shy away from historical circumstances, but works to incorporate the historical particularities of a Scripture into a coherent whole. I would put it even more directly: a responsible biblical theology must do so. The issue before us, then, is how to incorporate these various dimensions into a full biblical theology: OT context(s), NT contexts(s), Second Temple/Hellenistic developments, and contemporary praxis. Developing a unified field theory of theology (to borrow a term from physics), in which disparate factors can be brought together like this, is a project to be hoped for in Christian theology — evangelical or otherwise.

All of this is to illustrate that the differing theologies of Qohelet and Jesus are historically conditioned, but this does not mean this state of affairs is outside God's design, nor that it therefore lies outside biblical theology. On both counts, the opposite is the case. With regard to the issue of death, the afterlife, and eschatology/apocalyptic, I have attempted here to respect these various factors as valued and necessary elements of a true biblical theology. As I see it, the differences between Jesus and Qohelet are largely a function of their historical moment. For Qohelet that moment is understood as a function of his despair over the exile and its aftermath and the fact that he was not yet living at a time when death and the afterlife came to be the more deliberate topic of Jewish self-understanding. For Jesus that moment is one where the eschatological train had, after a long journey, pulled into the station, carrying with it cargo it had picked up while going through the Second Temple tunnel. It is up to biblical theologians to respect those differences while also articulating a theory (for that is what it really is) for how, in view of these differences, the parts cohere.

47. Ibid., 27-28 n. 36. See also Helyer, "Necessity, Problems, and Promise," 598.

Ecclesiastes and the People of God

Suffering and Doubt

As we have seen earlier, the words of Qohelet are not merely the publication of the private musings of a depressed Israelite, but words of a king-figure meant to be seen by others — not as an act of emotional voyeurism but as a statement with broader, nationalistic importance. Likewise, the words of Jesus are not simply reflections on the life of one person, however important he may be. The ultimate purpose of the NT is not to tell simply the story of Jesus, but the story of those who follow him, who are united to him in his death and resurrection. As Richard Hays has so well articulated, the NT is an "ecclesiotelic" document.[48] As we have seen before, Christ is to be understood as the goal (τέλος/*telos*) of the OT. He is the one in whom the OT finds its dramatic climax. That climax is a surprise ending (a messiah who dies on behalf of his people), but regardless, Jesus is the one in whom the OT finds its ultimate coherence. Hays rightly expands this notion to apply to the church. The NT may be described as a series of documents that address two issues: (1) Who is Jesus? (2) What does Jesus have to do with me? The second question follows upon the first. The OT drama may come to a climax in the person and work of Christ, but the purpose for which Christ came was to build a new people of God — Jew and Gentile — united by faith in Israel's crucified and risen Messiah.

This is why the church is called the body of Christ. The church is the extension, the continuation, of what Christ adumbrated in his life and inaugurated in his death and resurrection. A messianic hope narrowly considered is not the focus of the OT, as odd as that might seem for some Christian readers. Rather the focus is on the creation of a people who would be used by God to bring reconciliation to the world. Christ embodies the ideal of Israel: he, as the true Israel, brings to completion what historical Israel did not. Corporate Israel is realized in the one Israelite, the Davidic king, the Messiah, Jesus of Nazareth. But his job is not done until, through him, a new people is raised up to be the new, corporate Israel. This is a point that can be missed, at least in popular understandings of the gospel. Jesus did not die and rise again merely to save his people from eternal punishment. He died and rose in order to complete God's missional project, which finds its root in Abraham's call to be blessed and to be a blessing to the nations (Gen 12:1-2).

This close connection between Jesus and his people is described in the

48. Hays, "On the Rebound," 77-78.

Pauline corpus as "union" with Christ (Rom 6:5; 1 Cor 6:17; Phil 2:1). Another way of putting it is that the life of Jesus is played out in his people. Jesus died, as do his people in baptism; Jesus rose from the dead, as those who believe in him have risen (conversion) and will rise (bodily resurrection; Rom 6:1-14); Jesus ascended to the right hand of the Father, as have and will his people (Eph 2:4-7). The life of the church parallels the life of Christ. Christ journeys first and the church follows in union with him.

This union with Christ includes not just the high times but the low as well. Jesus suffered and was in his passion immersed in doubt — and he promised the same for his people. Again, true followers of Christ will eventually experience a dark night of the soul, as was so well articulated by the sixteenth-century Roman Catholic mystic St. John of the Cross. Christians have those dark times not — as is still too often advertised by charlatan preachers — because we are somehow out of God's favor or have failed to reach a sufficient stage of spiritual maturity. The biblical truth of the matter, corroborated over two millennia of common Christian experience, is precisely the opposite. Christians suffer *because* they are united to Christ and his purpose is to make his people ever more conformed to his image. When Christians suffer they are privileged to do so, because then they are more like Jesus. I do not say this lightly, for many people suffer indescribably. I am trying to communicate how counterintuitive the Christian faith is, and how even the most horrific suffering has a truly constructive, redemptive dimension according to the gospel.

It will helpful if we first review Jesus' suffering. As is well known to Christians, Jesus' suffering was vicarious — he suffered in our place. Jesus was the king, the Messiah, the Son of God — not only in keeping with OT royal imagery, but he was also "one with the Father," in a way none before was. Analogous to Qohelet, no one had it as good as Jesus. No one had so much at his disposal. Hence no one was able to suffer and despair to the extent that King Jesus did. When one grasps the sufferings of Christ, one says, along with the frame narrator, "The end of the matter." Nothing can be added. Jesus has gone over the edge to the true state of being abandoned by God — and returned. This does not minimize Christian suffering but puts it in a larger context. The sufferings of Christ's people cannot match those of the King, but those sufferings are nevertheless real. The task of the Christian in that suffering is to follow and obey. Jesus' suffering has both a supreme and a representative character vis-à-vis his people, much as we saw with Qohelet.

Jesus suffered, and it was a real suffering. It sometimes creeps into popular understandings of the gospel that, because of Jesus' incarnate status, his sufferings were somehow less real, but, of course, nothing could be further from the truth. If his sufferings were not real, then the very foundation of the gospel is called into question: Jesus bore sin; he suffered. Also, the depth of his suffering matches the loftiness of his pedigree. Truly, his suffering is more profound *because* of his incarnate status. Now, if we are not careful we may find ourselves sidetracked by a lengthy discussion of Christology, and that would take us very far afield. Still, a basic reminder of who Jesus was according to the heart of Christian thought will clarify the meaning of his suffering.

Think first of his temptation in the wilderness (Matt 4:1-11 par.). Was this a real temptation or just a show? For it to be a temptation, Jesus needed to have been tempted — really. We should let that sink in a bit. Jesus was solid in his response to Satan, but that response has teeth only to the extent to which he bore up under actual temptation. As the Son of God, it is not so much that Jesus had an edge over his people to resist temptation "easily." Rather, he was "made like his brothers in every way," and so "suffered when he was tempted" (Heb 2:17-18 NIV), but we miss the mark if we draw a simplistic equation. His lofty pedigree made the temptation *more* tempting. To put it another way, followers of Christ could not be tempted to the same degree that Jesus was. The lesson to be learned from the temptation narrative is not that Christians too should be on the lookout for similar temptations in their daily lives. The lesson is that the king has gone before, bore a deep unrepeatable temptation, and, like the warrior-hero-king he is, arose with victory. Those who follow him are able to repeat neither the depth of the temptation nor the height of the triumph (he is the king, after all), but they do participate in both his suffering and glorification.

Temptation meant that Jesus suffered (Heb 2:18), and the wilderness temptation at the outset of Jesus' ministry serves as a frame for his life. In Gethsemane and on the cross, Jesus nearly crumbles under the weight of what is about to happen. In the garden, he asks that the burden be lifted. On the cross, he cries out in the Aramaic words of Psalm 22, "*Eloi, Eloi, lama sabachthani?*[49] — which means, 'My God, my God, why have you forsaken me?'" (Matt 27:46; Mark 15:34 NIV). This depth of his suffering has inspired theologians and artists for two millennia, and is at the heart of the Christian faith. The only point I wish to focus on here, again, is that the depth of the suffering is matched by the loftiness of the pedigree. Jesus' suffering is, to be sure, a model for the church, but it is much more. It is a demonstration of the extent to which the Father will go to ensure that his people do not have to suffer like this. His followers *cannot* match the suffering of King Jesus. He suffered so that they would not have to.

---

49. The Hebrew version of Ps 22:2 has the root עזב/ʿzb, whereas the Aramaic has שׁבק/ šbq.

All of this brings us to the curious juxtaposition of (1) Jesus' necessarily unique suffering as the Son of God, and (2) the union of his followers with him, so that their lives follow Jesus' pattern. The NT speaks much of Jesus' suffering, not only in the Gospels but in the Letters as well. What is stressed is the foundational role that Jesus' suffering and death play in the *redemption* of God's people. But also we see a great emphasis placed on the *sufferings* of God's people as being connected somehow to Jesus' suffering. If we think back on Ecclesiastes, with the frame narrator's positive evaluation of Qohelet and his admonition to "fear God and keep the commands," the frame narrator's purpose is now to address the "son" on the basis of this evaluation. The sufferings of Qohelet are for the benefit of the son in the sense that he can now see his own sufferings in a larger perspective.

This is also what we see in the NT. The suffering of Jesus' followers is spoken of freely in the NT. It is to be expected because Jesus suffered. But Christian suffering is more than simply an imitation of Jesus' suffering (though see 1 Pet 2:19-21; 4:1). In suffering Christians *participate* in Jesus' suffering. As we read in Philippians, those who know Christ are part of a fellowship that shares in his sufferings (3:10). Not only "the power of his resurrection" but suffering is what connects Jesus to his followers. "Knowing Christ," as we read, means being united to Jesus both in his resurrection power (by which we have been raised to a new life) and by being like him in his suffering. Indeed, in v. 11, the suffering of v. 10 — by which followers become "like him in death" — is tied to the hope of somehow attaining "the resurrection from the dead." Whether this is hyperbole may be a matter of discussion, but I see here a much deeper and sustaining theological truth: suffering is part of the call of Jesus' followers — an important one, an expected one. Suffering has a redemptive dimension.

Now, this NT view on suffering goes well beyond what we read in Ecclesiastes, but that is to be expected. We gain greater clarity of God's ways in light of the gospel. But a general theological overlap remains: neither Ecclesiastes nor the NT rejects in any way the "rightness" of suffering. Again, Qohelet's words, which grate on us, perhaps, are not the whining of a weak-minded Israelite, but the words of the king that are said to be wise by the frame narrator. The frame narrator says, "See the suffering — now, follow Yahweh." So too the gospel teaches us, "See the suffering of the Messiah. This is your calling, too, as you follow in Jesus' footsteps." For both, it is by accepting the suffering, not skirting it, that one finds true depth of faith. Amazingly, that suffering includes the honest cry of the soul when God's presence is nowhere to be found.

The value of suffering is similarly mentioned elsewhere in the NT. In

Romans Paul remarks that sharing in Christ's suffering means that we will share in his glory (8:17-18). In 2 Cor 1:5 he speaks of his readers as sharing "abundantly in the sufferings of Christ." Suffering "for" Christ is something that is "granted" to those who believe (Phil 1:29). Suffering is something that is accompanied by joy, not joy despite suffering but joy *in* the suffering (1 Thess 1:6). One of the more mysterious and gripping comments, however, is found in Col 1:24. There we read that one's suffering on behalf of fellow Christians fills what is "still lacking in regard to Christ's afflictions." We may extrapolate from this comment that suffering is more than imitating Christ (although it is that); it is also more than sharing in his sufferings. It has a redemptive property. Paul seems to be saying that his own afflictions were "essential to the well-being of his converts."[50] This is not the place to unravel the deep mystery of Col 1:24. I do not think that the argument here is that Christ's sufferings were somehow insufficient. But I do think that Christian suffering is so closely connected to that of Christ that perhaps, as he gropes for words, this phrase finds its way to the writer's pen. The end result of this observation is that the suffering of the saints *matters* in a way that is almost too deep to express in words. This is a point that Ecclesiastes as a whole does not contradict. Indeed, it is supported in that ancient Hebrew work. But, as the gospel reveals, the role of suffering in the Christian life is even more than Ecclesiastes bargains for.

Fear and Obedience

"Trust and obey, for there's no other way. . . ." This line from the popular hymn captures well the final message of Ecclesiastes. These two principles sum up the heart of both Israel's wisdom and legal traditions, for both covenant reverence and submission are components of wisdom and law.

It is important to remember that the issue in Ecclesiastes is not Qohelet's disobedience, concerning which he is told to obey. He is not chided for disobedience but praised for his wisdom. The son is not told to fear and obey in order to be distinguished from Qohelet's failure to do so. Fear and obedience, rather, are the proper response in the face of skepticism and despair. Such an understanding of Ecclesiastes is also reflected in the NT, where

---

50. Dunn, *Colossians and Philemon*, 115. Dunn also adds that the completion of Christ's suffering reflects Paul's understanding that Christ's death "activated the first trigger" of cosmic renewal. The suffering of the saints continues Jesus' Suffering Servant role and will bring about the "second and final trigger" (116). In other words, like other aspects of Christ's work, Christ's suffering is to be understood against the backdrop of the two-age eschatological scheme.

God's people are encouraged to maintain a posture of fear and obedience despite the very real and difficult situation the church finds itself in. This has tremendously important practical implications for today, as we will glimpse in the final chapter of this commentary.

We see this posture reflected in Jesus' own behavior toward entering Jerusalem to be crucified. Throughout the Gospels, as opposition to Jesus' ministry mounted, Jesus began to confide in his disciples that he would meet his death in Jerusalem (Matt 12:40; 16:21; 17:22-23; 20:17-19; 26:1-2 par.). Knowing what entering Jerusalem would mean for him, Jesus nevertheless entered, not secretly, but with much Davidic fanfare (Matt 21:1-11 par.). In doing so, Jesus was demonstrating concretely his commitment to going where God required him to be, regardless of personal cost and the accompanying depth of doubt and despair he would feel at the prospect of dying a criminal's death. The temptation narrative is relevant here as it was above. Jesus really was tempted to forsake his calling and take an easier way out (or so it would seem). What Satan held before Jesus in the wilderness was attractive to Jesus, or else the temptation would have no teeth. Jesus fought against this temptation; it was not easy. He was tempted to throw it all away — but he remained obedient, as he says, "Away from me, Satan! For it is written 'Worship the Lord your God, and serve him only'" (Matt 4:10, citing Deut 6:13). Worship God and serve him — Jesus' version of "fear God and keep the commandments."

Jesus' preaching took on a similar tone of obeying God regardless of what one might be going through at the moment. The Sermon on the Mount in particular reflects this. Jesus comments on the types of people that are called blessed: poor in spirit, mourning, meek, hungering and thirsting for righteousness, merciful, pure in heart, peacemaking, persecuted (Matt 5:3-10). But the world will not meet such behavior with resounding applause: persecution will come in the face of such displays of character, and even there you are blessed by God. Jesus does not say, "Blessed are the poor, and so on, until you are under pressure to throw in the towel." The gospel is the harder road to take. It does not devalue in any way the daily stresses, internal and external, that befall those who are trying to follow Jesus. It tells them to maintain the path of obedience whatever the circumstances. So too with respect to unjust treatment. To be subject to malice is psychologically unnerving. It is natural to seek to make it right, normally by bringing the other to justice (or at least our own version of justice). And, as followers of Christ, an added dimension comes into play. The question is raised, as it was throughout Israel's literature of lament, why doesn't God do something about it? But, as we see in Matt 5:38-48, evil must be met with kindness, and one's enemies are to be loved. The counterintuitive tone of it all should not escape our notice. No matter what the circumstances, those who follow Jesus are to act as if they, well, follow Jesus. The circumstances do not determine the behavior. "Fear God and keep the commandments" rules what a follower of Christ does regardless of how one feels.

What Jesus says in Matthew 5 is reflected again in 18:21-35. One of the central Christian character traits is to forgive those who inflict personal injury. This does not mean pretending nothing happened. It does not mean eliciting a particular response from the offender. To forgive means to cease planning how one will mete out justice; it means letting it go and getting on with other matters. Jesus exemplified such a level of forgiveness when he forgave those who crucified him. In Matt 18:22 Jesus tells Peter to forgive those who sin against us, not seven times (a goodly number in its own right), but "seventy-seven times" (or perhaps, "seventy times seven"). In other words: a lot, more than one can count — always. One may feel horribly treated. One may be plunged into anger, despair, and every emotion in between as a result. One may in time doubt the mercy and justice of God. No matter. Forgive more than you can count. This is what it means to follow Jesus, to do the unspeakably courageous thing regardless of what the present circumstances seem to allow. Even if what is required is an affront to reason — especially then — Christians must do what the Master requires. As we have seen in the frame narrator's summation, we are to pass through (not around) the most desperate of times while maintaining the singular focus of "fear and obey."

Throughout the NT Letters, a major theme is that of a Spirit-led life, one where followers of Jesus are encouraged to press forward regardless of outward circumstances. Often those circumstances involve some type of persecution or resistance with respect to God's people, and so are only tangentially related to the theme under consideration here, fear and obedience in the face of deep doubt and despair. Still, even with respect to persecution and resistance, it is not a terribly long leap to see that part of what needs encouraging is the inner turmoil of the Christian in the face of such outward resistance. Remaining steadfast is not a call simply to outward strength in the face of opposition, but to inward strength in the face of one's psychological trauma, that is, not allowing the circumstances to drive one to despair. In that sense the call to "fear and obey" God is one that absolutely permeates the NT Letters and Revelation, and many episodes could be drawn into this theme.

The call of the gospel involves the call to remain steadfast not only in one's beliefs but in one's actions as they reflect those beliefs (as James remarks so famously in Jas 2:14-26). The underlying, and usually unstated, notion here is that it is not at all easy to follow Jesus. This world is one barrier after another, and so those who follow Christ are to be vigilant and disciplined on their spiritual journeys. Sometimes, as I said, those barriers are erected by those who intend harm to Christians, a very real issue in the early church. Elsewhere, the barriers are the result of followers of Jesus failing to live in such a way that reflects their high calling — sin stands in the way. This last situation is not at all relevant to Ecclesiastes, but other places in the NT Letters dovetail well with the theme we see in Ecclesiastes. These are passages where believers are expected to act in such a way that is contrary to what one may be inclined to do, what for all intents and purposes seems right and just. Every instinct they may have would lead them in one direction, but the gospel demands another.

For example, with respect to suffering, Paul writes in Rom 5:1-5 that followers of Jesus are to rejoice in suffering, knowing that such suffering leads to perseverance, character, and then hope. And such hope does not disappoint us, for the Holy Spirit is with us. Now, the frame narrator does not go this far in his final comments in Eccl 12:13-14, but consider Qohelet's predicament and the frame narrator's evaluation. For both Paul and the frame narrator, the suffering involved is neither minimized nor discounted. Indeed, it is by passing through the suffering well that one learns the final lesson. For both Paul and the frame narrator, that lesson is one of ultimate covenant faithfulness on God's part. For the latter that is expressed in the tried and true categories of Israel's faith — "fear God and keep his commandments." Remain steadfast. For the former it is the Spirit of God present with the believer that brings the believer through the suffering, not around it. The redemptive dimension of suffering is certainly clearer with Paul, as one might expect in view of his post-Easter reality, but the theological overlap between the two remains. It is also true that the suffering Paul refers to is likely something more systemic, a persecution of some sort, and not the emotional unhinging that we see with Qohelet (so perhaps "in tribulations" or "afflictions" in Rom 5:3 is a better translation of ἐν ταῖς θλίψεσιν/*en tais thlipsesin*). But remember too that personal suffering, in the OT as well as in postbiblical Judaism, was often assumed to be (rightly or wrongly) a sign of God's displeasure. Paul, however, turns this on its head, not simply by tolerating suffering or "making the best of it," but by proclaiming its positive role in the development of Christian character.[51] Now, I want to be clear that I do not see this happening explicitly in Ecclesiastes, but the echo is more than faint. There too the sufferings of Qohelet represent what Israelite readers experience in their own limited way.

---

51. Dunn remarks that the tribulations of 5:3 can also have an eschatological overtone, namely that Christians share in the sufferings of Christ in this period of eschatological overlap, and so are able to endure it (*Romans 1–8*, 249-50).

And when they do, the call to "fear and obey" takes on a richer, even unimpeachable, function in the spiritual growth of any ancient Israelite.

Paul utters a similar notion in Rom 8:18-27. There is much happening here, and it will not do to reduce the richness of this passage to a single dimension (or two). But with respect to our theme, we see that Paul remarks at the groaning of the faithful (v. 23) as they endure their present sufferings (v. 18). And, as they "wait eagerly" for the redemption of their bodies (v. 23), they remain in a posture of patience (v. 25) as the Spirit himself intercedes on their behalf (v. 27). The general scenario that Paul is laying out here is one of perseverance of hope, by the Spirit, in a state of suffering, a suffering that causes groaning — so much that the Spirit himself joins along. Perhaps we should allow this picture to become clearer. The Christian life is characterized by dissatisfaction with how things are. Paul does not detail for us just what causes this suffering. Indeed, v. 18 seems to begin somewhat abruptly, following as it does on v. 17, where sharing in Christ's sufferings is tied to sharing in his glory. These sufferings seem to be connected in some way to the believer's "obligation" to resist the "sinful nature" (v. 12) and the cosmic groans of "frustration" and "bondage to decay" to which it has been subjected (vv. 20-21). In other words, as I see it, the sufferings Paul refers to likely have some connection to the "decay" of creation, one of its manifestations being the daily struggle to resist being controlled by the sinful (i.e., preconversion) nature.

On that note, I will resist the temptation to link v. 20, "creation was subject to frustration, not by its own choice, but by the will of the one who subjected it" (NIV), to Ecclesiastes. I do not think for one minute that Paul here is lodging a complaint against God, as Qohelet does, for being unjust. Paul is more likely alluding to Gen 3:17-19, where God cursed the ground and made labor difficult. The reason, though, that Ecclesiastes is sometimes adduced is because of the use of the noun ματαιότης/*mataiotēs*, which is most often found in the LXX in Ecclesiastes and translates Hebrew הֶבֶל/*hebel*.[52] Regardless, at least one of Paul's points is that the Christian perseveres by and with the Spirit in the midst of a suffering that has cosmic proportions. Things *are* horrible, but Paul's Christ has himself passed through an even more unspeakable suffering, and so, as Paul writes at the beginning of this section, "I consider that our present sufferings (τὰ παθήματα τοῦ νῦν καιροῦ/*ta pathēmata tou nyn kairou*) are not worth comparing with the glory that will be revealed in us" (v. 18). That glory is no doubt the resurrection body (2 Cor 5:1-10), a decidedly eschatological hope, but it is the present work of the Spirit that applies that future hope in principle to us today. As Paul explains, it is in the res-

---

52. See Longman, *Ecclesiastes*, 39-40.

urrection of the Messiah that the future hope has broken into the present, thus giving followers of Christ a very concrete reason for hope. The Spirit is "a deposit, guaranteeing what is to come" (2 Cor 5:5). It is this knowledge that provides the stability for Christians here and now. It is not "pie in the sky" hopefulness, but God breaking into the present sufferings of his creation. Christians are to keep moving in this life, not simply because a better one awaits them, but because the future has already begun. And this future breaking into the present, applied to the believer by the Spirit, is at the heart of the Christian's ability to live in a world where things have gone horribly wrong and where, with a moment's reflection, it would seem absurd to continue. It is into this kind of situation that the gospel provides followers of Jesus with a way forward. Paul's theology is, in my view, much richer than what we find with the frame narrator, but the basic theological instincts are the same: no matter how bad things look, keep moving because God is still here.

We could explore numerous other NT avenues that exemplify this theme, on one level or another, but the point is illustrated well enough. Ecclesiastes is not a book about the faithlessness of a disobedient Israelite, whining about how bad things are and told at the end by the narrator to buck up. The wise king Qohelet has seen it all and is at the end of his rope. However striking and unsettling his words may be, they are to be understood as statements of utter despair that are taken quite seriously by the frame narrator. Qohelet's sense of how life should be is violated. With Paul, what we see is an augmentation of the depth of the despairing circumstances of this world as well as the augmentation of God's role in leading his people through it. Qohelet's anger is turned against God, and the frame narrator says in effect that God's solution to even this level of despair is the fully counterintuitive admonition to keep acting as if you trust God, keep acting like an Israelite — fear and obey. In the gospel it is Jesus himself on whom the grand dysfunction of the cosmos is placed, and the true depth of the human condition is paraded before all: sin. There is, ultimately, no security for any of us — Jew or Gentile. It is only in God's act of correcting the dysfunction that there is a true way forward. The frame narrator says of Qohelet, "What you are saying is true, but there is more." The gospel responds similarly to the book of Ecclesiastes: "What the frame narrator says, 'fear and obey,' is true, but there is more. The problem is deeper than you realize, and the way forward is more glorious."

The Significance of Ecclesiastes
for Theology and Praxis Today

We will take two avenues in considering the contemporary significance of Ecclesiastes. The first — a less traveled avenue — is what Ecclesiastes communicates to us with respect to the nature of Scripture. In what way is Ecclesiastes Scripture for the church today? How does Ecclesiastes contribute to our understanding of what Scripture actually is? These are intensely practical questions to ask, since so much of the church's theology and praxis are based on models of Scripture and how those models connect to everyday life.

The second avenue, the more familiar, concerns the theological trajectories of Ecclesiastes and how they connect with contemporary Christian faith. This is a question that we must address in the context of the biblical-theological discussion of the previous chapter, since, as the body of Christ, we do not "apply" Ecclesiastes apart from our understanding of how Jesus and his gospel leave their imprint on our understanding not simply of Ecclesiastes, but of the entire OT and the church's eschatological hope.

This last point might benefit from some further explanation. The gospel expands the scope of Ecclesiastes beyond the borders of the OT book itself. We understand it differently in light of the cross and resurrection than we might have if we lived in the pre-resurrection cosmos. The nature of that expansion can only be appreciated — and therefore the theological significance of that expanded meaning — if we take with utmost seriousness the meaning of the original utterance in its historical moment (as best as we can approximate it). We then can ask what effect Ecclesiastes has on our understanding of the depth of the gospel *and* what effect the gospel has on how we can appropriate the penultimate theology of Ecclesiastes in light of the ultimacy of God's revelation to Israel, the death and resurrection of the Son of God.

This is what I have laid out in the previous chapter, but now the question turns to the application of biblical theology to a people living in a time and place far, far removed — culturally, linguistically, politically, and every other way — not only from the first-century setting of the gospel, but from the even more remote moment of the writer of Ecclesiastes. As I see it, the foundation upon which the church's appropriation of Scripture rests is in its union with the risen Christ in whom all of God's promises — somehow, mysteriously — find their final "yes" and "amen" (2 Cor 1:20). For Christians, it is in Christ that Israel's Scripture is brought to completion, and we "participate in Scripture" not because we will it or because we respect it, but because we are united to Christ, of whom Christians confess Scripture ultimately speaks. By looking not just at Ecclesiastes but at the whole of the OT with Christian eyes, we *continue* the expansion of Qohelet's words, in Christ, to contemporary issues that the NT, let alone Ecclesiastes, never envisioned. N. T. Wright has articulated well this theological task vis-à-vis Scripture.[1] The church has in Scripture a five-act play (creation, fall, Israel, Jesus, church). We are living in the fifth act, but the script has only been partially written. We are called to continue "writing" the fifth act in a way that is faithful to the content of the first four acts and the trajectories already laid out in the fifth act (the NT Letters) and cognizant of the hints of the end in such places as Revelation. But this process requires creativity and innovation. The play as it is written does not dictate the precise forms that performance will take in our moment, although today's actors are expected to study the play and align the contemporary performance to its themes and trajectories.[2]

This is a helpful metaphor for understanding the church's present theological task. The church's application of Scripture today (as in any other day in the history of the church) is an attempt to be faithful to Scripture while also recognizing that our moment differs from those who were part of the original play. With respect to the OT, the theological issue takes on an added dimension. Not only are we far removed from the historical moment of Ecclesiastes, but, in seeking to interact responsibly with this book, we also have the NT to account for, where a broad vision for what it means to be the people of God is laid out and summed up in the Messiah. The historical distance between the church today and NT times is very real and obligates us to invest our theological energies into understanding more and more of the time in which the NT writers wrote.

---

1. Wright, *Last Word*, 115-42, esp. 121-27.

2. Brueggemann's memorable metaphor, somewhat similar to Wright's idea, is that of a compost pile (*Texts under Negotiation*, 61-62). The church's theology grows out of the fertile stuff of Scripture. It is not equated with Scripture, but grows out of it, i.e., goes necessarily beyond it. Christian theology does not simply guard the compost pile or tend it for its own sake, but nourishes that which can be grown from it.

Although the historical distance is great, the church today, by virtue of its union with Christ, shares in the same eschatological moment as that of the first-century church. In other words, just as the post-Easter church was working through the implications of the gospel for understanding Israel's Scripture and the significance of the resurrection, the church today participates in the same theological project. But there is one crucial difference: because of the unique canonical role of the NT, our "performance" of Ecclesiastes or any other OT book must itself be in conversation with the theological trajectories set out in the NT. The dilemma before us (which I feel we are called to embrace, not neuter through hermeneutical sleight of hand) is that, more than prescriptive principles, the NT gives the church examples of early moves to align the gospel and Israel's Scripture. This means that there is more to following the NT's use of the OT today than copying their exegesis of particular passages; it means sensing, exploring, and following the hermeneutical trajectories embedded in the writings of their cultural moment.

We could continue this discussion, but that would take us increasingly far from the specific question of the application of Ecclesiastes within a biblical-theological framework. The main point I wish to stress is that our act of application is a faithful extension of what we see happening on the pages of the NT itself. We might say that application is an extension of typology. How we use Scripture today is an extension of the theological/hermeneutical trajectories set down in the NT itself.

With this in mind, I will address first the effect that Ecclesiastes has on how we think about the nature of Scripture and its interpretation, followed by a discussion of the church's application of Ecclesiastes today.

Ecclesiastes and Scripture

Counterpoint as a Type of Scripture

What strikes any reader of the OT is the different literary genres represented under the title "Scripture."[3] There are various historical writings (which themselves vary in how they report historical events), laws, prophetic texts, songs and poems of various types, wisdom texts, and other variations on

---

3. Many of these issues have been addressed by Goldingay in two complementary volumes: *Models for Scripture,* and *Models for Interpretation of Scripture.* These are excellent sources to begin exploring the richness and diversity of Scripture and the accompanying richness and diversity in its interpretation.

these themes. These various genres are confessed by the church to be inspired by God, however one understands that concept. Despite the manifold ways in which Christian theologians have attempted to articulate Scripture as an inspired product, what is generally accepted as a function of inspiration is that Scripture is God's book, that it comes from God for his people. So far so good, but the question becomes more complicated when we turn to the matter of the *interpretation* of Scripture as an authoritative standard for life and practice in light of this fundamental conviction. We will leave that specific question to the side for the moment.

What occupies us here is that Scripture itself contains numerous types of writing. Some of those types fit more easily under rubrics familiar to Christians: authoritative, infallible, and so on. For example, we may think here of legal and prophetic sections, both of which have a top-down orientation: Moses speaking for God from a mountaintop and prophets saying "thus says Yahweh." Even though these genres hardly clarify the *nature* of that authority for contemporary readers, these texts nevertheless present themselves as the "voice of God" in a more immediate sense than what we see in other genres. Leviticus, Isaiah, and Judges are different genres and so function differently as Scripture. With many of the Writings, we have yet another "type" of Scripture before us, which includes poetic expressions of various kinds: a hymn of praise to God does not function as Scripture in the same way Deuteronomy does. With respect to Ecclesiastes, however, we have a type of Scripture, paralleled roughly in the lament psalms and in Job (as discussed earlier), that is in a different category altogether. As mentioned in the previous chapter, Brueggemann refers to these and other portions of the OT as Israel's countertestimony,[4] and I have suggested the parallel term "counterpoint." Whatever we call it, the fact is that portions of Scripture are not only in suggestive tension with other portions of the same Scripture, inspired by the same God, but are openly critical of those Scriptures — and even of God himself.

This presence of core testimony and countertestimony, point and counterpoint, in the same body of literature that comes from the same God is a topic of considerable importance. How does one articulate a view of Scripture that takes this dynamic into account? Brueggemann puts the matter more directly:

> The tension between the core testimony and the countertestimony is acute and ongoing. It is my judgment that this tension between the two

---

4. Brueggemann, *Theology of the Old Testament*, 315-403.

belongs to the very character and substance of OT faith, a tension that precludes and resists resolution. The conventional attitude of ecclesial communities, Christian more than Jewish, is to opt for the core testimony of faithful sovereignty and sovereign fidelity and to eliminate or disregard the countertestimony of hiddenness, ambiguity, and negativity from the horizon of faith. Such a process yields coherent faith, but it requires mumbling through many aspects of lived experience that evoked the countertestimony in the first place.[5]

Brueggemann's observation is very important for understanding Ecclesiastes, and it brings us into conversation with the polyphonic nature of Scripture.

Most biblical interpreters today will quickly affirm that Scripture speaks in different, though ultimately harmonious, voices.[6] Those voices can be seen either in the variety of genres represented in Scripture or in Scripture's various theological perspectives. In either case it is affirmed that we must respect rather than mute these voices. Proper biblical interpretation, in other words, means allowing the text to speak through "wrestling with its plurality of voices."[7] As Kevin Vanhoozer puts it, "The canon is a *complex simplex* — a chorus of diverse voices that nevertheless all testify to the same multifaceted reality: God's word-act in Jesus Christ."[8] Timothy Ward is also correct to work out an understanding of the diversity of Scripture that sees its polyphony as an expected character trait of its being God's word; and seeking support from such thinkers as M. M. Bahktin, Roland Barthes, and Paul Ricoeur only strengthens his point.[9]

In other words, discussions of biblical polyphony typically understand the voices to be "mutually supplementary,"[10] even amid tensions and dissonance. Polyphony is certainly an important point to consider with respect to Ecclesiastes as countervoice. But the type of polyphony described above does not quite address the hermeneutical offense of Ecclesiastes — an offense that Brueggemann articulates so well in the quote above. Qohelet's words do not simply contribute a particularly discordant voice to Scripture's ultimately harmonious polyphony. He does not seek to add a dissonant note to a complex chord, thus producing an unexpected and richer harmony. His presenta-

---

5. Ibid., 400.
6. Elsewhere Brueggemann refers to the pluralistic character of the OT as "irascible" (ibid., 64).
7. Thiselton, "Dialogue, Dialectic," 749.
8. Vanhoozer, *Drama of Doctrine*, 287.
9. Ward, "Diversity and Sufficiency."
10. Ibid., 213.

tion of God, which is his considered and final opinion on the matter, calls into question the very notion of harmony. He neutralizes rather than adds to Scripture's polyphonic testimony. He does not wish to be in conversation with other voices; he wishes to overtake them, to silence them. Synthesizing Qohelet and other voices is not just difficult — Qohelet would consider it foolishness.

This tension cannot be dismissed by looking beyond Qohelet's words and appealing to the frame narrator. By claiming that Qohelet is wise, the frame narrator legitimizes Qohelet's efforts. The frame narrator offends any sense of the ultimate rational hermeneutical — and doctrinal — resolution of Qohelet's voice. Ecclesiastes bends our imaginations toward the inscrutability of God by endorsing Qohelet's shrill voice without offering to resolve the intellectual tension. Harmony is to be sought elsewhere — not hermeneutically but by faith. And for Christians the object of that faith, wherein resides that higher, inscrutable, synthesis that includes even Qohelet's voice, is Christ. Christ provides the proper analogy for expecting nothing less from Scripture than polyphony, and confessing by faith that it is in Christ that even Qohelet's voice is resolved. Ward puts the matter well: "If a unique hypostatic union of human and divine natures really did take place in the person of Jesus of Nazareth as the culmination of a process of divine action in history, anything less diverse than the canon of Scripture we have might be thought to be simplistic to speak of such a reality."[11] Similarly, Vanhoozer affirms, "there is something about the event of Jesus Christ that makes *just these literary forms* particularly appropriate for rendering its reality."[12]

I agree with Ward and Vanhoozer, but would add only that the canon, with its diverse literary forms, which both writers affirm, includes and embraces a voice that seeks to cancel out other voices. The full significance of this Christological model for understanding *this* type of polyphony must account somehow for the unbearable tension introduced by Qohelet's view of God, a view that is embraced as wise by the frame narrator. Ward's analogy with the hypostatic union and Vanhoozer's Christ-centered theo-drama are fundamentally correct, but they require us to embrace the normativity of contradiction, which, as the frame narrator reminds us, is not to be resolved intellectually, but lived.

All of this means that Ecclesiastes has applicatory implications beyond how we can view despair, suffering, God, and so on. Wrestling with Ecclesiastes will also affect how we today as Christians understand the nature of Scrip-

---

11. Ibid., 212.
12. Vanhoozer, *Drama of Doctrine*, 287-88.

ture and what, as a result, we are to do with it — that is, how do we read Scripture? If our model of Scripture is defined by too restrictive articulations of divine authority, infallibility, or even polyphony, we may run afoul of the contrastive power of books like Ecclesiastes.

Another way of putting all this is to ask to what extent Scripture's counterpoint should even affect our overall view of the nature of Scripture, or whether "the nature of Scripture" is not touched by such stubborn texts. Perhaps it is best to let the counterpoint be subsumed under a "doctrine of Scripture" that is based on privileging some proof texts and marginalizing more reluctant portions of Scripture. Of course, I realize that to ask the question this way is to answer it, and I am not doing a very good job of concealing my own thoughts on the matter. All of Scripture should provide the church with its theological and doctrinal substance as it continues to articulate a doctrine of Scripture.

The reason I feel this is so important is that, when we marginalize portions of Scripture (or worse, mishandle them to fit into certain models), we are manipulating Scripture, and, ironically, actually undermining the very doctrine of Scripture we seek to promote. Also, by failing to account for Scripture's own overall behavior in promoting a doctrine of Scripture, we do not do well in preparing thoughtful generations of Christians from whom such obvious inconsistencies cannot long be hidden. The counterpoint of Scripture is part of Scripture and hence should be very much part of any discussion of Scripture and its role in the church. To think otherwise betrays common sense. It is important, therefore, to remember that the counterpoint must be incorporated into a doctrine of Scripture *as counterpoint*, however offensive or challenging that might be. The theology of Ecclesiastes or Job or the lament psalms must be allowed to provide their own diverse voices to the discussion. They cannot be tamed in the interest of familiar or comfortable formulations. The people of God are neither served nor protected by such a move, and God is not honored. A real belief in biblical authority cannot help but be doctrinally submissive to all of Scripture. The task is to try to understand *how* counterpoint functions as Scripture.

The practical value of taking such an approach to Scripture is in my opinion manifold. By allowing the counterpoint to have its say, we are allowing Scripture to embody for the church a disposition that, apparently (if one takes inspiration seriously), God himself seems very interested to have embodied. What is embodied in Scripture by the presence of counterpoint? It is a posture of *conversation and honest engagement with life and with God himself.* This is no small matter for anyone who has lived long enough to see the very practical challenges to one's faith that are so common to all Christians.

Scripture is not simply a top-down document that reveals to us God's will. It is also a God-authorized, documented, painful articulation of what is in store for those who follow God. Counterpoint is built into the nature of Scripture itself — regularly and often — and this cannot help but be a genuine factor in the church's cogitating over such basic questions as, What is our Bible like? What is it there to *do* for and to the church? What does it mean when we say "word of God"?

I am not suggesting that these questions are wholly up for grabs, only that other models of Scripture are often taken as somehow more "basic," and so the scriptural "value" of less amenable genres such as we find in Ecclesiastes is assessed on the basis of these other, allegedly more foundational, forms. This is perhaps one reason why for some there is no choice but to interpret Ecclesiastes either as affirming Israel's wisdom tradition or to put the theology of Ecclesiastes in its place, to tuck it safely under the "authority" of what we otherwise "know" Scripture to be (i.e., Qohelet is a misguided speculator — with occasionally orthodox glimpses such as the carpe diem passages — but the frame narrator essentially corrects him). The assumption is made that Ecclesiastes is certainly inspired, but just what can or cannot be considered inspired is determined by legal and prophetic models of Scripture. Hence much energy is invested in reading Ecclesiastes in such a way as to make it conform to a doctrine of Scripture that subverts the book's contents. Since Ecclesiastes *is* Scripture, and since it is known that Scripture behaves "this way, and not that way," there is little choice in the matter but to reread Ecclesiastes with these doctrinal concerns in mind.

What is lost in such a move, however, is an appreciation of what the counterpoint can add to our understanding of the nature of Scripture. If the wise God wills that his people would have *this* Scripture that says *these* kinds of things, might that not be a valuable piece of information for us as we come to terms with what it means when we say "word of God"? If the Psalms reflect Israel's praise and laments, if Proverbs records sage observations of the social order, if Ecclesiastes shows us an influential Israelite in the throes of despair, and if we understand these and others forms of Scripture, as Scripture, to have every bit as much right to be included, as of equal value, for addressing the question not only of the doctrine of Scripture but of the doctrine of God, then it follows that our thinking about Scripture overall will have to reflect such a diverse portrait.

Some are motivated to articulate a doctrine of Scripture that will help protect its identity as God's word and to prevent its abuse. I understand the motivation, but it is worth pointing out that Scripture itself may be a bit more "risky" a product than its protectors are willing to see — and Ecclesiastes drives the point home. Counterpoint shows that Scripture includes but is more than a collection of writings that can be described by a legal or prophetic model. Part of God's "authoritative communication" to his church includes a robust and highly varied articulation of the journey of believers. It stands to reason, therefore, that Scripture presents itself in such a way that cannot be described as simply a code of conduct, code of law, revelation of God's will, and so on. Rather *Scripture articulates both the divine initiative and the human response.* Neither dimension is less Scripture than the other, neither is less borne along by the Spirit than the other. This means that, as we look to Scripture, there is more there than the revelation of the divine will. There is also the inclusion of how those who are bound to God will struggle in discerning and following that revelation. In other words, Scripture is not simply an authoritative guide but a *covenantal document* that shows how seriously God takes the *relationship* he has with his people. Thus Scripture truly becomes a source of comfort and companionship to God's people in their spiritual journeys throughout their lives. When we read Scripture, we see not only God but ourselves *as God willingly sees us* — and it is good to know that God cares enough about the latter perspective to weave it so strongly into the fabric of Scripture.

A view of Scripture that embraces the counterpoint shows us how comfortable God is in the vicissitudes of life, and how willing and eager God is, in his mercy, to meet his people then and there. On one level, we see this throughout the historical books with their own type of theological diversity. That diversity is largely, though not exclusively, a function of the changing historical circumstances of the writers. The very significant and important differences between the Chronicler's telling of Israel's history and that of the Deuteronomistic Historian are a function of their different purposes in the context of their different historical settings. This type of developmental change is apparently not outside God's purposes, and so any doctrine of Scripture that does not embrace this dynamic characteristic is not rigorously biblical or God-centered.

On a more basic level, all of Scripture is God's condescension to the circumstances of life, since it is by his initiative that he speaks to and is involved in human affairs. This shows us much more than the fact that God condescends to us, or that he is involved in human affairs. It shows us how deeply he cares for his people, those who suffer and despair. Indeed, he is so intent on seeing this happen that he allows biblical writers to present him in a way that may not be altogether flattering. He allows himself to be interrogated and along the way to be misrepresented by his own creatures. *In Scripture itself* (let that sink in) he shows how willing he is to be presented as limited and distant. Scripture does not speak of God anthropomorphically (in human terms) — but even the less desirable of human traits are foisted upon God. The analogy with Christ is self-evident: he became not only human but despised and rejected among humans. So too in Scripture God allows to have ascribed to him the limited and fallen view of his creatures. In doing so, God thus makes the giving of Scripture an act of fatherly kindness and love to his people, the demonstration of the willingness of God to be like us — a divine initiative that finds its fullest articulation in Christ. To reduce this dynamic to one of "biblical authority" like an owner's manual or how-to book fails to do justice to what even a surface reading of Scripture demonstrates.

Models of Interpreting Scripture

In addition to making us think differently about Scripture, the counterpoint also helps us see different models for interpreting Scripture. This can be seen in the hermeneutical influence of the wisdom genre in general as well as those particular portions of Scripture that highlight suffering and despair. The latter issue is something we have already touched on, that the counterpoint can cause us to reflect more broadly on the nature of Scripture as the word of God. But beyond that, such an expanded understanding of the nature of Scripture will also — obviously — affect how we go about interpreting it: doctrine affects practice. So, hermeneutically speaking, knowing that Scripture itself regularly remarks on the human journey through suffering and despair should make us pause a bit when we consider what it means to handle Scripture properly. Briefly put, we do not see in Scripture a purely *prescriptive* type of communication, but a wonderfully *descriptive* one as well — where we see God at work in the life of his people and how his people work through this fact. Our expectation, therefore, of how Scripture is to function hermeneutically in the life of the church must take this into account. I mean more than simply a matter of acknowledging that some portions of Scripture are (regrettably) "merely" descriptive, knowing that they are, and then moving along to the more important prescriptive portion. I am asking, rather, whether the counterpoint should affect our hermeneutics overall, even in those prescriptive portions of Scripture, so that wherever we find ourselves in Scripture we are cognizant of the fact that we are in conversation with the text — where God is meeting his people, where the transcendent embraces human particularity.

Again, I fear I am not doing a very good job of hiding my opinion on the matter. Perhaps the point can be illustrated more concretely by looking at wisdom in general and its hermeneutical implications. Think of Proverbs and the diversity and flexibility this corpus of wisdom sayings includes. We have seen earlier that the situational character of Proverbs suggests that one must be wise in reading the situation and not simply the text. Again, this seems to be at least one problem with Job's friends. Their condemnation of Job is legitimate but only superficially so: they proof-text rather than discern the moment to consider whether the scriptural notion of immediate retribution should be applied mechanically. This "it depends" factor, as I named it earlier, is of paramount importance in handling wisdom literature. The question I am asking here is whether this "hermeneutic of wisdom" is one that can and should be applied to Scripture as a whole. Does knowing the circumstance affect how one might approach texts that are of different genres, namely of the legal, prophetic, or narrative kind?

Yes it does. For example, when Jesus gives the *command* to turn the other cheek, does it not take wisdom to know how and when that should be done? Does the situation affect how or even whether this admonition should be adhered to? Some strong pacifists might argue that the circumstances are irrelevant, but many (dare I say most) Christians would likely affirm quite readily that this admonition is not one that carries over to national concerns or protection of the innocent. (One does not turn the other cheek when Pearl Harbor has been bombed, nor when you are in a position to stop a child-killer.) I do not want to appear simplistic, nor do I want to express anything other than deep respect for the peace traditions of the church. But the fact remains that we have a hermeneutical problem here. What Jesus *says* is clear (sort of), but how Jesus' words should be applied is a matter of wisdom. Likewise, when Paul says, "Children, obey your parents" (Eph 6:1), does he mean absolutely, all the time? Even though he is citing the fifth commandment, written in stone by the finger of God, is Paul arguing that no hint of disobedience is ever acceptable? What if the parents are corrupt or engaged in heinous behaviors? Is not wisdom necessary for understanding and applying what Paul says?

Paul's writings seem about as propositional as any we encounter in the NT. Moreover, it is his patient and powerful exposition of the gospel that undergirds so much of Christian theology, particularly Protestant theology. What should not be forgotten, however, is the undeniable situational dimension of Paul's letters — being, as they are, *letters*.[13] Paul is not so much giving his readers timeless truths (as a legal or prophetic model might imply for

---

13. It is sometimes quipped that reading the NT letters is "reading someone else's mail." This does not imply, of course, that one should therefore not read them. It is, however, a reminder to be ever conscious of the situational dimension of the NT letters lest we mishandle them. Such an acknowledgment is nothing more than a central element of grammatical-historical exegesis.

some) as he is bringing together the particular situations of his readers with the context of the revealed gospel. It is this situational dimension that helps us grasp why Paul's writings do not display a systematic precision on matters that pertain to, for example, the law or the status of women in the church. The gospel is not negotiable for Paul, but each letter of his is a communication to a particular people with whom he has a particular relationship. Some of his readers have an antinomian tendency, and so Paul's view of the law is more traditional. Others elevate the law (especially circumcision) to a soteriological category, and so Paul comes down very hard on them and puts the law in its place. We honor Scripture not by taking one strand of passages, privileging them and holding others in their grip, or by aligning all of Paul's statements into one "coherent" theology. We honor Scripture by taking the time to read it wisely, knowing the situation so that we can discern (likewise an application of wisdom) how and to what extent these words apply to other situations.

In other words, there is more to reading the Bible than reading the Bible. One must also read the situation, and the Bible itself models for us frequently this hermeneutical posture. Such an approach to biblical interpretation is an application of Gerald Sheppard's thoughtful thesis that "at a certain period in the development of OT literature, wisdom became a theological category associated with an understanding of canon which formed a perspective from which to interpret Torah and prophetic traditions. In this sense wisdom became a hermeneutical construct for interpreting sacred Scripture."[14] Consider, for example, several instances in the book of Acts. There is certainly a "prophetic" quality to apostolic activity in the first-century church, but a wisdom dimension shines through as well. In Acts 6:1-7 the apostles are to choose from among them seven men to serve as deacons. They are chosen on the basis of whether their lives are known by them to be full of the Spirit and wisdom (v. 3). They are not chosen by direct revelation, but by the application of wisdom, and as a result "the word of God spread" (v. 7).

Likewise, in chapter 15 we read of the Jerusalem Council. Such a council was needed to exercise wisdom and discernment concerning the issue of Gentile believers, particularly the issue of whether Gentiles are to be circumcised as an entryway to becoming Christians. As we read in vv. 28-29, the Gentile believers are charged in the following manner.

> It seemed good to the Holy Spirit and to us not to burden you with anything beyond the following requirements: You are to abstain from food

---

14. Sheppard, *Wisdom as a Hermeneutical Construct*, 13.

> *sacrificed to idols*, from *blood*, from the *meat of strangled animals* and
> from *sexual immorality*. You will do well to avoid these things. Farewell.
> (NIV, italics added)

What is important for us, first of all, is the seemingly innocent phrase "It
seemed good to the Holy Spirit and to us." The conclusions of the council were
not a matter of employing the Urim and Thummim, or receiving some other
direct divine revelation — even at this crucial moment in the life of the early
church. Rather, what they exercised was wisdom, which is a quality of Spirit-
led, mature Christians. Also, it would be a grave mistake to read this fourfold
charge as a list of the "four most important laws Gentiles should keep." Jews
had learned to distance themselves from particular kinds of Greco-Roman behavior, and the council expected the same of Gentile converts. The issue is not
one of an abstract keeping of the law, but purity among followers of Christ in a
Greco-Roman context. The Gentiles are not being charged to hold on to at
least some laws, to be legalistic without going too far. Why take a stand against
such a central Jewish requirement as circumcision simply to introduce other
laws into the equation? What is at work here, rather, is the wise application of
Israel's legal tradition to Gentiles in the context of Greco-Roman practices so
as not to offend unnecessarily their Jewish brothers and sisters, all for the advance of the gospel.[15] The council's admonition is a wisdom move.

In Acts 15:5 the issue of Gentile circumcision is clearly stated and the Jerusalem Council gives its answer. But what is of further interest is how situational even that conclusion can be. For example, in Gal 5:11-12 Paul famously
declares that those who see circumcision as necessary for entry into the family of God should just go on and castrate themselves. This reflects the negative
view of circumcision of the Jerusalem Council, and one would think that Paul
would have little tolerance for an alternate view on circumcision. But consider Paul's own activity in Acts 16. Following on the heels of the Jerusalem
Council, Paul circumcises Timothy (16:3). The reason Paul does this is not because he is unaware of the event recounted in the previous chapter. Rather, he
circumcises Timothy so as not to present a stumbling block to the Jews in that
area when Timothy accompanied Paul on his journeys.[16] They knew Timothy's father was Greek, and they would be less open to Paul's preaching if he
had in tow a young, uncircumcised, Greek male.

---

15. The purpose of the decree "was to provide a minimal platform for sacramental fellowship in communities where at least some believers of Jewish background had qualms about
dietary matters" (Pervo, *Acts*, 376).

16. The stark contrast between the decree of the Jerusalem Council and Paul's act here is
"motivated by prudential considerations" (Johnson, *Acts*, 284).

Paul's posture here is similar to what we see in Acts 21:20-26. He arrives in Jerusalem, but the Jewish brothers have a concern. It seems that the gospel is making some headway there. Many thousands have believed, "and all of them are zealous for the law" (v. 20) — a curious way of explaining faith in Christ. Now, anyone familiar with Paul's temperament in his letters might guess that he would respond quickly with some comment about the inadequacy of the law in view of Christ's death and resurrection, and so on, but he does not. Rather, in an effort to convince the Jews that he is not telling his Jewish converts (i.e., "Jews who live among the Gentiles") to "turn away from Moses" (v. 21), he enters into a Jewish purification rite with four other Jews so as to demonstrate for all to see "there is no truth in these reports about you, but that you yourself are living in obedience to the law" (v. 24). Again, one might think that the apostle to the Gentiles should be less willing to support a program that he elsewhere criticizes so strongly. The reason, however, that Paul has Timothy circumcised and then later joins in a Jewish purification rite is that "mission drives theology." The issue of Jewish offense is at work in all of these cases, that is, not wanting to show disrespect to Jews by showing contempt for the law. Even though the law has no soteriological significance, it has a tremendous sociological benefit in the goal of forming one people of God, made up of Jew and Gentile. The Jerusalem Council and Paul exercised wisdom in negotiating a situation that, otherwise, might have been far more explosive than it already was.

We might also glance at 1 Cor 9:21-23 in the context of these passages in Acts. There Paul famously declares,

> To those not having the law I became like one not having the law (though I am not free from God's law but am under Christ's law), so as to win those not having the law. To the weak I became weak, to win the weak. I have become all things to all men so that by all possible means I might save some. I do all this for the sake of the gospel, that I may share in its blessings. (NIV)

Here Paul makes clear that even a central element to his teaching elsewhere, the law, is subservient to the mission of the gospel.[17] The larger point for us to consider, however, is that this very process of being as one who is or is not under the law is a wisdom exercise. There is no Bible verse to follow, nothing to exegete that will provide the answer. There is only the leading of the Holy Spirit at work in the lives of those who are in Christ, who are trying

---

17. To be sure, Paul is not advocating lawlessness but coming out from under the law that marked Jewish identity (Fee, *First Corinthians*, 429-30).

to see themselves in that grand synthesis of Scripture, tradition, and contemporary life. We are all, as perhaps Paul was here, working things out, driven by a Spirit we cannot control, discerning the circumstance we did not foresee, and then acting on what we think is best. We are at every moment, to expand the imagery of Prov 26:4-5 discussed earlier, deciding whether to answer a fool or not. Making those decisions is an exercise of wisdom.

Throughout the NT we see writers applying wisdom to their own situations, but this is more than a casual observation on our part of how Scripture behaves. We not only see their own hermeneutic at work, but their hermeneutic challenges us to consider our own. For example, in Romans 12–16 we see a series of admonitions by Paul. These all may be characterized as "living according to wisdom in a post-resurrection world." But we fail to grasp the point of Paul's admonitions if we ignore the very situational nature of his words. For example, in Romans 13 Paul admonishes his readers to submit to authorities. To be sure, Paul's words here are in no small way influenced by the fact that he wishes this group of Roman Christians to behave in such a way as to increase the influence of the gospel at the hub of ancient civilization. He is certainly not suggesting that always and at all times one is to submit to authorities, otherwise the early Christians would have reverted back to some sort of Caesar worship when told to renounce Christ.

But more importantly for us, the question is how a passage like Romans 13 applies to us, or is "authoritative" for us. What is the synthesis between Paul's ancient words and our contemporary situation? I do not think it is to be found in a slavish repetition of the literal sense of Paul's words (what American would quibble with this, founded as we are out of rebellion?), nor is it in abstracting some "principle" from the passage (what is the "principle" of Rom 13:1 if not "submit to authorities?!"). Rather, Paul's wise words here, driven as they are by his own synthesis of the gospel and its particular application, are valuable for the church today in this sense: they demonstrate for us the very work we are to do as we seek to be ever-faithful followers of Christ, imbued with the Spirit, and thoroughly immersed in Scripture. Such an interaction does not give us infallible information at every moment, but it is the calling of every Christian.

Examples could be multiplied here, but the point remains the same. *The practice of Christianity is a matter of wisdom and the very word that serves as our guide to all matters pertaining to faith and life exhibits this very same wisdom dynamic.* This is hardly to devalue Scripture, as some might conclude. It is, rather, a very sober — and, I might add, biblical — articulation of what our Scripture is and how it is to be handled. And it is an assessment of the nature of Israel's wisdom tradition that opens up this avenue of exploration.

All of this can be tied back to Ecclesiastes specifically. As an example of both wisdom and counterpoint, Ecclesiastes provides all sorts of challenges for Christians today who are seeking to discern its relevance. But we must remember just that very point: it is an act of discernment. The Bible is surprisingly resistant to attempts to reduce its hermeneutical complexity to a series of quick affirmations and denials. When one has such a posture, one can certainly understand the need to come to a quick resolution about whether Qohelet is right or wrong. "The word of God — as we know — cannot be so ambiguous. It simply *must* speak to us — plainly, quickly." This is misguided. If anything, a glance at the synchronic and diachronic diversity of biblical interpretation in the history of Christianity (not to mention Judaism) will reveal quite readily that the Bible is not so amenable to our control. The Bible is deep and rich, and if we want to access it, it is going to take some time and effort, and we are likely going to miss the mark at least as often as we hit it.

Ecclesiastes, especially, seems aimed more at unsettling readers than comforting them. But here too we see the word of God. What makes Ecclesiastes the word of God is not simply a nod to its inspired status, nor its alleged Solomonic authorship, nor the simple fact that it is "in the canon" (since this begs the question of why it is in the canon). In my opinion, what makes Ecclesiastes Scripture is not how it came about or who wrote it. Rather, it is the role it plays in God's purposes to challenge his people to think more deeply about the nature of life "under the sun," and — perhaps more importantly — *to affirm the normalcy and benefit of being in a state of struggle, despair, and disorientation in one's relationship with God* at certain stages in our spiritual journeys.

In this sense, the necessity of wisdom for understanding and applying Ecclesiastes is almost self-evident. And, by having such a hermeneutically mature view of things, we can quickly see how important this "wisdom hermeneutic" is for understanding not only Scripture as a whole but the very practice of Christianity. How is Scripture to be applied *here?* This is a question every generation is called to work out. Biblical interpretation is, in this sense, a journey, a pilgrimage, not a fortress. Mature biblical interpretation recognizes how embedded both we and the biblical writers are in our respective contexts — and that we should thank God for it. It recognizes that, as situations change, new interpretive challenges arise, and so sees the importance of both progress and maintenance in our use of Scripture. Wisdom is not a concept restricted to some books of the OT and maybe James in the NT. It is a central concept in how we understand the nature of Scripture and its use. It is also, therefore, central to how we live out the Christian life.

Ecclesiastes and Praxis

The Bible is not an owner's manual, and the Christian life is more complex than the application of a few biblical principles. Indeed, much of the Christian life is connected, at best, only tangentially to "biblical teaching." In vain do we "look to Scripture" to provide "answers" to some of the most basic issues confronting us today. I have heard it said many times that the most pressing challenge of the nineteenth century to Christians and the authority of the Bible for their lives was not the many discoveries (e.g., Babylonian creation myths) and theories (e.g., Wellhausen's Documentary Hypothesis) about the Bible and its origins that began to surface during that century. It was, in the United States at least, slavery.[18] Here was an issue of indescribable moral importance, and the country was divided, with both sides citing Scripture in defense of polar opposite opinions. Can it be that, on even so pressing and "clear" an issue, we cannot rely on Scripture to help us?

This situation contributed to the overall "authority crisis" Christians were feeling during this time. If anything, we are reminded once again that there is more to "applying the Bible" than reading what it "says" and doing it. Rather, it is a process that involves often unstated and deeply held instincts about how Scripture ought to be handled, not to mention, unfortunately, an unstated deep commitment to one's own position that one "knows" to be correct and then "applying" the Bible to make the point. But when we take the time to observe the connection between what Scripture "teaches" and the ups and downs of our own daily existence, we see that there is often more disconnection than anything else. One might say that a fair amount of the Christian life is improvisation in the Spirit. We are in the process of making split-second decisions at nearly every turn where no biblical command, admonition, or proverb seems to relate.

This sense of disconnection between what we experience in our daily lives may not be all-encompassing or ever-present, but it is certainly there, as anyone can attest who has been a Christian for more than a brief time. Like Qohelet, we look around and — perhaps with the despair knob turned down from ten to five — wonder whether all this really makes sense. Do I really believe what I say I believe? Is God really there? Is there any good reason to keep on? Who of us has not asked these questions, perhaps in the quiet of our own

18. See Noll, *Civil War*. Noll argues that biblical interpretations clashed irreconcilably before and during the Civil War, and that some foreign commentators, especially Roman Catholics, understood this as a crisis in biblical authority, not just biblical interpretation. The clash of interpretation led to pondering biblical authority after the war. See Oshantz, "Problem of Moral Progress."

minds, when we can grab a quiet moment alone, at the end of the day, after the dust has settled and we have a moment to think?

The good news, I suppose, is that when we are in that difficult place, we are in good company with Qohelet, Job, the lament psalms — even Jesus himself. Like the frame narrator of Ecclesiastes, I do not mean to appear in any way dismissive of the struggle. Indeed, my aim is to affirm it. The Christian life is tough for reasons that, if we take a moment to reflect, are not all that different from what Qohelet was uttering: I am doing my best, but it seems that God is nowhere to be found. I am angry with God for doing this (who else is to blame?), and I am not sure what the sense is to keep going.

Honesty in the Faith Journey

If I gather anything from reading Ecclesiastes and the other counterpoint portions of the Bible, it is the value of being honest with one's struggles, even if — especially if — they pertain to God. I remember well an incident when my son was six years old. We had just moved from one state to another and into our first house. Our family routines were disrupted for a while, and when we settled a bit, we resurrected one of those routines: a brief Bible reading and prayer before bedtime. I turned to the garden of Eden story and began reading. Adam, Eve, a talking serpent — familiar and full of drama, a safe place to resume our routine. As I read, my son kept sighing, as if annoyed. I ignored him and kept reading. He kept sighing. I stopped and asked him what was wrong.

"Daddy, snakes can't talk."

I ignored him.

"Daddy, snakes can't talk."

This was clearly on his mind, so I stopped reading, wondering where all this might go. I asked him what he meant, and he began telling me what amounted to a faith crisis. The final blow was when he said, "I just don't know if I believe in God anymore."

I had failed as a parent. That was where my head went immediately. I teach the OT for a living, and here is my six-year-old heretic son, questioning the Bible and declaring that now he has trouble believing that God is real because the Bible opens up with a story — not unlike some cartoons he watches — of two naked people in a magic garden having a casual conversation with a snake.

My first instinct was to hush him up: "Shhhhhh! Don't say that! God may hear you." Wouldn't want to rock the boat, now would we? Thankfully I resisted that impulse. Not only is the notion of keeping our feelings from God somewhat silly (and arrogant), one only has to glance at the Bible to see that, even at the age of six, my son was in pretty good company. Rather, I told him: "You don't really believe in God anymore? Okay, well, tell *him*." He was not expecting this response, but I think it is one that has good biblical precedent. Let's not talk *about* the problem; tell God *he* is the problem. Be honest with him. It is by being honest, laying out where we really are with God, that true growth can come. Consider, again, the writer of Psalm 73. He was struggling mightily with God's justice, so much so that he had nearly lost his foothold (v. 2). He did not understand until he "entered the sanctuary of God" (v. 17). If you have a problem with God, the only good thing to do is to march right up to God and address him directly. Like the frame narrator, if one is struggling with the core issue of what it means to be an Israelite in covenant with God, the response is to go on and be an Israelite even more ("fear God and keep his commandments").

Qohelet's response to his human condition is one that may generally be called a "theodicy of protest," where despair leads to dissent, which is addressed by asking what God will do in the future (a matter that the epilogue raises succinctly in 12:14).[19] There is much to be gained from looking at Ecclesiastes from this perspective. Shaking one's fist at God is part of the Israelite experience and has been revisited throughout the Jewish and Christian dramas. With respect to practical theology, it is indeed good to see how that protest has a place in the Christian life, and that Christianity does not supersede Israel's protest as much as recasts it in view of the passion and resurrection of Christ. On the other hand, I do not think "theodicy" captures either Qohelet's tone or that of the frame narrator. A true theodicy seeks to legitimate God's actions in the face of evidence to the contrary. It seeks to provide some answer. It is not a theodicy if the answer is assumed in the very quest — as is the case with Qohelet.[20]

Qohelet does not seek to legitimate God — Qohelet blames him. He is not concerned with the "problem of evil" but with the absurdity of life. What bothers Qohelet is not newspaper headlines of tragedies or violent and senseless deaths. It is that faith in Israel's God has no explanatory power for the ev-

---

19. This notion is developed in Roth, "Theodicy of Protest."

20. Roth describes further this theodicy of protest as an "antitheodicy" for its resistance to explaining all suffering as simply deserved or to assuring the sufferer that there will be a happy ending by "appealing to God's unfathomable wisdom and goodness" (ibid., 17). Schoors echoes this view: "Qohelet offers no rationally acceptable solution of the problem of theodicy . . . he does not even try to find a theoretical solution, so that we might say that he simply does not have a theodicy" ("Theodicy in Qohelet," 403).

eryday things that occupy our time: building, working, marrying, saving money, and especially our own inevitable mortality. Qohelet does not ask why God does what he does (or better, fails to do what he should). He simply declares that God cannot be counted on to bring coherence to his life. It is clear to Qohelet that God is oblivious to what Qohelet's religious heritage prescribes God to be. Nor do the frame narrator's closing comments seek to legitimate God. As Thiselton puts it, Ecclesiastes as a whole does not address the question of God's responsibility for evil in the world. Rather, the author is writing a "confessional act."[21] By legitimating Qohelet's dissenting observations and then admonishing his readers to continue down the very path Qohelet has been protesting against (fear and obedience), the frame narrator is making a statement of faith.

Most Christians, at least in my experience, can identify with this notion of protest and dissent — and to see this endorsed in Scripture can be a breath of fresh air. Ecclesiastes encourages such honesty, and it borders on simple common sense to acknowledge that we cannot hide our feelings from God, and it is perhaps best not to try. But in order to be honest with God it is necessary that we be fully honest with ourselves first. Never let it be said that theology is divorced from psychology and sociology. How we think of God, what we are willing to say, the questions we are willing to pose, are wrapped up in our own sociological identity and psychological frame of mind. If we are honest with ourselves, we may find we are far less in control of things than we think, and we may find a God who is far less interested in being controlled than we want. It is very hard work knowing oneself, but fear of standing out, of not fitting in, of losing one's social identity, is a strong factor. We pull back from full disclosure, true honesty and authenticity, in order to preserve our identities. For a variety of complex reasons, we often act as if everything is fine when in fact all is not well.

It is my experience, and I am sure of many others, that life in the Christian community can sometimes feel like a show. We do not always know one another very well, let alone ourselves, and we are very concerned to put on appearances. To think this way is a great injustice to the Christian faith. It cheapens it as yet another commodity to be controlled and manipulated for personal gain. It ceases being that which gives us our true identities to become that which is manipulated, along with everything else, to hold on to our false selves. But the gospel is transformative, from the inside out, and so it stands to reason that a failure to be honest with oneself and therefore with others (especially God) is a fundamental barrier to true spiritual growth.

21. Thiselton, "Dialogue, Dialectic," 749.

Growth is frightening, to be sure. It hurts — much like the goads and firmly embedded nails of a shepherd (Eccl 12:11).

We can conjure up many reasons for maintaining a posture of dishonesty toward oneself and God. Perhaps we have achieved a position of some power, either academically or ecclesiastically, and to open up to others how dark our soul really is may jeopardize that standing. Perhaps we are so intoxicated by that power that we are not even truly aware of how out of touch we are with our own state. For others, the failure to utter before God where we really are and what we are really thinking may be a function of how we were taught to think of the faith — that real Christians have it together and simply do not go to such dark places, and to do so would disappoint God. Frankly, a glance at the Bible should cure us of this nonsense, but there you have it. In what is perhaps one of the more ironic twists we can think of, the gospel becomes a motivation to hide from our true selves rather than the prompting to be more real than the world could ever allow. The God of Scripture is a no-nonsense God who is not interested in our wearing masks or maintaining well-scripted roles. He is not interested in how "together" we can appear, but in how much we truly belong to him. Books like Ecclesiastes show us how it is done.

We often speak of having a relationship with God without our accounting for the fact that truly healthy relationships are founded on trust and honesty. A relationship with God is one where trust and honesty reach a depth that we, in our carefully orchestrated social networks, may not be prepared to handle. In this sense, the despairing cry of Qohelet or a psalmist is about as real and honest as it gets. No, one is not required to remain there, but these moments are a necessary step to go through in order to achieve greater intimacy. In human relationships we often hear that there can be no deep connection between two people without going through very difficult times, where the masks come off and we are more vulnerable and more truly known by others. This is what happens when we risk our false sense of self-control and tell God exactly what we think. And this is why we are to consider it a joy when we are in such a difficult place that requires such gut-wrenching honesty.

Qohelet's words are not a hermeneutical or theological problem to be overcome. They are a path to spiritual growth. Qohelet is not a villain. He is our hero.

Suffering

One of my favorite authors is Stephen Lawhead. His novels largely center on medieval themes and always have a Christian undercurrent without being heavy-handed. I like his books because they help me to think of my faith outside contemporary trappings. One of his novels, *Byzantium*,[22] is set in medieval Ireland and recounts the journeys of a young scribe, Aidan, living in an Irish monastery. He is chosen by the order to accompany some monks to Byzantium to present a gift to the emperor. The journey turns out to be more than he bargained for. Along the way he is captured and enslaved by Vikings, and his trek to Byzantium takes a long and distant detour.

At the end of the book, Aidan is back in his native land when a lookout sees the Sea Wolves (Vikings) approaching. The abbey is in a state of panic, scurrying about to hide the treasure. They send Aidan to meet them, hoping his facility with the language would dissuade them from bringing their warring ways to their peaceful abbey. As they come closer, Aidan recognizes one of the Vikings as his old friend Gunnar. Soon he finds himself in a reunion with those who first enslaved him and then came to be his close friends.

As it turns out, the Vikings have come to Aidan's land not to plunder and pillage but to seek out their friend. Throughout their journeys together Aidan had opportunities to respond with Christian love to those who at first meant him only harm. The Vikings come bearing a very expensive gift (a solid silver book cover embossed with the image of a cross) — only it is no gift but a first installment of a trade agreement. The Vikings want to build "a church for the Christ" and they want Aidan, who introduced them to Christianity, to come back with them to oversee the project.

Unfortunately, in the meantime, Aidan's struggles have brought him to a point of despair, unbelief, and he chides his visitors for trusting in a God who "cares nothing for us." But Gunnar responds that it is *their* gods who "neither hear nor care." What makes the Christian God different is that he came to live among the fisherfolk and was hung up on a tree to die. "And I remember thinking," says Gunnar, "this Hanging God is unlike any of the others; this god suffers, too, just like his people. . . . Does Odin do this for those who worship him? Does Thor suffer with us?"

This episode illustrates what is so disarming — and sometimes underemphasized — about the gospel. Christians claim that their God, manifested in Christ, knows suffering and has in some true sense experienced it.[23] The Christian faith is counterintuitive. When we suffer, God

22. Lawhead, *Byzantium*. The pages cited and alluded to below are 856-63.

23. I do not mean to raise here the very involved issue of whether the Father suffers, or the way in which he suffers, in the crucifixion. Unraveling this ball of yarn would require a deeper understanding of the incarnation than we will ever have. As far as I am concerned, it is enough to confess that our suffering is not foreign to God, and the cross demonstrates the fact. To what extent the Father participated in the Son's suffering is a theologically generative ques-

knows and understands. Indeed, it is more than this: he understands better than we do, for his suffering was deeper. In his suffering, Christ was like us; in our suffering, we become more like him. The Vikings understand what every reader of Scripture should recognize immediately: suffering will come but God's participation in suffering is, as Gunnar concluded, "good news."

Suffering is a central NT theme — both the suffering of Christ and the suffering promised to those who follow him. Understanding the purpose of suffering should be front and center in our Christian training and education. As many know, a theme of some popular expressions of the gospel (TV preachers, Christian self-help books) is that suffering is evidence of a lack of faith or of God's withdrawn blessing. Thus, when those who hold to such views address books like Ecclesiastes, they assume at the outset that something must be wrong with Qohelet, and thankfully the frame narrator neutralizes such a faithless perspective. I do not wish to discuss what might motivate such thinking, but I am certain that it can stem from honest (yet mistaken) impulses as well as dishonest ones. What Christian has not asked, at some point in his/her life, Why is this happening to me? Why is God doing this? Why is God acting this way? Have I done something to deserve this? These are normal questions, but they all seem to stem from the same faulty premise, that suffering is somehow unusual, unexpected, abnormal, and that someone is at fault, and so some sort of explanation is required.

I want to make clear that I am in no way minimizing suffering or suggesting that we should simply behave stoically, take it as our lot in life, and move on. Nothing could be further from a gospel-centered understanding of suffering. Suffering is a deep, deep state of being where we are perhaps more real than at other times in our lives. We should suffer honestly, loudly, openly, not shy away from it. Jesus' agony and even doubt were displayed for all to see, and are even recorded for us in the Gospels. We should do no less. But we must also try to recall, sooner or later, that our suffering is what forges the closer tie between us and our Creator, who through his suffering in Christ has also become the Redeemer. I do not claim to understand it, nor do I claim to have reached a point in my own life where I accept this. Still, this is the truth of the gospel. This is the mystery and even offense, if also comfort, of the gospel: our suffering has redemptive value, both for us as well as for others.

When we are truly suffering — to the point where we, like Qohelet, the psalmists, and Job, question God himself — we are engaged in something truly meaningful for our own spiritual development (i.e., our true development as

---

tion, and in other contexts a very important one to investigate, but it is not something that needs to be settled in this discussion concerning Ecclesiastes.

human beings created in God's image). Suffering is what propels us on the road to great maturity. Our suffering does not redeem us as does the Savior's, but it does contribute to our total redemptive process, which includes our completion, a process often referred to as sanctification. It is through suffering that we are being saved every day, so to speak. It is through the disconnect we all feel, as did Qohelet, that the life we live here and now does not seem to match up very well with the glimpse we caught, by virtue of our union with the resurrected Christ, of what God's world ought to look like. Our suffering somehow prepares us to be more fully human, that is, more fully Christlike.

Likewise, when we suffer we are most like Jesus to those around us. As Paul wrote, "For just as the sufferings of Christ flow over into our lives, so also through Christ our comfort overflows" (2 Cor 1:5). Our suffering prepares us to help others in similar situations. And this is more than simply a matter of helping them limp along. If that were all there were to it, one might easily ask why God does not just stop all the suffering rather than find suffering people to comfort the suffering. But this brings us back to the central point of all this. It is not simply that by our suffering we can comfort others. Rather it is by our suffering that we can *be Jesus* to others. Our own sufferings have a redemptive impact on others. This is quite startling if we pause to think about it. When we suffer we are only *then* in the position to truly comfort others, because our suffering makes us more like Jesus so we can act more like Jesus toward the other. Like most Christians, I have been at the end of my rope more than once in my life. Thankfully, I have always had access to fellow travelers to help me through it. These are people who, amazingly, have gone through very similar episodes, and they are poised and primed to participate in my suffering and offer true comfort and wisdom. If we can learn anything from the honesty of Qohelet or of Jesus himself, it is that by opening up the inner world of our own pain we can be equipped to be used by God to show Jesus to others. It is, in a word, a tragedy when Christians — either knowingly or unknowingly — mute this very important aspect of the Christian life.

We can take another cue from Qohelet. Despite the tendency — at least as I see it — to privilege the physical dimensions of suffering, we must also pay attention to the emotional/psychological, even intellectual, dimensions of suffering in our world. To be sure, we should never forget the many heinous ways human beings conjure up to inflict physical suffering on other humans, but, especially in the Western world, we are not always exposed to such things. But this does not mean that suffering is not there. With physical suffering there is, obviously, a deeply emotional component as well. For others, however, the suffering takes on an exclusively emotional dimension — as it did with Qohelet.

It is my point of view that *any* suffering a Christian endures, no matter what its source or expression, has redemptive value. There is something unique about martyrs, those who die for the faith, but we do an injustice if we conclude that Christian suffering cannot also be considered on a broader scale. Any suffering a Christian endures is Christian suffering in that it all contributes to conforming us more to the image of Christ. So, when a Christian suffers from depression, as many quietly do, this is more than a problem that we need to get over with Jesus' help. There is also in the struggle something redemptive happening, for oneself and others. When we lose all we have through an accident, an "act of God," or a plummeting economy, and it causes us great stress and anguish, that too is a suffering of redemptive value. These are times when God shows us how concerned he is with us to bring us back to the basics in order to redirect our lives. We may be kicking and screaming along the way, as was Qohelet. We may say all sorts of things along the way, as did Qohelet, but none of it diminishes the ultimate redemptive value of what is happening.

We all know that these kinds of life experiences can threaten to drive us away from God, but we also know that those dark times eventually begin to brighten when we catch glimpses of God's redemptive purposes. Scripture's counterpoint reminds us of the inevitability of suffering and depths of its purpose. Suffering is not the occasional bump or roadblock that impedes our growth; it is the preferred path by which we achieve that goal. It is not the problem to be overcome; it is that through which we overcome. Such suffering is truly a "dark night of the soul," although not in the sense in which that famous phrase of St. John of the Cross is often misunderstood. As psychiatrist Gerald May puts it, " 'dark night of the soul' has become a catch phrase in the circles of pop spirituality, where it is used to describe all kinds of misfortunes from major life tragedies to minor disappointments."[24] Instead, what St. John was after is a sense of the redemptive value of suffering, where suffering instigates "a deep transformation, a movement toward indescribable freedom and joy," where one is "liberated from attachments and compulsions and empowered to live and love more freely."[25]

What makes this liberation "dark" is that our suffering is out of our control. We do not choose how to suffer and when. It happens to us. Our choice is how to respond, and out of that comes that transformation of which St. John speaks. In this respect, the "answer" to suffering is, as Harold Kushner puts it, not so much "explanation" as it is "response."[26] Is this not also the frame nar-

---

24. May, *Dark Night of the Soul*, 4.
25. Ibid., 4-5.
26. Kushner, *When Bad Things Happen*, 147. Similarly, Viktor Frankl's "will to meaning,"

rator's "answer" to Qohelet's despair, to "respond" to it by continuing to live in harmony with God, despite appearances? I do not understand all of this, nor do I necessarily like it. I would be very careful not to pass this along in a frivolous, unwise manner, to those whose nerves may be so raw they are not in a position to hear it. I am simply remarking that Scripture itself — not to mention the example of Jesus — puts the matter before us with consistency and intensity. Once again, Qohelet is one of our heroes along the way, even if we are put off and even a bit offended by what he says. He is an honest sufferer, and we should honor that a part of his journey is put on display for us.

Keep Moving Anyway

The theological richness of Ecclesiastes, particularly when placed in its broader canonical context, is worthy of much further reflection and exploration than I can muster in the ending pages of a commentary. But, for me, one of the most gripping points that can be gleaned from the book is seen in 12:13 in the interplay between the frame narrator and Qohelet.

As we have seen in the introduction, the phrase כָּל־הָאָדָם/*kol-hā'ādām* appears four times in the book. In 3:13 and 5:18 it is found on Qohelet's lips as he describes what sums up humanity's daily task: to find enjoyment in one's daily existence amid all the absurdity. Then in 7:2 he states that it is for all humanity to die. In other words, what is the "whole duty of man" (as the NIV translates the phrase in 12:13)? Enjoy what you have, then die. The fourth occurrence of the phrase is in 12:13, where the frame narrator takes this expression and, while never refuting Qohelet, nevertheless does not leave the reader in such a state of despair. His solution to Qohelet's dilemma, rather, is to put his finger on what the real "duty of humanity" is, namely, "fear God and keep his commandments." In other words, for the benefit of his son (12:12), the frame narrator's response to the portrait Qohelet paints is, "Yes, but keep being an Israelite anyway."

I am reminded here of that wonderful scene in C. S. Lewis's *Silver Chair* (in the *Chronicles of Narnia*). The Green Witch has kidnapped and bewitched Prince Rilian and hidden him in her underground kingdom, waiting to reveal him at the right moment to rule all Narnia through him. Puddleglum, Jill

---

a response to suffering worked out in his experiences in Auschwitz, teaches individual responsibility in the face of suffering *(Man's Search for Meaning)*. One responds to suffering by choosing to construct meaning from it rather than be a victim. These experiences formed the basis for Frankl's unique therapeutic technique, Logotherapy (meaning-centered psychotherapy), which advocated the client's active decision to change one's outlook rather than the more introspective methods of conventional psychotherapy.

Pole, and Eustace Scrubb find themselves captured by the witch, and in a free moment find Prince Rilian (known to them only as "the Knight") masked and bound to a silver chair. They do not know, however, that he is the very prince they have been charged to find, thinking that he is simply one of the witch's underlings. He himself had warned them that, for one hour a day, he must be bound to a chair, as he raves madly and says all sorts of things — but they are not to believe him, no matter what he says. The truth is, however, that it is only during that one hour that the witch's spell holds no power over him, and it is then that he is in his right mind. But he warns his captives not to untie him under any circumstances, no matter what he says. If they do, he will kill them all.

Earlier in the story Aslan had charged Jill with "four signs" to guide them on their quest, and said they will know they are on the right track when they heed them. The fourth sign is most important: "You will know the lost prince (if you find him) by this, that he will be the first person you have met on your travels who will ask you to do something in my name, in the name of Aslan." When Prince Rilian came to his senses that one hour, he pleaded and pleaded with the three to release him from the bonds. He pleaded, cajoled, and even threatened them — as anyone in a similarly desperate situation might do. This continued for some time, and the three seemed resolute that releasing the prince would be tantamount to suicide, and so they refused to be taken in by all his tricks — that is, until the captive spoke one last time:

"Once and for all . . . I adjure you to set me free. By all fears and all loves, by the bright skies of Overland, by the great Lion, by Aslan himself, I charge you —"

They were sure the knight was going to kill them the moment he was released — but here was the fourth sign. They began to rationalize, thinking that perhaps it was an accident, or the witch knew of the signs and taught them to the knight in order to trick the would-be rescuers. How could they know that this was actually the fourth sign?

"Oh, if only we knew!" said Jill.

"I think we do know," said Puddleglum.

"Do you mean to think that everything will come right if we do untie him?" said Scrubb.

"I don't know about that," said Puddleglum. "You see, Aslan didn't tell Pole what would happen. He only told her what to do. That fellow will be the death of us once he's up, I shouldn't wonder. But that doesn't let us off following the sign."

Puddleglum is the frame narrator and Jill (Pole) and Eustace (Scrubb) are the son addressed in 12:12. Puddleglum does not minimize their fear.

Rather, he is quite certain that unbinding the Knight will mean death. But what one perceives, or what one thinks will happen, has no bearing on following the sign.

At the end of the day, I think the ultimate point about Ecclesiastes is to keep moving forward, no matter what. Whatever we are going through, however we see the world around us — even if we come to the point of blaming God for the whole mess — the final biblical answer is to push forward. And we do so not by ignoring or whitewashing the pain. We are not to play make-believe that everything is okay and real people of faith should not be going through this. To the contrary, the admonition to "keep moving" has teeth only because of the pain. It is only by moving through the pain that "fear God and keep his commandments, *anyway*," can take hold of us in our deepest distress. It is easy to believe, easy to act as you do, when things are going well. But when they are not, that is where real growth happens. And like a garden plant, we cannot grow tall unless our roots are deep in the manure.

The admonition to "keep moving anyway" is one that takes all control out of our hands. We are stripped down to nothing and then asked, "Are you going to follow or not? I understand that everything you hold dear has been taken away, and nothing that once made sense now does. I know that you hold me responsible for everything, that I am not just or good. I will not defend myself. The only matter before you is to follow or not follow. What will you do?" Those who, in the midst of such anguish, continue to follow, can be stopped by nothing else. If someone, feeling as Qohelet did, can rise from the ashes and continue down the path, that person has become indestructible. And if we have someone who has gone down that path before us, with more anguish than we can understand, who himself has emerged victorious, having conquered death itself (the very enemy Qohelet so feared) — then, as Gunnar said, this is truly good news.

No, Ecclesiastes does not sound the note as clearly as does the gospel, but the tone is evident nonetheless. Describing what one sees in unflinching terms is not an act of rebellion or faithlessness. It is wisdom. But even more wise is knowing that such wisdom does not explain all. The one who is truly wise will continue to trust and follow God, even when he/she is weary and worn from trying to make sense of God. He is never more our God than when he bids us to follow, even when we have every good reason not to. And we are never more his servants than when we obey — regardless.

Bibliography

Aland, B., et al., eds. *The Greek New Testament.* 4th ed. Stuttgart: Deutsche Bibelgesell-schaft, 1993.

Albertz, R. "The Sage and Pious Wisdom in the Book of Job: The Friends' Perspective." In *The Sage in Israel and the Ancient Near East.* Ed. J. G. Gammie and L. G. Perdue, 243-61. Winona Lake, IN: Eisenbrauns, 1990.

Alonso Schöckel, L. "Sapiential and Covenant Themes in Genesis 2–3." *TD* 13 (1965) 3-10.

Backhaus, F. J. *"Denn Zeit und Zufall trifft sie alle": Studien zur Komposition und zum Gottesbild im Buch Qohelet.* BBB 3. Frankfurt am Main: Anton Hain, 1993.

Balentine, S. E. *Job.* Smyth & Helwys Bible Commentary. Macon, GA: Smyth & Helwys, 2006.

Bartholomew, C. *Reading Ecclesiastes: Old Testament Exegesis and Hermeneutical Theory.* AnBib 139. Rome: Pontifical Biblical Institute, 1998.

Bastiaens, J. C. "The Language of Suffering in Job 16–19 and in the Suffering Servant Passages of Deutero-Isaiah." In *Studies in the Book of Isaiah: Festschrift Willem A. M. Beuken.* Ed. J. van Ruiten and M. Vervenne, 421-32. BETL 132. Leuven: Leuven University Press, 1997.

Beckwith, R. *The Old Testament Canon of the New Testament Church.* Grand Rapids: Eerdmans, 1985.

Blenkinsopp, J. "Ecclesiastes 3.1-15: Another Interpretation." *JSOT* 66 (1995) 55-64.

———. "The Sage, the Scribe, and Scribalism in the Chronicler's Work." In *The Sage in Israel and the Ancient Near East.* Ed. J. G. Gammie and L. G. Perdue, 307-15. Winona Lake, IN: Eisenbrauns, 1990.

———. *Wisdom and Law in the Old Testament: The Ordering of Life in Israel and Early Judaism.* Oxford: Oxford University Press, 1983.

Brichto, H. C. "Kin, Cult, Land and Afterlife — A Biblical Complex." *HUCA* 44 (1973) 1-54.

Brueggemann, W. *Texts under Negotiation: The Bible and Postmodern Imagination.* Minneapolis: Fortress, 1993.

———. *Theology of the Old Testament: Testimony, Dispute, Advocacy.* Minneapolis: Fortress, 1997.

Buhlman, A. "The Difficulty of Thinking in Greek and Speaking in Hebrew (Qohelet 3.18; 4.13-16; 5.8)." *JSOT* 90 (2000) 101-8.

Burkes, S. *Death in Qoheleth and Egyptian Biographies of the Late Period.* SBLDS 170. Atlanta: SBL, 1999.

Burkitt, F. C. "Is Ecclesiastes a Translation?" *JTS* 23 (1921-22) 22-26.

Carasik, M. "Qohelet's Twists and Turns." *JSOT* 28 (2003) 192-209.

Christianson, E. *A Time to Tell: Narrative Strategies in Ecclesiastes.* JSOTSup 280. Sheffield: Sheffield Academic Press, 1998.

Collins, J. J. "Wisdom, Apocalyptic, and Generic Compatibility." In *In Search of Wisdom: Essays in Memory of John G. Gammie.* Ed. L. G. Perdue et al., 165-85. Louisville: Westminster/John Knox, 1993.

Cooper, A. "The Suffering Servant and Job: A View from the Sixteenth Century." In *"As Those Who Are Taught": The Interpretation of Isaiah from the LXX to the SBL.* Ed. C. M. McGinnis and P. K. Tull, 189-200. SBL Symposium 27. Atlanta: SBL, 2006.

Crenshaw, J. *Ecclesiastes: A Commentary.* OTL. Philadelphia: Westminster, 1987.

——. *A Whirlpool of Torment: Israelite Traditions of God as an Oppressive Presence.* Overtures to Biblical Theology. Philadelphia: Fortress, 1984.

Davidson, R. M. *Flame of Yahweh: Sexuality in the Old Testament.* Peabody, MA: Hendrickson, 2007.

——. "Theology of Sexuality in the Song of Songs: Return to Eden." *Andrews University Seminary Studies* 27 (1989) 1-19.

de Jong, S. "A Book on Labour: The Structuring Principles and the Main Theme of the Book of Qohelet." *JSOT* 54 (1992) 107-16.

——. "God in the Book of Qohelet: A Reappraisal of Qohelet's Place in Old Testament Theology." *VT* 47 (1997) 154-67.

Delitzsch, F. *Song of Songs and Ecclesiastes.* Trans. M. G. Easton. 1877. Repr. Grand Rapids: Eerdmans, 1982.

Dell, Katherine J. "Ecclesiastes as Wisdom: Consulting Early Interpreters." *VT* 44 (1994) 301-29.

Deutsch, C. M. *Lady Wisdom, Jesus, and the Sages: Metaphor and Social Context in Matthew's Gospel.* Valley Forge, PA: Trinity Press International, 1996.

Dunn, J. D. G. *The Epistles to the Colossians and to Philemon: A Commentary on the Greek Text.* New International Greek Testament Commentary. Grand Rapids: Eerdmans, 1996.

——. *Romans 1-8.* WBC 38. Dallas: Word, 1988.

Ehrman, B. D. *God's Problem: How the Bible Fails to Answer Our Most Important Question — Why We Suffer.* San Francisco: HarperOne, 2008.

Eichrodt, W. *Theology of the Old Testament.* Trans. J. A. Baker. 2 vols. Philadelphia: Westminster, 1961-67.

Enns, P. "Apostolic Hermeneutics and an Evangelical Doctrine of Scripture: Moving beyond the Modernist Impasse." *WTJ* 65 (2003) 263-87.

——. *Exodus Retold: Ancient Exegesis of the Departure from Egypt in Wis 10:15-21 and 19:1-9.* Harvard Semitic Monograph 57. Atlanta: Scholars Press, 1997.

——. *Inspiration and Incarnation: Evangelicals and the Problem of the Old Testament.* Grand Rapids: Baker, 2005.

———. "Wisdom of Solomon and Biblical Interpretation in the Second Temple Period." In *The Way of Wisdom: Essays in Honor of Bruce K. Waltke*. Ed. J. I. Packer and S. K. Soderlund, 212-25. Grand Rapids: Zondervan, 2000.

———. "כל-האדם and the Evaluation of Qohelet's Wisdom in Qoh 12:13 or 'The "A Is So, and *What's More*, B" Theology of Ecclesiastes.'" In *The Idea of Biblical Interpretation: Essays in Honor of James L. Kugel*. Ed. H. Najman and J. H. Newman, 125-37. Journal for the Study of Judaism Supplement 83. Leiden: Brill, 2004.

Evans, C. A. "Jesus and the Continuing Exile of Israel." In *Jesus and the Restoration of Israel: A Critical Assessment of N. T. Wright's Jesus and the Victory of God*. Ed. C. C. Newman, 77-100. Downers Grove, IL: InterVarsity Press, 1999.

Fee, G. D. *The First Epistle to the Corinthians*. NICNT. Grand Rapids: Eerdmans, 1987.

Fischer, S. "Qohelet and 'Heretic' Harpers' Songs." *JSOT* 98 (2002) 105-21.

Fox, M. V. *Ecclesiastes*. JPS Commentary. Philadelphia: JPS, 2004.

———. *Qohelet and His Contradictions*. JSOTSup 71. Sheffield: Sheffield Academic Press, 1989.

———. "Review of Craig Bartholomew, *Reading Ecclesiastes*." *Int* 54 (2000) 195-98.

———. *A Time to Tear Down and a Time to Build Up: A Rereading of Ecclesiastes*. Grand Rapids: Eerdmans, 1999.

Frankl, V. E. *Man's Search for Meaning: An Introduction to Logotherapy*. Trans. I. Lasch. Repr. Boston: Beacon, 2006.

Fredericks, D. C. "Life's Storms and Structural Unity in Qoheleth 11.1-12.8." *JSOT* 52 (1991) 95-114.

———. *Qoheleth's Language: Re-evaluating Its Nature and Date*. ANETS 3. Lewiston, NY: Mellen, 1998.

Fuller, M. E. *The Restoration of Israel: Israel's Re-gathering and the Fate of the Nations in Early Jewish Literature and Luke-Acts*. Beihefte zur Zeitschrift für die neutestamentliche Wissenschaft 138. Berlin: de Gruyter, 2006.

Gault, B. P. "A Reexamination of 'Eternity' in Ecclesiastes 3:11." *BSac* 165 (2008) 39-57.

Goldingay, J. *Models for Interpretation of Scripture*. Grand Rapids: Eerdmans, 1995.

———. *Models for Scripture*. Grand Rapids: Eerdmans, 1994.

Gordis, R. *Koheleth — The Man and His World: A Study of Ecclesiastes*. 3rd ed. New York: Schocken, 1968.

———. "The Original Language of Qohelet." *JQR* 37 (1946-47) 67-84.

Green, W. H. *Old Testament Literature: Lectures on the Poetical Books of the Old Testament*. Princeton: Princeton College, 1884.

Gunkel, H. *The Psalms: A Form-Critical Introduction*. Trans. T. M. Horner. Philadelphia: Fortress, 1967.

Hartley, J. E. *The Book of Job*. NICOT. Grand Rapids: Eerdmans, 1988.

Hays, R. B. "On the Rebound: A Response to Critiques of Echoes of Scripture in the Letters of Paul." In *Paul and the Scriptures of Israel*. Ed. C. A. Evans and J. A. Sanders, 163-89. Journal for the Study of the New Testament Supplement 83. Sheffield: JSOT Press, 1993.

Helyer, L. R. "The Necessity, Problems, and Promise of Second Temple Judaism for Discussions of New Testament Eschatology." *JETS* 47 (2004) 597-615.

Hermisson, H.-J. "Observations on the Creation Theology in Wisdom" (trans. B. Howard).

In *Israelite Wisdom: Theological and Literary Essays in Honor of Samuel Terrien.* Ed. J. G. Gammie et al., 43-57. Missoula, MT: Scholars Press, 1978.

Hirshman, M. "Qohelet's Reception and Interpretation in Early Rabbinic Literature." In *Studies in Ancient Midrash.* Ed. J. L. Kugel, 87-99. Cambridge: Harvard University Press, 2001.

Isaksson, B. *Studies in the Language of Qoheleth, with Special Emphasis on the Verbal System.* AUUSSU 10. Stockholm: Almqvist & Wiksell, 1987.

Japhet, S. *I and II Chronicles.* OTL. 1993. Repr. Louisville: Westminster John Knox, 2000.

———. *The Ideology of the Book of Chronicles and Its Place in Biblical Thought.* BEATAJ 9. Frankfurt: Peter Lang, 1989.

Jarick, J. "The Hebrew Book of Changes: Reflections on *hakkōl hebel* and *lakkōl zĕmān* in Ecclesiastes." *JSOT* 90 (2000) 79-99.

Johnson, L. T. *The Acts of the Apostles.* Sacra Pagina 5. Collegeville, MN: Liturgical Press, 1992.

Krüger, T. *Qoheleth: A Commentary.* Trans. O. C. Dean Jr. Hermeneia. Minneapolis: Fortress Press, 2004.

Kugel, J. L. "Qohelet and Money." *CBQ* 51 (1989) 32-49.

Kugel, J. L., and R. A. Greer. *Early Biblical Interpretation.* Library of Early Christianity 3. Philadelphia: Westminster, 1986.

Kushner, H. S. *When Bad Things Happen to Good People.* New York: Avon, 1981.

Lambert, W. G. *Babylonian Wisdom Literature.* Oxford: Oxford University Press, 1960.

Lawhead, S. R. *Byzantium.* New York: HarperPrism, 1996.

Lindblom, J. "Wisdom in the Old Testament Prophets." In *Wisdom in Israel and in the Ancient Near East: Presented to Professor Harold Henry Rowley.* Ed. M. Noth and D. Winton Thomas, 192-204. VTSup 3. Leiden: Brill, 1955.

Lo, A. "Death in Qohelet." *JANES* 31 (2008) 85-98.

Lohfink, N. *Qoheleth.* Trans. S. McEvenue. Continental Commentary. Minneapolis: Fortress, 2003.

Longman, T., III. *The Book of Ecclesiastes.* NICOT. Grand Rapids: Eerdmans, 1998.

———. *Proverbs.* Baker Commentary on the Old Testament: Wisdom and Psalms. Grand Rapids: Baker, 2006.

Machinist, P. "Fate, *miqreh,* and Reason: Some Reflections on Qohelet and Biblical Thought." In *Solving Riddles and Untying Knots: Biblical, Epigraphic, and Semitic Studies in Honor of Jonas C. Greenfield.* Ed. A. Berlin et al., 159-75. Winona Lake, IN: Eisenbrauns, 1995.

May, G. G. *The Dark Night of the Soul: A Psychiatrist Explores the Connection between Darkness and Spiritual Growth.* San Francisco: HarperSanFrancisco, 2004.

McCarter, P. K., Jr. "The Sage in the Deuteronomistic History." In *The Sage in Israel and the Ancient Near East.* Ed. J. G. Gammie and L. G. Perdue, 289-93. Winona Lake, IN: Eisenbrauns, 1990.

McCartney, D. "The New Testament's Use of the Old Testament." In *Inerrancy and Hermeneutic: A Tradition, a Challenge, a Debate.* Ed. H. N. Conn, 101-16. Grand Rapids: Baker, 1988.

McNeile, A. H. *An Introduction to Ecclesiastes.* Cambridge: Cambridge University Press, 1904.

Michel, D. *Untersuchungen zur Eigenart des Buches Qohelet.* BZAW 183. Berlin: de Gruyter, 1989.

Miller, D. "Qohelet's Symbolic Use of הבל." *JBL* 117 (1998) 437-54.

Mitchell, D. C. *The Message of the Psalter: An Eschatological Programme in the Book of Psalms.* JSOTSup 252. Sheffield: Sheffield Academic Press, 1997.

Mowinckel, S. "Psalms and Wisdom." In *Wisdom in Israel and in the Ancient Near East: Presented to Professor Harold Henry Rowley.* Ed. M. Noth and D. Winton Thomas, 205-24. VTSup 3. Leiden: Brill, 1955.

———. *Psalms in Israel's Worship.* Trans. D. R. Ap-Thomas. 2 vols. Nashville: Abingdon, 1962.

Muntingh, L. M. "Fear of Yahweh and Fear of the Gods according to the Books of Qohelet and Isaiah." In *Studies in Isaiah.* Ed. W. C. van Wyk, 143-58. OTWSA 22-23. Pretoria: NHW Press, 1981.

Murphy, R. E. *Ecclesiastes.* WBC 23A. Dallas: Word, 1992.

———. *The Tree of Life: An Exploration of Biblical Wisdom Literature.* 3rd ed. Grand Rapids: Eerdmans, 2002.

Newman, C. C., ed. *Jesus and the Restoration of Israel: A Critical Assessment of N. T. Wright's Jesus and the Victory of God.* Downers Grove, IL: InterVarsity Press, 1999.

Noll, M. A. *The Civil War as a Theological Crisis.* Chapel Hill: University of North Carolina Press, 2006.

Ogden, G. S. "The 'Better'-Proverb (Tôb-Spruch), Rhetorical Criticism, and Qoheleth." *JBL* 96 (1977) 489-505.

Oshantz, M. "The Problem of Moral Progress: The Slavery Debates and the Development of Liberal Protestantism in the United States." *Modern Intellectual History* 5 (2008) 225-50.

Packer, J. I. "Theology and Wisdom." In *The Way of Wisdom: Essays in Honor of Bruce K. Waltke.* Ed. J. I. Packer and S. K. Soderlund, 1-14. Grand Rapids: Zondervan, 2000.

Pahk, J. Y. S. "A Syntactical and Contextual Consideration of 'šh in Qoh. IX 9." *VT* 51 (2001) 370-80.

Parsons, G. "Guidelines for Understanding and Proclaiming the Book of Ecclesiastes, Parts 1-2." *BSac* 160 (2003) 159-73, 283-304.

Paulson, G. N. "The Use of Qoheleth in Bonhoeffer's *Ethics.*" *WW* 17 (1998) 307-13.

Perdue, L. G. "Cosmology and the Social Order in the Wisdom Tradition." In *The Sage in Israel and the Ancient Near East.* Ed. J. G. Gammie and L. G. Perdue, 457-78. Winona Lake, IN: Eisenbrauns, 1990.

———. *The Sword and the Stylus: An Introduction to Wisdom in the Age of Empires.* Grand Rapids: Eerdmans, 2008.

———. *Wisdom and Creation: The Theology of Wisdom Literature.* Nashville: Abingdon, 1994.

Perry, T. A. *Dialogues with Kohelet.* University Park, PA: Pennsylvania State University Press, 1993.

Pervo, R. I. *Acts: A Commentary.* Hermeneia. Minneapolis: Fortress, 2009.

Pfeiffer, E. "Die Gottesfurcht im Buche Kohelet." In *Gottes Wort und Gottes Land: Hans-Wilhelm Hertzberg zum 70. Geburtstag.* Ed. H. G. Reventlow, 133-58. Göttingen: Vandenhoeck & Ruprecht, 1965.

Phua, M. "The Wise Kings of Judah according to Ben Sira: A Study in Second Temple Use of Biblical Traditions." Ph.D. diss. Westminster Theological Seminary, 2008.

Pixley, J. "Qoheleth: A Teacher for Our Times." *CurTM* 26 (1999) 123-35.

Prior, J. "'When All the Singing Has Stopped': Ecclesiastes: A Modest Mission in Unpredictable Times." *International Review of Missions* 91 (2002) 7-23.

Provan, I. *Ecclesiastes, Song of Songs.* NIVAC. Grand Rapids: Zondervan, 2001.

Rad, G. von. "The Joseph Narrative and Ancient Wisdom." In *The Problem of the Hexateuch and Other Essays.* Trans. E. W. Trueman Dicken, 292-300. Edinburgh: Oliver & Boyd, 1966.

————. *Old Testament Theology.* Trans. D. M. G. Stalker. 2 vols. San Francisco: Harper & Row, 1962-65.

————. *Wisdom in Israel.* Trans. J. D. Martin. Nashville: Abingdon, 1972.

Reicke, B. *The Roots of the Synoptic Gospels.* Philadelphia: Fortress, 1986.

Reitman, J. S. "The Structure and Unity of Ecclesiastes." *BSac* 154 (1997) 297-319.

Roth, J. K. "A Theodicy of Protest." In *Encountering Evil: Live Options in Theodicy.* Ed. S. T. Davis, 1-20. Louisville: Westminster John Knox, 2001.

Rudman, D. "A Contextual Reading of Ecclesiastes 4:13-16." *JBL* 116 (1997) 57-73.

————. *Determinism in the Book of Ecclesiastes.* JSOTSup 316. Sheffield: Sheffield Academic Press, 2001.

————. "Woman as Divine Agent in Ecclesiastes." *JBL* 116 (1997) 411-27.

Sandberg, R. N. *Rabbinic Views of Qohelet.* Mellen Biblical Press Series 57. Lewiston, NY: Mellen Biblical Press, 1999.

Schoors, A. *The Preacher Sought to Find Pleasing Words: A Study of the Language of Qoheleth.* OLA 41. Leuven: Peeters, 1992.

————. "Theodicy in Qohelet." In *Theodicy in the World of the Bible.* Ed. A. Laato and J. C. de Moor, 375-409. Leiden: Brill, 2003.

————. "Words Typical of Qohelet." In *Qohelet in the Context of Wisdom.* Ed. A. Schoors, 17-39. BETL 136. Leuven: Leuven University Press, 1998.

Seow, C. L. *Ecclesiastes: A New Translation and Commentary.* AB 18C. New York: Doubleday, 1997.

————. "Linguistic Evidence and the Dating of Qohelet." *JBL* 115 (1996) 643-66.

————. "Qohelet's Autobiography." In *Fortunate the Eyes That See: Essays in Honor of David Noel Freedman.* Ed. A. Beck et al., 275-87. Grand Rapids: Eerdmans, 1995.

————. "Qohelet's Eschatological Poem." *JBL* 118 (1999) 209-34.

————. "The Socioeconomic Context of 'The Preacher's' Hermeneutic." *PSB* 17 (1996) 168-95.

————. "Theology When Everything Is out of Control." *Int* 3 (2001) 237-49.

Shaffer, A. "The Mesopotamian Background of Qoh 4:9-12" [Hebrew]. *ErIsr* 8 (1967) 246-50.

————. "New Information on the Origin of the 'Threefold Cord'" [Hebrew]. *ErIsr* 9 (1969) 159-60.

Sharp, C. J. "Ironic Representation, Authorial Voice, and Meaning in Qohelet." *BibInt* 1 (2004) 37-68.

Shead, A. G. "Reading Ecclesiastes 'Epilogically.'" *TynBul* 48 (1997) 67-91.

Sheppard, G. T. *Wisdom as a Hermeneutical Construct: A Study in the Sapientializing of the Old Testament*. BZAW 151. Berlin: de Gruyter, 1980.

Shields, M. A. "Ecclesiastes and the End of Wisdom." *TynBul* 50 (1999) 117-39.

————. *The End of Wisdom: A Reappraisal of the Historical and Canonical Function of Ecclesiastes*. Winona Lake, IN: Eisenbrauns, 2006.

————. "Qohelet." In *Dictionary of the Old Testament: Wisdom, Poetry, and Writings*. Ed. T. Longman III and P. Enns, 635-40. Downers Grove, IL: InterVarsity Press, 2008.

————. "Re-examining the Warning of Eccl. XII 12." *VT* 50 (2000) 123-27.

Siegfried, C. *Prediger und Hoheslied*. HAT 2nd series, 3/2. Göttingen: Vandenhoeck & Ruprecht, 1898.

Silva, M. *Biblical Words and Their Meaning: An Introduction to Lexical Semantics*. Rev. ed. Grand Rapids: Zondervan, 1994.

Sneed, M. "(Dis)closure in Qohelet: Qohelet Deconstructed." *JSOT* 27 (2002) 115-26.

Spangenberg, I. J. J. "Irony in the Book of Qohelet." *JSOT* 72 (1996) 57-69.

Thiselton, A. C. "Dialogue, Dialectic and Temporal Horizons: 'Polyphonic Voices and Theological Fiction' and 'Temporal Horizons in Hermeneutics' (1999)." In *Thiselton on Hermeneutics: Collected Works with New Essays*, 747-67. Grand Rapids: Eerdmans, 2006.

Torrey, C. C. "The Question of the Original Language of Qoheleth." *JQR* 39 (1948-49) 151-60.

Vanhoozer, K. J. *The Drama of Doctrine: A Canonical-Linguistic Approach to Christian Theology*. Louisville: Westminster John Knox, 2005.

Van Leeuwen, R. C. *Context and Meaning in Proverbs 25–27*. SBLDS 96. Atlanta: Scholars Press, 1988.

Verheij, A. "Paradise Retired: On Qohelet 2.4-6." *JSOT* 50 (1991) 113-15.

Vos, G. "Eschatology of the Psalter." *Princeton Theological Review* 18 (January 1920) 1-43. Repr. in *Pauline Eschatology* (Grand Rapids: Baker, 1979), 323-65.

————. *The Pauline Eschatology*. Repr. Grand Rapids: Baker, 1979.

Waltke, B. K. *Proverbs*. 2 vols. NICOT. Grand Rapids: Eerdmans, 2005.

Waltke, B. K., and M. O'Connor. *An Introduction to Biblical Hebrew Syntax*. Winona Lake, IN: Eisenbrauns, 1990.

Ward, T. "The Diversity and Sufficiency of Scripture." In *The Trustworthiness of God: Perspectives on the Nature of Scripture*. Ed. P. Helm and C. R. Trueman, 192-218. Grand Rapids: Eerdmans, 2002.

Weinfeld, M. *Deuteronomy and the Deuteronomic School*. Oxford: Oxford University Press, 1972.

Whitley, C. F. *Koheleth: His Language and Thought*. BZAW 148. Berlin: de Gruyter, 1979.

Whybray, R. N. *Ecclesiastes*. New Century Bible Commentary. Grand Rapids: Eerdmans, 1989.

Witherington, B., III. *Jesus the Sage: The Pilgrimage of Wisdom*. Minneapolis: Fortress, 1994.

Wright, N. T. *The Last Word*. San Francisco: Harper, 2005.

————. *The New Testament and the People of God*. Minneapolis: Fortress, 1992.

————. *The Resurrection of the Son of God*. Minneapolis: Fortress, 2003.

————. *Surprised by Hope: Rethinking Heaven, the Resurrection, and the Mission of the Church.* San Francisco: HarperCollins, 2008.

Young, I., ed. *Biblical Hebrew: Studies in Chronology and Typology.* JSOTSup 369. London: T & T Clark, 2003.

Zimmerli, W. "Concerning the Structure of Old Testament Wisdom." Trans. B. W. Kovacs. In *Studies in Ancient Israelite Wisdom.* Ed. J. L. Crenshaw, 175-207. New York: Ktav, 1976.

Zimmermann, F. "The Aramaic Provenance of Qohelet." *JQR* 36 (1945-46) 17-45.

Index of Authors

Index of Ancient Literature